Montréal & Québec City
For Dummies® 1st Edition

W9-CCA-744

Montréal Métro

2 Henri-Bourassa
Sauvé
Crémazie
Jarry

5 Saint-Michel

Honoré-Beaugrand **1**
Radisson
Langelier
Cadillac
Assomption
Viau
Pie-IX
Joliette
Préfontaine
Frontenac
Papineau
Beaudry

D'Iberville
Fabre

Jean-Talon
De Castelnau
Parc

Beaubien
Rosemont
Laurier
Mont-Royal
Sherbrooke

2 Côte-Vertu
Du Collège
De la Savane
Namur
Plamondon
Côte-Sainte-Catherine

Edouard-Montpetit
Acadie
Outremont
Université-de-Montréal
Côtes-des-Neiges

5 Snowdon
Villa-Maria
Vendôme
Place-Saint-Henri

Saint-Laurent
Place-des-Arts
McGill
Peel
Guy-Concordia
Atwater

4

Berri-UQAM

Champ-de-Mars
Place-d'Armes
Square-Victoria
Bonaventure
Lucien-L'Allier
Georges-Vanier

St. Lawrence River

Pont Jacques-Cartier

Jean-Drapeau

Lionel-Groulx
Charlevoix
LaSalle
De l'Eglise
Jolicoeur
Monk
Verdun

Pont Victoria

Longueuil **4**

1 Angrignon

Pont Champlain

For Dummies: Bestselling Book Series for Beginners

Montréal & Québec City For Dummies, 1st Edition

Cheat Sheet

A Glossary of French Terms

Parlez-vous français? Most of the people you encounter in Montréal and Québec City work in the tourism industry and speak English quite well. But if you venture outside the cities, you may find this simple glossary quite helpful.

English	French	French Pronunciation
Yes	*Oui*	Weeh
No	*Non*	Nonh
Please	*S'il vous plaît*	Sill-vooz-PLAY
Thank you.	*Merci*	Mer-SEE
You're welcome.	*De rien*	DUH-ree-en
Good day/Good evening	*Bonjour/Bonsoir*	BON-jewr/BON-soih-re
Do you speak English?	*Parlez-vous anglais?*	Par-LAYS vooz ONG-lay
I do not speak French.	*Je ne parle pas français*	Je neh PARL pah fran-SAYS
Where is...?	*Ou est...?*	Ooh eh
Is there a tourism office nearby?	*Est-ce qu'il y a un bureau de tourisme près d'ici*	Eh skill ee ah unh BOO-roh de toor-EEZME pres duh EE-see
Can we exchange money here?	*Changez-vous de l'argent ici?*	SHAWN-jayz vooz duh LARGE-anh ee-see

Accommodations, dining, and shopping

English	French	French Pronunciation
Do you have...?	*Avez-vous...?*	AH-veyz vooz
How much is this?	*Ça coûte combien?*	Sa koote com-BEE-en
I would like...	*Je voudrais...*	Je VOO-dreh
Do you serve breakfast/lunch/dinner/drinks	*Servez-vous le déjeuner/le dîner/le souper/à boire?*	Ser-VAY vooz leh DAY-jun-ay/leh DI-nay/leh SOO-pay/ah BOI-re
A cup of coffee/tea/hot chocolate	*Une tasse de café/thé/chocolat chaud*	Oon tass duh cah-fay/tay/cho-CO-la sho
A glass of water/wine/beer	*Un verre d'eau/de vin/de bière*	Unh ver d-oh/duh vain/duh bee-air
The wine list	*La carte des vins*	Lah kart dehs vain
An appetizer	*Une entrée*	Oon en-TRAY
A main course	*Un plat principal*	Unh plaa prince-uhl-pal
I am a vegetarian.	*Je suis vegetarian(nne).*	Je swees veh-GEH-TA-ree-en(ne)
Do you have any rooms available?	*Avez-vous des chambres de libre?*	Av-ay vooz dehs SHAM-breh duh LEE-breh
How much is a room per night?	*À combien est une chambre pour la nuit?*	Ah com-bee-en eh oon SHAM-breh poor lah nwit

For Dummies: Bestselling Book Series for Beginners

FOR DUMMIES®

The fun and easy way™ to travel!

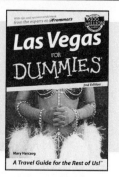

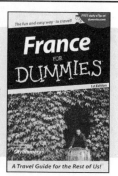

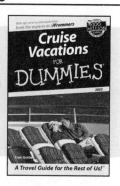

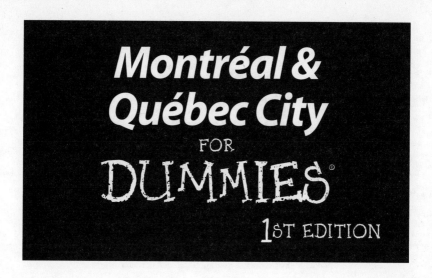

Montréal & Québec City

FOR

DUMMIES®

1ST EDITION

by Julie Barlow and Austin Macdonald

WILEY

Wiley Publishing, Inc.

Montréal & Québec City For Dummies®, 1st Edition

Published by
Wiley Publishing, Inc.
111 River St.
Hoboken, NJ 07030-5774
www.wiley.com

Copyright © 2004 by Wiley Publishing, Inc., Indianapolis, Indiana

Published simultaneously in Canada

No part of this publication may be reproduced, stored in a retrieval system, or transmitted in any form or by any means, electronic, mechanical, photocopying, recording, scanning, or otherwise, except as permitted under Sections 107 or 108 of the 1976 United States Copyright Act, without either the prior written permission of the Publisher, or authorization through payment of the appropriate per-copy fee to the Copyright Clearance Center, 222 Rosewood Drive, Danvers, MA 01923, 978-750-8400, fax 978-646-8600. Requests to the Publisher for permission should be addressed to the Legal Department, Wiley Publishing, Inc., 10475 Crosspoint Blvd., Indianapolis, IN 46256, 317-572-3447, fax 317-572-4447, or e-mail permcoordinator@wiley.com

Trademarks: Wiley, the Wiley Publishing logo, For Dummies, the Dummies Man logo, A Reference for the Rest of Us!, The Dummies Way, Dummies Daily, The Fun and Easy Way, Dummies.com and related trade dress are trademarks or registered trademarks of John Wiley & Sons, Inc., and/or its affiliates in the United States and other countries, and may not be used without written permission. Frommer's is a trademark or registered trademark of Arthur Frommer. Used under license. All other trademarks are the property of their respective owners. Wiley Publishing, Inc., is not associated with any product or vendor mentioned in this book.

For general information on our other products and services or to obtain technical support, please contact our Customer Care Department within the U.S. at 800-762-2974, outside the U.S. at 317-572-3993, or fax 317-572-4002.

Wiley also publishes its books in a variety of electronic formats. Some content that appears in print may not be available in electronic books.

Library of Congress Control Number: 2004102604

ISBN: 0-7645-5624-X

Manufactured in the United States of America

10   9   8   7   6   5   4   3   2   1

1B/RZ/QU/QU/IN

WILEY

About the Authors

Julie Barlow (julie.barlow@sympatico.ca) is a magazine journalist and travel writer who spent several years living in Paris. She recently published *Sixty Million Frenchmen Can't Be Wrong,* a sort of travel guide for Americans who are puzzled by the French. In it, she explains why the French think, act, and organize themselves the way they do. At the moment, she is based in Montréal, where she writes regularly for the French-language magazine *L'actualité,* but she will soon be heading back to France to work on her next book, *The Story of French.* When she's not traveling, she's cooking, eating, drinking, and enjoying this North American corner of the French-speaking world as much as possible.

Austin Macdonald (austin_macdonald@yahoo.com) first came to Montréal for school. For three summers, while studying English Literature at McGill University, he worked as a tour guide in both Montréal and Québec City. Since teaching English in Tokyo, counting down the millennium in Rio, and having a series of misadventures in the dot-com world, Austin has been working as a freelance writer concerned with urban affairs at large. His work has been published in Canadian magazines such as *Toronto Life* and *Azure* and in newspapers, including *Globe and Mail,* the *National Post,* and the *Montréal Gazette.*

Publisher's Acknowledgments

We're proud of this book; please send us your comments through our Dummies online registration form located at www.dummies.com/register/.

Some of the people who helped bring this book to market include the following:

Editorial

Editors: Tere Drenth, Lorraine Festa

Cartographers: Roberta Stockwell, Nicholas Trotter

Editorial Manager: Michelle Hacker

Editorial Assistant: Elizabeth Rae

Senior Photo Editor: Richard Fox

Front Cover Photo: Catherine Karnow Photography

Back Cover Photo: Fairmont Le Château Frontenac, Québec City: J.A. Kraulis/ Masterfile

Cartoons: Rich Tennant, www.the5thwave.com

Production

Project Coordinator: Ryan Steffen

Layout and Graphics: Andrea Dahl, Lauren Goddard, Denny Hager, Michael Kruzil, Jacque Schneider, Julie Trippetti

Proofreaders: Laura Albert, David Faust, TECHBOOKS Production Services

Indexer: TECHBOOKS Production Services

Publishing and Editorial for Consumer Dummies

Diane Graves Steele, Vice President and Publisher, Consumer Dummies

Joyce Pepple, Acquisitions Director, Consumer Dummies

Kristin A. Cocks, Product Development Director, Consumer Dummies

Michael Spring, Vice President and Publisher, Travel

Brice Gosnell, Associate Publisher, Travel

Kelly Regan, Editorial Director, Travel

Publishing for Technology Dummies

Andy Cummings, Vice President and Publisher, Dummies Technology/General User

Composition Services

Gerry Fahey, Vice President of Production Services

Debbie Stailey, Director of Composition Services

Contents at a Glance

Maps at a Glance

Table of Contents

Chapter 12: A Shopper's Guide to Montréal...........................159

Chapter 13: Living It Up After the Sun Goes Down:
Montréal Nightlife...169

Chapter 14: Exploring Beyond Montréal:
Three Great Day Trips...185

Introduction

· ·

*E*uropean flair and French *joie de vivre* — you'll definitely find these elusive Old World qualities in Montréal and Québec City.

Visiting Montréal is like escaping into a little corner of Europe, except that you don't have to cross the Atlantic to get there. And Montréal doesn't feel European only because life and business is carried out mostly in French. Things are really different here. People eat later (and, may we add, better), they party differently (ditto), and life is infused with a touch of European style. Montréalers seem to keep one eye on Paris all the time.

Visiting Québec City is like slipping into the past without actually leaving the present. One of the oldest, most picturesque cities in North America, Québec City has preserved all its historic charm while hanging on to its vibrant and distinct culture.

Yet make no mistake. Both cities have their feet firmly planted in North America. Distinct as they are, Montréal and Québec City feel familiar, too: The road system looks similar, telephones work the same way, and people here smile at strangers. You'll feel a *je ne sais quoi* about both cities, but people here won't leave you scratching your heading, wondering what planet they're from.

Now it's time for confessions. Years before we wrote this book, we each left the *belle province,* thinking life would be more interesting somewhere else. Well, guess what? We quickly saw what we were missing and high-tailed it back. We even missed the latent tension between English and French culture. We love these cities — with their great restaurants and their worldly spirit. As born-again Québeckers, we think we're in a particularly good position to tell you what's so great about both cities. And that's what we do in this book.

About This Book

By no means is *Montréal & Québec City For Dummies* an encyclopedia about the two cities. Although we've scoured the cities, this book highlights the best of Montréal and Québec City, not the most. We assume you have only so much time and need to cut to the chase. With that in mind, we've organized the chapters in this book to answer your questions roughly in the order they pop up — from figuring out whether you really want to visit these cities to knowing when to go, planning a budget, deciding where to stay and eat, and figuring out what to see and do.

Of course, you may not have the same questions in the same order, so feel free to read the chapters in any order you want. Who are we to judge? In these pages, you find a fair bit more information about Montréal than Québec City, but that's not because we're choosing favorites. Montréal is a much bigger city, with much more to see and do (and many more places to eat!). To give you the best of Montréal, we have to give you more. But if you decide to skip Montréal, don't worry, because we cover all the bases in Québec City, too.

Conventions Used In This Book

Montréal & Québec City For Dummies uses a few conventions to help you find information quickly.

All prices in this book are shown first in Canadian dollars, then in U.S. dollars. The dollar signs are preceded by "C" or a "US," so that you know which is which. (As we write this book, C$1 is worth US75¢, and all prices were converted at the rate. That may change by the time you read this and when you travel to these cities.)

In the hotel sections, the prices we give are the *rack rates* (the official rates the hotel publicizes) for one night for a double room, during the high season of tourism: May to October. The price you end up paying may be significantly lower if you travel off-season or with a package deal.

In the restaurant sections, we give you the price range of a main course at each establishment. In most cases, these are the prices of dinner entrees, but if a restaurant doesn't serve dinner, we give you the price of a lunch entree. We use dollar sign symbols ($) in both the restaurant and hotel sections. These signs give you the price range of a night's stay at a hotel (non-discounted standard rates) or a restaurant meal (including drinks and tips). Check out the following table to decipher the dollar signs:

Cost	Hotel	Restaurant
$	less than C$100 (US$75)	Less than C$10 (US$7.50)
$$	C$100–C$200 (US$75–US$150)	C$10–C$20 (US$7.50–US$15)
$$$	C$200–C$300 (US$150–US$225)	C$20–C$30 (US$15–US$22.50)
$$$$	more than C$300 (US$225)	More than C$30 (US$22.50)

Prices can change. Generally, they go up as time goes by. And sometimes, this price increase can happen quite quickly, even over the course of a few months. Keep that rule in mind when you're making restaurant or hotel reservations. Before you commit to a particular lodging, restaurant, or attraction, call ahead of time to confirm prices.

We also use abbreviations for credit cards, so that you can quickly see how you can pay for hotels and restaurant. They are as follows:

AE	American Express
DC	Diner's Club
DISC	Discover
MC	MasterCard
V	Visa

In addition, we keep the addresses of hotels, restaurants, and attractions in French, because that's what you'll see on street signs — we hope this simplifies finding your way around. Here's the rundown of French street terminology:

French Term	*U.S. Equivalent*
rue	street
bd.	boulevard
av.	avenue
Est	east
Ouest	west
Nord	north
Sud	south

You may sometimes see the odd street name starting with *place.* Some street names also start with *côte,* which means hill, so at least you know what to expect before you get there (don't worry, though, most hills are just gentle slopes). Also, many streets are named for saints, whose given names are preceded by "Ste" (female) or "St" (male). *Vieux* means old, as in Vieux-Montréal and Vieux-Québec, the older sections of the cities, which are loaded with character.

We also keep names of buildings and sites in French, except where they are very frequently referred to in English.

Otherwise, we translate French words and expressions into English as much as possible. However, some terms just don't translate very well, and when that happens, we leave the words in French and put them in italics. For a list of handy French expressions, see the Cheat Sheet at the front of this book.

Foolish Assumptions

We make a few assumptions about you, dear reader. You probably fall into one or more of these categories:

- **You're a first time visitor to Montréal or Québec City.** Or you stopped here briefly, say, on business, got a taste of it, and want to come back for more. We don't want to give you a comprehensive course on these cities. We simply show you how to enjoy them with the least work possible.

- **You're busy.** Perhaps you're an experienced traveler, but you don't have a ton of time to spend planning trip or you don't have loads of time to spend in Montréal and Québec City after you get there. You want expert advice on how to maximize your time and enjoy a hassle-free trip.

- **You don't want to spend your whole trip reading a guidebook.** This a quick and easy read, and it tells you everything you need to know for the kind of trip you want to take.

How This Book Is Organized

Montréal & Québec City For Dummies is both a planning guide to help you prepare your trip and a travel guide that gives you all the information you need after you get there. Our philosophy is to give you the information you need *before* you leave, so that you don't waste time looking for information when you could be enjoying the sights. As such, this book is organized into five parts, discussed in the following sections.

Part 1: Getting Started

This part introduces you to Montréal and Québec City. We describe the main attractions for each city, tell you what the weather is like, and give you ideas of what's going on throughout the year. Then we start helping you plan your trip. We tell you how much everything costs, give you tips on how to plan a budget, and help you decide whether to use cash, credit, travelers' checks, or ATMs. Finally, we give specialized advice for gay and lesbian travelers, people traveling with kids, travelers with disabilities, and senior citizens.

Part II: Ironing Out the Details

In this part, we help you plan your trip and buy tickets. We explain the ins and outs of using travel agents, buying package tours, and planning your trip on your own. We also tell you how to find the best airfare and explain alternate means of travel to Montréal and Québec City. We give you tips on selecting a neighborhood, choosing a hotel, and finding the best prices possible. Finally, we tell you what to expect crossing the border, what kind of paperwork you have to take care of before you leave, what kind of insurance you need. We give you the pros and cons of renting a car and suggest what kind of reservations you may want to make ahead of time. In a nutshell, this part gives you enough information to get you to either city.

Part III: Exploring Montréal

We start this part by explaining what to do when you arrive in Montréal and where to get the information you need to visit the city. The chapters in this part also give you lists of the best hotels, restaurants, and attractions in the city. We list the best nightspots in Montréal and also describe the best day trips, in case you want to get out of the city for an afternoon.

Part IV: Visiting Québec City

Moving up the river, we tell you how to get to Québec City and explain how to get oriented after you're there. In this part, we describe the neighborhoods you want to spend time exploring. We also give you a list of our top hotel picks, recommend what to see and do, and direct you to the best food in town — whether you want fine French cuisine or just pizza. Finally, we suggest some sample itineraries that let you explore different themes in the city.

Part V: The Part of Tens

One thing to never forget when you travel is your sense of humor. In this part, we tell you how to have fun in Montréal and Québec City. Some of our advice is practical. Some of it is whimsical — just an indirect way of poking fun at our cities and their inhabitants. You be the judge.

Icons Used in This Book

To help you find information as quickly and easily as possible, every *For Dummies* book includes a series of icons that serve as little road signs, alerting you to pleasures and dangers ahead — or just alerting you, period. In this book, we add an icon of our own to tell you what's really, truly, unique about this French-speaking corner of the continent.

 Think traveling with kids is hard work? Okay, you're right. But we try to make the process easier by using this icon when a hotel, restaurant, or attraction happens to be particularly well-suited for your pint-size companions.

 This icon alerts you to special, insider advice on everything from dealing with Québec's extreme weather to exchanging money and finding the best rate on accommodations.

 Traveling in Canada used to be a real steal for Americans, thanks to the weak Canadian dollar. Those days are over, at least in the short term, so you have work a little harder to cut corners off your travel budget. We use this icon to make that job easier for you.

 Even among polite and congenial Canadians, a few bad apples may try to squeeze more cash out of you than you should rightly part with. This icon warns you when to beware of a rip-off.

 Some of the sites, foods, and activities in Montréal and Québec City wrap up what's unique about Québec. We don't want you to miss out on these or accidentally overlook them, so we flag them with this icon. *Vive le Québec!*

Where to Go from Here

Time to dig in and do some reading. You won't find any fixed rule about which chapters to read first. We've organized them in what we thought was a logical sequence, but you're free to wander in and out of them to your heart's content, in whatever order suits you. You may actually want to read about attractions and restaurants before you dig into the nitty-gritty about planning a trip and buying air tickets — just to see what fun stuff is in store for you.

Don't worry, though. Regardless of the order in which you plan this trip, you'll be amply rewarded when you arrive. So start reading!

Part I
Getting Started

The 5th Wave   By Rich Tennant

"Here's something. It's a language school that will teach you to speak French for $500, or for $200 they'll just give you an accent."

In this part . . .

*P*lanning a trip may sound like a lot of work, especially if you've never done it before. Don't worry, though. In this part, we tell you about the top events and attractions in Montréal and Québec City, so that you can decide when to go. We also tell you how much everything costs and how to make a budget for your trip. Finally, we give advice and information for travelers with special needs.

Chapter 1

Discovering the Best of Montréal and Québec City

In This Chapter

▶ Uncovering the distinct European flair of French North America

▶ Diving into Montréal's and Québec City's cultural and linguistic experiences

▶ Experiencing dining, nightlife, and festivals in both cities — winter or summer

*M*ontréal is fun, sexy, and sophisticated. It's a city with charisma; a place with flair. Even the people who live here think so. Is it the mix of French and North American cultures that is so appealing? Is it Montréal's tumultuous past as a battleground between English and French? Or is it just the great food and pulsing night and generally hedonistic ways of modern Montréalers? Actually, it's the combination of these and other qualities that give the city its unique beat.

Montréal has seen some dark days. A decade ago, the economy was in a slump, political tensions were at their peak, and morale hit rock bottom. It wasn't pretty. But the city made an amazing about-face — which means now is a great time to visit Montréal. The economy has seen a remarkable upturn in the last five years, so the city boasts more great restaurants, clubs, and attractions than ever. The city's festivals are getting bigger and more glamorous every year, attracting an amazing array of talent. Tensions between English and French feel like ancient history now. And best of all, this cultural and economic germination is really putting Montréalers in a good mood.

Québec City, with its quaint cobblestone streets, top-notch restaurants, beautiful vistas, and Old World charm, simply never goes out of style. In 2003, both *Travel & Leisure* and *Condé Nast Traveler* magazines ranked Québec City as one of the top five destinations in North America. And the city is in no danger of losing the title of North America's most romantic holiday destination. Just being in this fortified, cliff-top, port city is enough — although you can find plenty more to do than just soak up the view. For a small city, it offers an impressive roster of cultural events, exhibitions, performances, festivals, and more. The booming economy through Québec province hasn't done its capital city any harm, either.

Savoring the language

Before taking your trip, why not take some time to brush up on your French? Québec City is almost entirely French-speaking, and in Montréal, some of the most interesting parts of the city are predominantly French, as well. While you don't need to speak French to get around either city, knowing when to drop the occasional civility, such as "*bonjour*" and "*au revoir*," "*s'il vous plaît*" and "*merçi*," endears you to the locals. They may answer you in English anyway, but they'll be flattered by your effort. (The words and expressions we provide on the Cheat Sheet at the front of this book can definitely get you out of any tight spot.)

The question on most people's minds when they visit either city is: "Can I get by without French?" To be honest, you can have more fun if you master a few words of French, but you can get by just fine without it. While once upon a time, the English and the French were throwing rocks at each other in the streets of both cities, today, young Montréalers are often as comfortable speaking English as they are French — or Spanish or Italian, for that matter. In Québec City, the booming tourism industry has done its work in making English widely used and understood. You can always expect warmth and cordiality from Québeckers, but especially if you make an effort to speak their native tongue.

Soaking Up That European Flavor

That Québec and Montréal have preserved so much European flair isn't surprising. These are two of the oldest cities in North America — and definitely among the best preserved. In both, you can stroll cobblestone streets and gaze at stone buildings and churches that date back to the 1700s. The relaxed pace, late hours, and abundance of cafes only add to the illusion that you're somewhere in Europe. For maximum Old World impact, visit the port areas of both cities. In Vieux-Québec, don't miss **Le Petit Champlain.** In Montréal, la **rue Notre-Dame** or la **rue St-Paul** transport you back in time.

Following Your Stomach

Thanks to the ongoing French influence on local cuisine, Montréal and Québec City are both renowned for excellent restaurants and a refined approach to dining. And trust us, it's getting better every day. That said, Québeckers also eat their share of fast food, so you want to be selective about where you eat. Chapters 10 and 17 give you the low-down on the best food for every budget in both cities.

Excellent eateries can be found everywhere, but in some neighbor-hoods, you just can't get a bad meal. Québec's Old City houses many fine choices, like the **Café du Monde.** Montréal's Old Port area is actu-ally not the best place to eat, but streets like **rue St-Denis** and **boule-vard St-Laurent** offer impressive dining choices.

Experiencing the Festival Frenzy

Other cities may have summer festivals, but Montréal is famous for its festivals. Unlike elsewhere, this city shuts down large portions of downtown for a string of festivals lasting practically all summer long. An intoxicating mix of English and French permeates these widely attended festivities. The fact that party-hearty Montréalers attend the festivals in droves, not to mention various states of intoxication, cer-tainly doesn't hurt. There's definitely a *je ne sais quoi* about the dozens of summer events here, whether its the **Montréal International Jazz Festival,** the **Just for Laughs Comedy Festival,** the **International Film Festival,** the **Nuits d'Afrique** African music festival, or the **Francofolies.** (The last is the largest French-language music festival in the world.)

See Chapter 2 for a calendar of the major festivals in Montréal and Québec City.

Living It Up After Hours

Back in the 1920s, when the rest of North America was in the grips of prohibition, Montréal was known as the "City of Sin" for its freewheeling, immoral ways. Among modern-day Canadians, the city is still revered for late bar closings (last call is at 3 a.m.), public affection (couples get *very* cozy on benches in public parks), and general lack of political correctness — all of which can create a carnival-like atmosphere after dark. If you want to let your hair down or stay out all night, Montréal offers endless opportunities for entertainment. You can roam the hopping club scenes, concentrated along **boulevard St-Laurent, rue Crescent,** and **rue St-Denis.**

Checking Out the Many
Faces of Montréal

France isn't the only culture you taste in Montréal — and we mean that literally. Dozens of other nationalities have marked out distinct corners of the city and filled them with great restaurants. In sheer numbers of immigrants, Montréal doesn't compare to multi-cultural havens like Toronto and Vancouver, but Montréal's long-established ethnic neighborhoods have left a lasting mark and continue to play a vital role on the urban landscape. Have a cappuccino at **Café Italia** in Little Italy, pick up some bagels on **rue St-Viateur** in the heart of the Montréal's Orthodox Jewish neighborhood, or grab a souvlaki along **avenue du Parc,** with its concentration of Greek restaurants, and you see what we mean.

Many of these areas boast interesting architecture, as well, such as the famous winding staircases of the **Plateau** and **Little Italy,** winding cobblestone streets and graceful stone buildings of Vieux-Montréal, and the beautiful churches, basilicas, and cathedrals throughout the city.

Walking (and Skiing and Eating) in a Winter Wonderland

There's no denying winter in Montréal and Québec City, where temperatures can regularly dip to –5°F (–20°C) or lower for weeks on end. But while many North Americans live in denial of their semi-Nordic surroundings, Québeckers embrace winter. By April, locals have had enough of snow, slush, and those speeding sidewalk plows that terrorize pedestrians. But from November to March, locals whisk away the winter blues by dressing properly — and plenty stylishly — and then skiing, snowboarding, skating, snowshoeing, and, let's be honest, eating and drinking to their heart's content.

Québec history 101

The cities of Montréal and Québec City boast fascinating histories. The following are some highlights from the annals of two of the oldest cities in North America.

The French discovered Québec . . .

Looking for a quick passage to Asia, French explorer Jacques Cartier landed at the future site of Québec City in 1535. For some reason, he thought the ground was rich with diamonds. It wasn't, so he went back to France. In 1608, another French explorer, Samuel de Champlain, founded a fur trading post in Québec, which attracted French settlers. The British captured the colony from France in 1759 and began to settle it with Irish, Scottish, and English immigrants and American Loyalists. In the 19th century, when railroads began cutting into Québec's port business and economic prospects looked grim, the English-speaking population moved to Montréal, leaving Québec City almost entirely to French speakers.

. . . and then Montréal

Jacques Cartier also discovered Montréal in 1535, but again left without making much of an impression. In 1641, the French explorer Paul de Chomedey Maisonneuve founded a mission on the site and set out to convert natives to Christianity. Then, of course, the French ceded Montréal to the English in 1760. By the early 1800s, Montréal was the cultural and commercial capital of Canada, with a booming port business and a wealthy English population running the show, while the Catholic French-speaking majority did the grunt work for them.

. . . and then Québeckers took over

In the 1960s, Québec's French-speaking majority decided become their own bosses and shake off the influence of the Catholic Church in one shot. The period is known as the *Quiet Revolution*. Practically overnight, French-speaking Québeckers went from being mostly farmers and working poor dominated by the Catholic Church to being a modern, secular society.

Join the fun and dive right into the season by taking your trip during Québec City's **Winter Carnival** or Montréal's **Fête des Neiges** (Snow Festival), both in February. In either city, you're less than an hour from great skiing and snowboarding destinations, such as **Mont Tremblant** or **Mont Ste-Anne.** If you really can't take the cold, you can always retreat to Montréal's **underground city,** where you never have to leave the safety of central heating to visit a number of museums, shopping centers, skyscraper lobbies, and major hotels.

Chapter 2

Deciding When to Go

· ·

In This Chapter

▶ Choosing a steamy urban jungle or winter wonderland

▶ Examining the four seasons of each city

▶ Scanning Montréal's and Québec City's cultural calendars

· ·

*M*ontréal is always hopping — no matter when you decide to visit — but the weather is always an issue. During the year, Montréal's climate swerves between scorching summer heat waves and icy winter cold snaps. Between these extremes, spring and fall are as unpredictable as they are short.

Québec City is 250 kilometers (150 miles) up the St. Lawrence River from Montréal, and one degree of latitude to the north, so the winters tend to be a couple of degrees Fahrenheit colder. Snowfalls are heavier and more consistent than in Montréal. In fact, by the end of the winter, the accumulated snow in the streets can reach as high as the rooftops. Summers are a little cooler than those in Montréal, but they can still be surprisingly hot and humid. During summer evenings, a wind off the river can make you feel a bit chilly.

Autumn can be an extremely beautiful time of year to visit both cities. For two short weeks, usually starting at the end of September, the leaves are ablaze in vivid oranges, reds, and yellows. Visit Québec in mid-October, and you're almost certain to see the autumn glory. This is a great time to tour the countryside, ideally in a sporty European two-seater convertible; if not, any car will do.

Be aware when making travel plans that weather extremes and unpredictability are the general rules. The heat — or cold — can hit when you least expect it. Bring a sweater, even in July.

Revealing the Two Faces of Montréal and Québec City

Freezing temperatures, snowy conditions, and icy roads may intimidate some travelers, but for residents of Montréal and Québec City, winter's harsh conditions are merely facts of life. We simply don more layers, tread carefully over icy patches, and spend more time indoors. As soon as we have enough snow and the temperatures are low enough, we swing into hardy outdoor pursuits, such as ice hockey, cross-country skiing, skating, snowboarding, snowshoeing, snowmobiling — and even ice fishing, which is incredibly popular in Québec.

Fortunately, all these activities can be done within an hour's drive of either Montréal or Québec City. If you're tempted by the idea of trekking into the wilderness in winter, just remember that daylight hours are extremely short from November until March.

Quiet, midnight snowfalls and pristine snow banks never seem to lose their magic. Fresh snow turns Québec City, with its fortifications, cannons, French colonial architecture, and cliff-top setting next to the river, into a winter wonderland. For the first two weeks in February, the provincial capital celebrates its Nordic spirit with the **Québec City Winter Carnival,** the world's largest outdoor winter festival. In 2003, this *Carnaval de Québec* celebrated its 50th anniversary.

Come March, however, all that snow turns into salty gray-brown slush that coats both cities and drives everyone nuts. Navigating through slush ponds is an arduous, nerve-jangling task, whether you're driving or walking, and the salt city officials dump on the roads to thaw the ice stains pant legs and ruins shoes.

Seemingly endless Montréal winters leave most urbanites aching to break out when the spring thaw finally arrives, but spring is slow in coming. The odd warm spell in March can make even the most weather-jaded Montréalers start stripping off their outer layers, but don't you be fooled: Winter almost never ends for good until the end of April.

When spring comes, it's short, partly because Montréalers interpret any warm weather as proof that summer has begun. At the first sign of a parasol on a *terrace,* locals hit the streets and start tearing off their clothing. Really.

From the grease, glitz, and green light of the **Formula One Canadian Grand Prix** in early June to the last curtain of the **Montréal World Film Festival** in September, outdoor events and festivals jam this city's summer schedule. By the end of June, Montréal is a steamy urban jungle, where throngs of locals and visitors flock the streets for free outdoor concerts, stand-up comedy shows, open-air film screenings, and more. Summer in Montréal is one long party.

In Québec City, spring brings glee, but it also brings tourists. Depending on the weather, the tourism season can be in full swing by the end of May and last well into September. Remember, Québec is a small city, and the part you want to see (the Old City) is even smaller, so reserve accommodations well ahead of time if you want to stay there.

The same holds true for Montréal's jammed-packed summer festival season, when hotel accommodations can be dear and scarce — if not entirely sold out. If you're planning to visit during this time, do your planning and book your room well in advance. (See Chapter 6 for our advice on deciding where to stay and Chapters 9 and 16 for our top hotel picks.)

Experiencing the Secret of the Seasons

The weather is always an issue when you're visiting Montréal or Québec City. Your tolerance for cold — or heat — is probably the first aspect to consider when planning your trip. In the following sections, we tell you what to expect from the seasons. If meteorological extremes don't faze you, consider other factors when timing your trip.

Spring

With the annual great thaw, excitement in both cities builds as snow and ice melt away:

 ✔ Days are longer, particularly after Daylight Saving Time.

 ✔ You encounter less snow, sleet, and cold.

 ✔ After a barren winter, life returns to the streets.

The dicey weather of the short transition between winter and summer, however, comes with its drawbacks:

 ✔ You usually can't put your coat, hat, and gloves away until the middle or end of April.

 ✔ As temperatures warm and the snow melts, expect a bit of everything, weather-wise. Definitely be prepared for some rain.

 ✔ Enormous slush ponds form at every street corner. Be prepared by wearing waterproof footwear or risk spending some of your stay with cold, wet feet.

Summer

After the heat of a summer day, the city's nightlife comes alive after the sun goes down:

- ✔ Expect festivals galore. Both in Montréal and Québec City, the summer season brings many special events.
- ✔ People in the streets bask in the glorious weather.
- ✔ Eating and drinking moves outdoors. People dine on their balconies. Restaurants open their patios, and the parks are filled with picnicking families (a popular option for travelers, too, because drinking wine and beer in parks is perfectly legal, as long as you accompany your drink with a meal).

On the downside, the heat and the crowds can get unbearable, so you may want to seek refuge in your air-conditioned hotel room, that is if you can find one. Here are some other drawbacks:

- ✔ The crowds of tourists and festival-goers, although loads of fun, can be enough to give you a mild fit of agoraphobia.
- ✔ The heat can be brutal — and it's not just the temperature. Montréal and Québec City can be unbearably humid in the summer.
- ✔ Booking a room, particularly during the major festivals, can be difficult.
- ✔ Rates at hotels and attractions are high.

During Québec's Construction Holidays, a major holiday in the last two weeks of July, many out-of-town accommodations and attractions are booked solid by Québeckers taking their summer holidays.

Fall

Brisk fall days are glorious, with the brilliantly colored leaves, harvest bounty at the markets, and temperatures that are typically ideal:

- ✔ The leaves change color.
- ✔ Temperatures are cooler and usually remain pleasantly warm until the end of September.
- ✔ You have an easier time finding accommodations.
- ✔ Restaurants keep their terraces open practically until the first frost.

However, autumn can start to turn nasty, as winter begins:

✔ Cold, unpredictable weather can set in as early as October. First you see frost, then the ground freezes, then you get snow.

✔ Most of the festivals are over and the winter activities haven't begun yet, so the cities can feel a tad drab.

Winter

Instead of seeing the snow and ice as impediments, your best bet is to regard them as opportunities for seasonal recreation and leisure. By braving the extreme conditions in the name of fun, or, *le fun* as locals are likely to say, you're taking part in Québec's Nordic spirit:

✔ It's sunny almost all of the time, and the days can be really exhilarating, even if your hands and feet are numb, your glasses are fogged, and you have hat head all the time.

✔ By the end of December, both cities usually offer enough snow and ice for all winter sports. Skaters at the artificially frozen rink in the **Bonsecours Basin** (Montréal's Old Port) are usually the first to hit the ice outdoors.

✔ Good food, not to mention drink, goes down that much better when you've worked up an appetite by braving the elements all day.

Lots of layers and defensive driving are the winter's watchwords:

✔ You need a hat, mittens, and a scarf — and not just as fashion accessories.

✔ Driving can be difficult. When it snows, roads become slippery or icy and visibility is poor.

Viewing Montréal's Calendar of Events

Montréal is definitely a four-season town — although one of its seasons can be brutally cold — so you get plenty of reasons to celebrate all year 'round.

January/February

Bundled-up kids celebrate the annual *Fête des Neiges* (literally, Snow Party) spread over three weekends in late January. The festival takes place on Île Ste. Hélène and features ice skating, ice sculptures, tube slides, dog sleds, mitten-making workshops, and more. Most activities are free of charge. For more information, visit www.fetedesneiges.com or call ☎ 514-872-6120.

The **Montréal High Lights Festival** is an adult version of the snow party, combining multimedia light shows, a performing arts program, and guest appearances by world-renowned chefs at the trendier downtown eateries. Visit www.montrealhighlights.com or call ☎ 888-477-9955 to see what else is cooking during these 11 days in February.

March

When the sap in Québec's maple trees starts to drip, it's **Sugaring-Off** time, and groups of friends and families flock to the countryside to visit sugar shacks where maple farmers boil the sap and make syrup. The main event on these excursions is a traditional meal in a mess hall where fresh maple syrup is used as a topping for everything — gulp, even fried pork fat. Back in town, outdoor stands at markets and on sidewalks sell *tire* (pronounced TEER), which is maple taffy that's made by ladling thick hot, unrefined syrup from a steaming caldron onto a bed of snow. When the syrup cools, you wrap the gooey stuff on a Popsicle stick and watch salivating kids devour it.

Everyone in Montréal is Irish on St. Patrick's Day, despite historic tensions between the English the French. Beginning at noon, thousands of onlookers line rue Ste-Catherine for Montréal's **St. Patrick's Day Parade,** a procession of floats, marching bands, and folk dancing. After the parade, the crowds get a little rowdy and roam the streets in search of green beer. The parade is the oldest and longest-running one of its kind in North America. For more info, not beer, visit Tourisme Montréal on the Web, www.tourisme-montreal.com.

May

The critically acclaimed biennial *Festival de théâtre des amériques* (☎ 514-842-0704 or www.fta.qc.ca) in Montréal offers two weeks of French-language theater productions from the Americas and Europe in odd-numbered years. Plays tend toward the edgy, and many make their North American debuts here.

Every year, the last Sunday of May in Montréal is **Museum Day.** Entry to select museums is free, as is a shuttle service running between them.

June

The **Formula One Grand Prix** makes its only Canadian stop at *Circuit Gilles Villeneuve* on Île Notre-Dame, where, at press time, homegrown F-1 hero Jacques Villeneuve has not finished a race on the track named after his father since his second place debut in 1996. In the weeklong festivities leading up to Sunday's race, fumes of motor oil and champagne mix freely on the main drags downtown. Call ☎ 514-350-4731 for more info or click on www.grandprix.ca for tickets on the hairpin turn.

The **Montréal Fringe Festival** offers off-off-Broadway type drama on boulevard St-Laurent — for ten days in the middle of the month. Call ☎ **514-849-3378** or visit www.montrealfringe.ca for more information. At the ***Mondial de la bière*** (World Beer Festival), visitors sample 250 liquid products, including beer, scotch, cider, and port, from around the world. It's one of the largest festivals of its kind on the continent (☎ **514-722-9640** or www.festivalmondialbiere.qc.ca).

The **Montréal International Jazz Festival** is the summer's main event. For two weeks, a boatload of international acts play free outdoor shows and world-class headliners top the bills at ticketed venues. Each year, well over a million and a half people swarm the downtown site of the festival, which takes place on the streets and parks surrounding *Place des Arts,* Montréal's main performing arts center. For information, visit www.jazzfest.com or call ☎ **514-523-3378.** At this time of year, it's always tough to choose between the Jazz Fest and the ***Mondial SAQ:* Montréal International Fireworks Competition.** The riverfront in Vieux-Montréal is an ideal place to watch the pyrotechnics, which go off at 10 p.m. every Saturday, from mid-June to late-July. For information, go to www.lemondialsaq.com or call ☎ **514-397-2000.**

July

For just a month, from mid-July to mid-August, a local theater troupe gives free outdoor presentations of the Bard's original plays during the annual **Shakespeare-in-the-Park.** Call ☎ **514-916-7275** for tickets or visit its Web site at www.shakespeareinthepark.ca for schedules. For ten days, right after the Jazz Fest, the ***Festival International Nuits d'Afrique*** (Nights of Africa Festival), showcases African and Caribbean musicians at paid venues downtown. *Nuits d'Afrique* is nearly two decades old, and by now, many of the greatest names in world music have participated. For info or tickets call ☎ **800-361-4505** or click on www.festivalnuitsdafrique.com.

Gory B-movies and improbable sci-fi action are the hallmarks of the **Fantasia Film Festival,** held in a state-of-the-art theater at Concordia University's downtown campus. Preview all the action at www.fastasiafest.com.

The **Just For Laughs Comedy Festival** in mid-July is another roaring success with locals and visitors alike. This outdoor festival has launched the likes of Jim Carrey, Ray Romano, and Tim Allen. It takes place on rue St-Denis south of rue Sherbrooke, where the scene turns into a veritable freak show, with clowns, street acts, and circus school students all vying for the attention of passers-by. Do your best not to end up as the victim of a gag on the festival's spin-off, candid-camera TV show. For further information, call ☎ **888-244-3155** or chuckle your way to www.hahaha.com.

Les FrancoFolies de Montréal is a two-week festival at the end of the July that features a bevy of French language musicians from across the planet. It takes place on the same site as the Jazz Festival (see the "June" section) and has a similar format, with a mix of free, outdoor, and paid indoor shows. For information, call ☎ **800-361-4595** or visit www.francofolies.com.

August

The Divers/Cité Festival is a weeklong celebration, early in the month, thrown by Montréal's gay community. It's capped off by the lesbian, gay, bisexual, and transgendered **Pride Parade** on the Sunday. It's an absolutely fab party, which has attracted 800,000 people in past years. For the lowdown, call ☎ **514-285-4011** or click on www. diverscite.org.

Tennis, anyone? Montréal hosts one-half of the **Tennis Masters Canada,** sharing it with Toronto. Each year, the women's and men's tournaments alternate between the cities. Because it's a warm-up for the U.S. Open, many top-ranked players make a show here. Call ☎ **514-275-1515** or click www.masters-series.com for your spot at center court. Mid-month, Park Maisonneuve, next to the Olympic Stadium, hosts *La Fête des enfants de Montréal* — a weekend festival for Montréal's kids. The information line is ☎ **514-872-0060.** Then, the **Molson Indy Montréal** (www.molsonindymontreal.com) brings another class of screaming racecars back to the Gilles Villeneuve track (also discussed in the "June" section). And if that's not fast track enough, movie stars and paparazzi descend on the city for the **World Film Festival,** which starts in late August and runs until the second week in September. Screenings, premiers, and parties abound. "What, I'm not on the list? Do *you* know who I am?" Crash the party by calling ☎ **514-848-3883** or click on www. ffm-montreal.org.

September/October

Warmly anticipated by Montréalers, cool weather brings the **Magic of Lanterns** to the Botanical Gardens, a dazzling annual display of over 700 handcrafted lanterns of silk and bamboo from Shanghai. For information, call ☎ **514-872-1400** or click on www2.ville.montreal.qc. ca/jardin/jardin.htm.

The **International New Dance Festival** is the highpoint of the Canadian modern dance community's annual calendar. The varied programming presents dance pieces that are daring and experimental. For information, call ☎ **514-287-1423** or click on www.find-lab.com.

Even more modern, the **Montréal International Festival of New Cinema and New Media** pushes the frontiers of high-tech art a little more each year, with its eclectic mix of provocative film and other digital arts. For more information, call ☎ **514-847-1242** or click on www.fcmm.com.

The Atwater Market's **Great Pumpkin Ball** is as close as Montréal gets to the Peanuts gang's *It's the Great Pumpkin, Charlie Brown*. In this case, kids see Pépo the Pumpkin in a play and meet Esmerelda, the Friendly Witch. For information, call ☎ **514-937-7754.**

Over 12,000 people of all persuasions attend the **Black and Blue Festival's Main Event,** an extravagant, mega-dance party with DJs and choreographed live performances, making it the largest AIDS benefit in the world. Everyone's there to dance into the wee hours of the morning for a good cause. For tickets and info, visit www.bbcm.org or call ☎ **514-875-7026.**

November

Mid-month, during the **Santa Claus Parade,** Montréalers bid *adieu* to the big guy just before he leaves for work in the North Pole. Yes, Santa spends his off-season in Montréal. Kids line up to watch the procession down rue Ste-Catherine, shivering with excitement until the very last float. For information, call ☎ **514-937-7754.** Montréal's documentary film festival, ***Rencontres internationales du documentaire de Montréal,*** takes place the last two weeks of the month, featuring the work of local, Canadian, and international documentary filmmakers. For information, visit www.ridm.qc.ca.

Checking Out Québec City's Calendar of Events

The fun doesn't end just because the temperatures are frigid. Some of the city's best events take place in the beginning of the year. But great events occur in the other seasons, too.

January/February

A red-sashed snowman known as the *Bonhomme du Carnaval* leads two weeks of festivities at the ***Carnaval de Québec.*** More than a million people brave the cold to join parades, concerts, and nightly winter balls in an ice palace. Many fortify themselves against cold with *caribou,* a Québec specialty consisting of red wine and pure alcohol, which in colonial times contained actual caribou blood. For information, call ☎ **418-626-3716** or visit www.carnaval.qc.ca.

March/April

Slurp up as much maple syrup as you can at the *cabanes à sucre* (sugar shacks) surrounding the city. In late April, the three-day *Festival de la Gastronomie de Québec/Coupe des nations* is a food-and-drink extravaganza and competition that showcases Québec's regional specialties. For more information, call ☎ **418-683-4150** or visit www. coupedesnations.com. **Images of the New World,** a pan-American film festival, screens over 100 short and feature-length films in Saint-Roch, a neighborhood just outside the Old City. For directions and more, **visit** www.festival-inm.com.

May

The *Manifestation international d'art de Québec,* a biennial exhibition taking place on the odd years (the next one is in 2005), showcases the newest and the best contemporary and multidisciplinary artists in Québec City. For more information, call ☎ **418-524-1917** or visit its bilingual site at www.meduse.org/manifestation.

June

June 24 is **St-Jean-Baptiste Day,** Québec's so-called national holiday. Named in honor of the province's patron saint, this holiday is taken very seriously in Québec City, which many Québeckers consider their "national" capital. For more information, call ☎ **418-640-0799** or visit www.snqc.qc.cq. The annual *Concours Hippique de Québec,* an equestrian event, takes place on the historic **Plains of Abraham,** where the French lost the decisive battle for their New World colonies. For more information, visit the event's Web site at www.concourshippique. quebecplus.ca.

July

The *Festival d'été de Québec,* held during the first two weeks of July, is one of the world's largest French-speaking cultural events, featuring more than 600 performers from 22 countries. For more information, call ☎ **888-992-5200** or visit www.infofestival.com. *Les grands feux,* a fireworks display choreographed to music, starts at the end of the month, on Wednesday and Saturday nights. For more information, call ☎ **800-923-3389** or visit its Web site at www.lesgrandsfeux.com.

August

The biennial *Festival des Troubadours et Saltimbanques* starts early in the month, but only in odd-numbered years. This medieval festival is a tip of the hat to the popular origins of street performance and public spectacle. For more information, call ☎ **418-622-3127** or visit its Web site at www.lefestival.info. The **Québec City International Festival of Military Bands,** an annual *tattoo* (military exhibition), gives marching bands a chance to perform somewhere other than parades and college football game halftimes. For information, call ☎ **418-694-5757** or visit www.fimmq.com.

September/October

When Québec's colorful autumn leaves start to fall, visitors lift their spirits with inspirational music at the **Québec Festival of Devotional Music,** which features internationally known gospel singers, Gregorian chanters, and a cappella groups. For information, call ☎ **418-525-9777** or visit its site at www.festivalmusiquesacree.ca.

Chapter 3

Planning Your Budget

* *

In This Chapter
▶ Making a budget

▶ Avoiding hidden expenses

▶ Finding ways to cut costs

▶ Deciding how to pay

* *

*O*n the whole, the living is easy in Montréal and Québec City. Like the French, Québeckers tend to consider eating at restaurants and going out more like a basic human right than a luxury. That attitude somehow keeps prices affordable. Plus, you can find plenty to do for free — strolling quaint streets, gazing at beautiful architecture, gawking at beautiful people. Factor in the still-favorable exchange rate for the U.S. dollar, and you have yourself a pretty amazing vacation for the money.

But there's a price to easy living throughout Québec: **steep taxes on sales and services.** Whenever you see a price, except on alcoholic beverages, add 15%. The other bit of bad news is that the value of the Canadian dollar is on the rise, making Canada less of a deal for you. At press time, C$1 was worth roughly US75¢.

Multicolored Canadian bills aren't like Monopoly money anymore, but you can still live it up here with limited damage to your pocketbook. The secret? Make yourself a travel budget and stick to it.

We give prices in this guide in both Canadian and U.S. dollars. To quickly calculate the U.S. equivalent of what you're paying, think of U.S. prices as about three quarters of the Canadian amount. So a C$40 meal is worth about US$30. A C$10 show is US$7.50. Remember the 15% sales tax, though, because until you get the hang of it, the tax will come back to haunt you every time you pull out your wallet.

Making a Budget

Planning a budget is a little bit like performing a juggling act. You have six vacation pins: accommodations, transportation, dining, attractions, shopping, and nightlife. You can't really afford to drop any of them (that is, unless you want to be truly Spartan), but you may want to throw some pins higher than others. First, decide ahead of time what's most important to you: Staying in a fine hotel? Eating gourmet meals? Hitting the chicest shops? After you set your priorities, look for ways to cut costs in other areas. To get you started, the following sections show you what to expect — and expect to pay — from each category of basic travel expenses.

Accommodations

Whether you like it or not, accommodations are your biggest expense. Before leaving on your trip, do your homework to find bargains and reserve rooms. Plan ahead, and you may save enough to stay another night! (See Chapter 6 for details on getting the best hotel deals.) The minimum you want to spend on accommodations per night is around C$100 ($75). Sure you can get better deals, but your comfort may be compromised.

Transportation

Here's an area where you can save. You don't need a car unless you want to take day trips around Montréal and Québec City. Driving in both cities can be a nightmare, and you don't need to put yourself through it. Québec's Old City is so small and compact you can walk everywhere. Montréal has a great **public transportation system,** with a subway that serves all major attractions, even the ones outside the city. A booklet of six tickets (valid for both buses and subway) costs C$10 (US$7.50) — less than the price of a single taxi ride across downtown.

If you're bent on **renting a car,** check Chapter 7 for details on getting a good rental deal. When you're doing your calculations, remember that gas is expensive in Canada. At press time, prices were at a summer holiday peak of C70¢/litre, or the equivalent of US$3.10/gallon. Nothing on the nightly news suggests prices will be dropping any time this century.

Montréal and Québec City (outside of the Old City) have an abundance of **taxis** that are easy to flag in case you're too tired to walk back to your hotel. Just find a busy street and raise your arm.

See Chapter 5 for ways to save on your trip to and from Montréal or Québec City. Booking your travel arrangements well in advance is one sure way to save money. Researching and comparing the prices of lots of different fare options, like discount airlines, seat-sales, courier fares, or flying standby, is another. Usually both of these factor into what you pay.

Dining

Dining is probably not the place to trim the fat in your budget. Look at it this way: Eating out in Montréal and Québec City is an entertaining, potentially evening-long activity. Splurge at the dinner table, and you won't need to spend money on entertainment for the rest of the night. With a little planning, you won't need to bust the bank to satisfy your palate, either. We suggest eating a big breakfast, then cutting back on lunch, either by grabbing a sandwich at a cafe or picnicking in a park.

You can get inexpensive lunches at many ethnic eateries for C$10 (US$7.50) per person. Prices at fast food restaurants are comparable to U.S. prices, so just factor in the exchange rate. See Chapters 10 and 17 for recommendations. In the evening, most fine restaurants offer a *table d'hôte* (also called a *menu*) that's usually a good deal with prices ranging from C$20 to C$65 (US$14–US$47) for a meal, not including drinks. For the higher-end places, expect to spend from C$30 to C$100 (US$23–US$75) per person for a complete dinner, including drinks.

Attractions

The adult admission price for most museums and attractions is between C$10 and C$12 (US$7.50–US$9). Pricier attractions like La Ronde set you back about C$28 (US$21) and C$17 (US$13) for kids under 12. Kids under 6 get into most attractions for free. See Chapters 11 and 18 for exact prices in each city.

Shopping

Shopping in Montréal and Québec City can be hazardous to your budget. With so much great stuff to buy — from clothes to art to home decorations — the abundance of merchandise may make you lose your perspective, not to mention your senses. We recommend that you give yourself a shopping allowance before you leave home, either a daily one, a weekly one, or one that's for the whole trip (if you're disciplined and do your accounting regularly). If shopping isn't your thing, you can save big bucks in this department.

Nightlife

Nightlife is another area where money can disappear before you know it. But you can indulge inexpensively. The cheapest time to visit a bar is during happy hour, or *cinq à sept,* as it's called in Québec. (The expression "five to seven" refers to the early evening hours, not the number of drinks you get for one price!) Drinks usually range between C$5 (US$4) and C$8 (US$6).

Tickets for shows start at C$10 (US$7.50) and go up to C$100 (US$75) for prime seats. The cabaret show at the Montréal casino costs C$39 (US$25). Movie prices range from C$9 (US$7) to C$13 (US$10). For details on the prices of outings, see Chapters 13 and 20.

Watching Out for Hidden Expenses

Planning a travel budget is like renovating a house. It always ends up costing more than you think. Both endeavors are laden with temptations. Trust us, if you're setting out to be a Spartan traveler, Montréal and Québec City will test your willpower. To help you stick to your budget, keep in mind the tips in the following sections.

Taxes

When you see a price, add approximately 15%. Canada's *Goods and Services Tax* (*Taxe de produits et services* or TPS in Québec) is 7% and applies to everything but alcoholic beverages. Québec's *Provincial Sales Tax* (TVQ) slaps another 7.5% on top of that.

Non-Canadians can get a refund on the GST/TPS if it adds up to more than C$14 (US$10) in tax or C$200 (US$144) in hotel bills. But unless you're an amateur accountant, the paperwork may prove to be more of a hassle than it's worth. Just make sure you keep original receipts. If you want to go after the refund, pick up a copy of the booklet "Tax Refund for Visitors to Canada" at duty-free shops, hotels, and tourist offices. Complete and submit the forms with your original receipts within a year of the purchases. Note that you have to attach your original boarding pass or travel ticket to the application. Complete instructions are available on the Canada Customs Web site: `www.ccra-adrc.gc.ca/tax/nonresidents/visitors/tax-e.html`.

Tipping

To tip or not to tip, and how much? These are the eternal questions when you find yourself in a strange land. In Québec, tipping waiters between 10 and 15 percent is the norm, and taxi drivers usually expect

10%. For bellhops, C$1 (US75¢) or C$2 (US$1.50) per bag does the trick. For hotel housekeeping, count C$1 (US75¢) per person per day. For valet parking, C$1 or C$2 (US75¢–US$1.50).

In restaurants, remember that you're tipping on the total price *before* taxes, not the total on the bottom of the bill. There's an easy trick to calculate a 15% tip. Just add up taxes, the TPS and TVQ, that appear above the total on the bill and equal 15% of the bill's subtotal.

Cutting Costs Painlessly

A little foresight and planning are all you need to cut down on your basic travel expenses. Follow these tips so that you can free up some extra funds for a shopping spree or a wild night on the town.

- ✔ **Go in the off-season.** You get better deals when you travel at non-peak times between November and April. For winter trips, avoid the Christmas season, New Year's Eve, and the school March break.

- ✔ **Travel midweek.** Flights are cheaper on Tuesdays, Wednesdays, and Thursdays. When you book your flight, ask which days have the best rates.

- ✔ **Check out package tours.** You may get airfare, hotel, and even ground transportation and attractions for less if you buy them all at once, through a packager. See Chapter 5 for details on finding package deals.

- ✔ **Reserve a room with a kitchen.** Doing a bit of cooking is an easy way to save on your food budget. Grab some basic food items, cereal, coffee, bread, and milk at a *dépanneur* (corner store) near your hotel. Make some sandwiches before you leave in the morning so that you can afford to splurge on some serious gastronomy in the evening.

- ✔ **Ask for discounts.** You may be eligible for deals and not know it. Membership in AAA, frequent flyer plans, trade unions, AARP, or other groups may qualify you for savings on hotels, airfare, car rentals, and meals. It never hurts to ask.

- ✔ **Bunk with your kids.** A room with two double beds usually doesn't cost more than one with a queen-size bed. Many hotels won't charge you extra if you put your little angels (usually under age 12) in the extra bed. If they do charge a surplus, it's still cheaper than renting another room. Fees for rollaway beds are usually C$10 to C$15 (US$7.50–US$12) per day.

- ✔ **Use ATMs.** Exchange rates are better when you withdraw Canadian cash directly from an automatic teller. In the unlikely case you have to ask around to find an ATM (they're everywhere), they're are called *guichets automatiques* in the province of Québec (pronounced GEE-shay o-to-ma-TEECK).

> While the exchange rate is good, the banking networks involved charge a fixed fee for the transaction. Find out from your bank what fee it charges you to withdraw on your ATM card abroad. You can absorb and limit this amount best by making a few larger withdrawals, rather than by many withdrawals for smaller amounts.
>
> ✔ **Stay away from exchange bureaus.** They charge a 1% commission or a minimum of C$3 (US$2.15) to exchange cash. Avoid them if you can.

Paying Up

Should you spend cash? Credit? Travelers checks? This section explains the pros and cons of the various options.

Cashing in with good 'ol greenbacks

Is there a place on earth that doesn't accept or exchange U.S. dollars? If there is, we've never seen it. But use them only if you're in a pinch. You get less bang for your buck when doing a cash exchange in a retail shop, because on most cash transactions, the exchange rate can be up to 10% higher for cash transactions. So one Canadian dollar would cost you US85¢ instead of US75¢. However you won't have any problem exchanging your greenbacks in Québec. Every major bank has an exchange service. Just walk in and ask. The exchange rate will be just, but not as good as using your ATM card. For details on the major banks in Québec, see the Appendix.

It's always a good idea to arrive in a foreign country with some local currency, even in Canada. Montréal's airport has a handy currency exchange desk situated to your right when you exit the baggage claim area into the waiting area. The rates here are as good, or slightly better, than you get at the bank. But who knows, you may be faced with a long line, the desk may not be open when you arrive, or you may be in a hurry to catch a cab. You can avoid a potentially stressful situation by exchanging $100 U.S. into Canadian funds at your bank at home before you leave.

Going for the guichet

All Québec banks have ATMs, called *guichets automatiques* (see the "Cutting Costs Painlessly" section for details on ATMs). User fees can be as high as C$1.50 (US$1.10), and you may be charged other fees on top, but you can absorb them best by withdrawing a chunk of money at a time. Almost all ATMs in Canada are linked to **Cirrus** (☎ 800-424-7787; www.mastercard.com/atms) or **Plus** (☎ 800-843-7587; www.visa.com/atms). You select the amount you want to withdraw in

Canadian funds, so do a quick conversion first to know the worth of what you're withdrawing. Despite the additional fees, the amount is deducted from your account at home at roughly the same rate you get from the bank.

 The main advantage of ATMs is that they are convenient. You get roughly the same rate of exchange you get at the counter of the bank, but at the bank, you're charged both a fee of up to C$3 (US$2.15) at the Canadian bank and whatever fee your local bank charges for withdrawing from an ATM. Check the fees for withdrawals from foreign ATMs before you leave.

The major banks in Montréal and Québec City and the bank-card system they honor are as follows:

- ✔ Bank of Montréal: Cirrus
- ✔ Banque Nationale du Canada: Cirrus
- ✔ Caisse populaire Desjardins: Plus
- ✔ CIBC: Plus
- ✔ Royal Bank of Canada: Cirrus and Plus
- ✔ Scotia Bank: Cirrus

Going the debit card route

You can also debit your bank account for retail transactions. You have to use a debit card and type your PIN into a small machine at the cash register. The debit system is widely used in Canada and considered safe. In some restaurants, waiters even bring hand-held debit machines to your table so you don't have to get up to type your PIN at the register. Note that most U.S. banks charge an extra fee for purchases made in Canada. Check with your local bank before leaving.

Using credit cards

Credit cards are an invaluable resource for any traveler. Don't leave home without at least one. Why? You can do anything with them: pay for hotels and restaurants, shop, authorize deposits if you rent something, and even get cash advances. They are your trusted back-up in case you have a problem with your cash supply. Stash an extra credit card in your suitcase.

Carrying traveler's checks

Traveler's checks are a dying breed of currency — but they're not extinct yet. If they make you feel more secure about your funds, by all means buy some. You can get them from any major bank. You can still use them as payment in many places — or redeem them for cash. Traveler's checks can be replaced if they are lost or stolen, so be sure to store a record of their serial numbers in a separate place. But these days, you're probably better off having an extra credit card stashed somewhere in your luggage.

American Express offers traveler's checks in denominations of C$10, C$20, C$50, C$100, and C$1,000. You pay a service charge ranging from 1% to 4%, although AAA members can obtain checks without paying any fee. You can also get **American Express** travelers check over the phone by calling ☎ **800-221-7282.** For addresses of American Express offices in Montréal and Québec City, see the Appendix.

Visa (☎ **800-732-1322**) also offers traveler's checks, available at Citibank locations across the country and at several other banks. The service charge ranges between 1.5% and 2%. **MasterCard** has its hand in the traveler's check market, too; call ☎ **800-223-9920** for details.

Dealing with money emergencies

Losing your wallet while traveling is everyone's worst nightmare, but you don't need to panic if it happens to you. Rule number one: Keep your cool. If someone else makes a purchase with your stolen card, the credit card company should cover the amount, as long as you've reported your card stolen.

Report a lost or stolen card as soon as you realize it's gone, so that fraudulent use of it won't be charged to your account. On the other hand, don't jump the gun. If you cancel the card and it turns up in the back pocket of those jeans you wore last night, it will be worth no more to you than the plastic it's made of. Expect to wait two days for a credit card company to ship you an emergency card. If you need cash to get you by until then, the credit card company can wire you a cash advance. Every credit card company has a toll-free number you can call to report a lost or stolen card. In Canada, these numbers are: **American Express** ☎ **800-268-9824, Diners Club** ☎ **800-336-8472, MasterCard** ☎ **800-826-2181,** and **Visa** ☎ **800-336-8472.**

Ever wondered how you report a stolen card when you can't remember your number? Not an easy task. Keep a sheet of paper with emergency numbers on it somewhere in your luggage and leave it at the hotel when you're out. That way, if you need to report stolen cards or ID, you have the numbers handy and can make the calls quickly.

Chapter 4

Tips for Travelers with Special Needs

* *

In This Chapter

▶ Surviving the trip with your pint-sized travelers

▶ Savoring refined pleasures if you're a senior traveler

▶ Overcoming disabilities on the road

▶ Living it up in gay Québec

* *

Montréal and Québec City are about as open-minded and welcoming as cities get. The fun factor is spread out across all groups, whether you're traveling with a family, you qualify for senior discounts, you travel with a disability, or you're a gay or lesbian traveler.

Advice for Families

Montréal is a safe, clean, relatively inexpensive city full of fun things for kids to do. And while Québec City is hardly Disney World, you can find plenty of activities and sights that interest kids, and the city is well organized to accommodate families.

Here are a few tips to keep in mind when you're planning your kid-friendly trip:

✔ **Find out what your kids want to do.** Look for kid-friendly activities before you travel and let the kids get in on the action by having them check Web sites, read brochures, and, well, dream of adventures to come.

✔ **Surf the Web for ideas.** Check out www.montreal.com for lists of kids' activities. The Montréal-based site www.yikeskids.com has an Ask the Experts link, where you can ask a local expert about entertaining little ones. Québec City's tourism site (www.quebecregion.com) doesn't have a specific kids section, but ask your kids to let you know what appeals to them.

✔ **Play up the history.** From bayonets and epic battles to fancy frocks and horse-drawn carriages, Montréal and Québec City have plenty of historical aspects that set kids' imaginations on fire.

✔ **Locate kid-friendly establishments.** Throughout this book, we identify kid-friendly hotels (see Chapters 9 and 16), restaurants (see Chapters 10 and 17), and attractions (see Chapters 11 and 18) with the Kid Friendly icon.

✔ **Visit tourism centers.** In Montréal, the **Infotouriste Centre** is downtown at 1000 Square-Dorchester (☎ **800-266-5687** or 514-873-2015). In Québec City, the **Bureau d'information touristique** is in the Old City at 835 av. Wilfrid-Laurier (☎ **418-649-2608**). Both centers distribute free **Official Tourist Guides** with special sections on activities for kids.

✔ **Have a Plan B.** As far as the weather goes, the only certainty is uncertainty. Abrupt rain cancellations can definitely send kids into a tailspin, so plan activities for rain, shine, heat, and cold. Plan indoor activities, like museums, on rainy days, for cold relief in winter, or when you need to avoid the noonday heat in summer. Outdoor activities like in-line skating or amusement parks are best in late afternoon or early evening.

✔ **Have a little talk about language before you leave.** Older kids may be miffed when they don't understand what people around them are saying. Explain that most people in Québec speak French and teach them a few words. *Bonjour* and *au revoir* will probably do (or check out the Cheat Sheet at the front of this book). You can turn it into a game and pick up a few words yourself.

Traveling with kids can be a riot, but sometimes it actually turns into one. If you want to leave the kids behind for a day — in trustworthy hands — some hotels offer baby-sitting services. Ask at the front desk. The **Montréal YMCA,** downtown on rue Stanley, offers educational day care for kids 18 months to 5 years (☎ **514-849-8393** or click on www. ymca.ca).

Advice for Seniors

Montréal and Québec City are both great cities for refined pleasures like fine dining and visiting museums and galleries. And, of course, if you're not in the mood for culture, you can always head to the Montréal Casino.

You can find plenty of bargains if you know where to look. Both Air Canada and the charter company Air Transat offer discounts for seniors, as do American Airlines, United Airlines, and US Airways. Most museums and attractions offer seniors' discounts, too. To get the best deals, join **AARP** (formerly the American Association of Retired Persons;

☎ **800-424-3410;** www.aarp.org). For a mere US$12.50 a year, you get discounts on airlines, car rentals, cruises, entertainment, hotels, tours, and more.

For the tech-savvy senior, a growing number of Internet sites can point you in the direction of travel deals. Like many a Web site, though, they come and go, so the best strategy is to type **senior travel** into the Google search site (www.google.com) and see what you come up with. Check out www.seniortravel.com for links to destinations and packages for seniors (☎ **800-564-3148**). You can also visit the Web site of *Travel Tips* magazine (www.traveltipsmagazine.com) for advice on traveling and on finding deals.

Several Canadian tour companies offer organized holidays for seniors. In Montréal, **Prométour Cultural Tours** is located in Vieux-Montréal (☎ **514-848-0766**). In Québec City, **Groupe Voyages Québec** is located right in the thick of it on Grande Allée (☎ **800-463-1598** or 418-525-4585).

If you need help or advice finding senior services, contact the **Fédération de l'age d'or du Québec** (Québec Golden Age Federation) in Montréal (☎ **514-252-3154**).

Advice for Travelers with Disabilities

Canada is a world leader in promoting the rights of people with disabilities. If you or someone in your party is traveling with a disability, you can find loads of resources and services to make your trip as hassle-free and fun as possible.

Worldwide resources

Check out *A World of Options,* a 658-page book with resources for disabled travelers. It is available from **Mobility International USA,** P.O. Box 19767, Eugene OR, 97440 (☎ **541-343-1284** voice and TTY; www.miusa.org).

Visit the Internet site of **Access-Able Travel Source** (www.access-able.com), which provides names and addresses of travel agents who specialize in disabled travel, as well as information on accessible destinations around the world. The Web site www.disabilitytravelexperts.com also has recommendations.

Vision-impaired travelers should contact the **American Foundation for the Blind,** 11 Penn Plaza, Suite 300, New York, NY 10001 (☎ **800-232-5463**).

Canadian resources

While visiting Montréal and Québec City, you may also seek the support of or information from these national sources.

Abilities Magazine is Canada's best magazine on disability lifestyles issues. The magazine's Web site, www.enablelink.org, offers links to a wide range of services in Canada for persons with disabilities.

The Active Living Alliance for Canadian with a Disability can direct you to resources and services in Canada (☎ **800-771-0663** or 613-244-0052).

Local resources

The best resource for disabled travel in Québec is an organization called **Kéroul.** Check out its tourism guide, *Accessible Québec,* for lists of accessible attractions. The group also provides travel packages for travelers with disabilities and a database of accessible places in the province (☎ **514-252-3104** or click on www.keroul.qc.ca).

Québec's **Recreation Association for People with Disabilities** (*Association québécoise pour le loisir des personnes handicappées*) also provides information on accessible leisure activities (☎ **514-252-3144** or click on www.aqlph.qc.ca).

Most large hotels in both cities have some accessible rooms, so call around. The **Hyatt Regency Montréal** (formerly the Wyndam Hotel), 1255 Jeanne-Mance, (☎ **514-285-1450**) in downtown Montréal provides information on its facilities for disabled travelers.

Also consider:

- ✔ Montréal Association for the Blind at ☎ **514-488-0043.**
- ✔ Office for Persons with Disabilities: In Québec City, call ☎ **800-567-1465.** In Montréal, call ☎ **888-873-3905.**
- ✔ West Island Association for the Intellectually Handicapped. In Montréal, call ☎ **514-694-7722.**
- ✔ Québec Society for Disabled Children at ☎ **514-937-6171.**
- ✔ **Access to Travel** (www.accesstotravel.qc.ca): This organization provides information on wheelchair-accessible transport in Québec.

Support while traveling to either city

In this section, we include the organization to call while traveling to and from Montréal and Québec City.

Air Canada (☎ 899-247-2262) and **Air Transat** (☎ 877-872-6782) offer wheelchair-accessible service.

Greyhound buses (☎ 800-661-8747) and **Orléans Express** (☎ 514-395-4000) offer wheelchair-accessible bus service between Montréal and Québec City.

Via Rail offers wheelchair-accessible service on some of its routes, but you have to reserve in advance (☎ 888-842-7245).

Support while traveling within cities

Montréal's transit commission has 456 low-floor, wheelchair-accessible buses on over 40 routes in the city (☎ 514-280-5100). Despite the good intentions of the public transport system, however, the buses are not actually that accessible, especially during peak periods.

Paratransit in Montréal offers free wheelchair-accessible minivan service, but you have to apply for the right to use it (☎ 514-280-8211). You can get the application from its Web site at www.stcum.qc.ca/ English/t-adapte/a-index.htm. Apply two months in advance. For wheelchair-accessible taxis, call **Taxi Boisjoli** (☎ 514-255-2815).

In Québec City, **Paratransit** also offers free wheelchair-accessible minibus service, but as in Montréal, you need to reserve in advance. Call ☎ 418-687-2641 several days before your departure to register for services. Note that these are public transportation services, and you may wait up to eight hours for your minibus.

Advice for Gay and Lesbian Travelers

Québeckers have an extremely tolerant attitude towards gay and lesbian travelers. This is a country where gays and lesbians can legally marry, after all. The gay community in Montréal is one of the largest in the world, and the city even has its own Gay Chamber of Commerce and a Gay Village Merchants Association. For a list of gaycentric activities, events, and accommodations, click on www.montrealplus.ca. In Québec City, you find fewer services and resources for the gay and lesbian communities, but that's because it's a smaller city, not because people are uptight.

The Montréal scene

According to Tourism Québec, Montréal's gay tourism industry is the third biggest draw to the city, after the Grand Prix and the Jazz Festival. With its circuit of bars, clubs, restaurants, boutiques, antiques shops, discos, bath houses, and more, there's plenty of action. Montréal's Gay Village runs along rue Ste-Catherine between rue Berri and rue Papineau, in gritty, but vibrant, south-central downtown.

Places to stay

Gay Village offers plenty of gay-friendly hotels and inns. For lesbians, there's **Pension Vallières,** 6562 rue de Lorimier (☎ **514-729-9552**), an all-women hotel. For men, there's the **Auberge Cosy,** 1274 rue Ste-Catherine Est (☎ **514-525-2151;** www.aubergecosy.com), **Bed & Breakfast du Village,** 1281 rue Montcalm (☎ **888-228-8455;** in Montréal, 514-522-4771; www.bbv.qc.ca), or **Le Chasseur B&B,** 1567 rue St-André (☎ **514-521-2238;** www.lechasseur.com).

Places to eat

Gay Village also has no shortage of great restaurants. We recommend **Area,** 1429 rue Amherst (☎ **514-890-6691**), for fine French cuisine and **Bazou,** 1310 bd. de Maisonneuve Est (☎ **514-526-4940**), for refined fare in a quirky "haute" flea market setting — where you can bring your own wine. Check out **La Piazetta,** 1101 rue Ste-Catherine Est (☎ **514-526-2244**), for good thin-crust pizza.

Bars and clubs

The hot spots of the moment in the gay village are **Sky Complex,** 1474 rue Ste-Catherine Est (☎ **514-529-6969**), and **Stereo,** 858 rue Ste-Catherine Est (☎ **514-286-0300**), which opens late and carries on until the next morning. You can also find dozens of clubs and bars just by walking around the Village at night.

Special events

The big yearly events in the gay and lesbian community are Montréal's **Gay Pride Parade,** which takes place at the beginning of August (call ☎ **514-285-4011** for info; visit www.diverscite.org/anglais/index.htm for info and tickets); the gay and lesbian film festival, **Image+Nation,** in September (visit www.image-nation.org for info only; no tickets); and the **Black and Blue Festival,** the world's largest gay and lesbian benefit event, in October (visit www.bbcm.org for info only; no tickets).

The Québec City scene

In Québec City, the gay community is centered on rue St-Jean, between rue Dufferin and rue St-Augustin, just outside the walls of the Old City. For accommodations, the most famous inn is **Le 253,** 253 rue de la Reine (☎ **418-647-0590**). Other good options are **Le Coureur des Bois,** 15 rue Ste.-Ursule (☎ **418-692-1117**) and **Guest House 727,** 727 rue d'Aiguillon (☎ **418-648-6766**).

Part II
Ironing Out the Details

The 5th Wave   By Rich Tennant

In this part . . .

Your planning is not quite over, but in this part, we give you the information you need to finish the job. This part tells you how to get to Montréal and Québec City, focusing especially on airfare deals. We explain how to choose your hotel and book your room, detail what kind of travel insurance you need, give you information on car rentals, tell you what to reserve ahead of time, and even let you know what to pack in your bag.

Chapter 5

Getting to Montréal and Québec City

In This Chapter

▶ Deciding whether to use a travel agent

▶ Choosing a package or escorted tour

▶ Making travel arrangements without any assistance

*Y*ou've made up your mind. You're ready for some Old World romance in the New World. The hardest decision is over, but you still have some work to do before you kick back on a sidewalk cafe and sip a glass of chardonnay. This chapter guides you through your options and helps you figure out whether to buy a package vacation or go on your own.

Finding a Good Travel Agent

A good travel agent is like a good mechanic or good plumber: hard to find, but invaluable when you locate the right one. The best way to find a good travel agent is the same way you find a good plumber or mechanic or doctor — word of mouth.

To get the most out of a travel agent, do a little homework. Read up on your destination (you've already made a sound decision by buying this book) and pick out some accommodations and attractions that appeal to you. If you have access to the Internet, check prices on the Web yourself (see the "Getting the cheapest airfare" section later in this chapter) to get a sense of ballpark figures. Then take this guidebook and Web information to the travel agent and ask him or her to make the arrangements for you. Because they have access to more resources than even the most complete travel Web site, travel agents generally can get you a better price than you can get by yourself. And they can issue your tickets and vouchers right at the agency. If they can't get you into the hotel of your choice, they can recommend an alternative, and you can look for an objective review in this guidebook.

Most travel agents work on commission. The good news is that you don't pay the commission — the airlines, accommodations, and tour companies do. The bad news is that unscrupulous travel agents will try to persuade you to book the vacations that nab them the most money in commissions. Over the past few years, many airlines and resorts have begun to limit or eliminate these commissions altogether. The immediate result has been that travel agents don't bother booking certain services unless the customer specifically requests them. (And some travel agents have started charging customers for their services.) To find an agent you can trust, ask around.

So how do you find an agent who can help you plan a memorable trip? Here are a few suggestions:

- ✔ **Get a reference.** The best place to start looking is in your own address book. Ask friends and family for recommendations.

- ✔ **Phone local travel agencies.** Ask about the destinations in which they specialize, or ask them to recommend an agency that knows your destination. Some agencies specialize in business travel, others in resort-type holidays, and others in international travel.

- ✔ **Call ASTA.** If all else fails, the American Society of Travel Agents (☎ 703-739-2782; www.astanet.com) is the organization to call. Tell ASTA where you live and where you want to go, and the organization can recommend an agent in your area.

Considering Escorted or Package Tours

Say the words, "escorted tour" or "package tour," and you may automatically feel as though you're being forced to choose: Your money or your lifestyle. Think again. Times — and tours — have changed.

An **escorted tour** does, in fact, involve an escort, but that doesn't mean it has to be dull — or even tame. You do, however, travel with a group, which may be just the thing if you're single and want company. In general, your costs are taken care of after you arrive at your destination, but you still have to cover the airfare.

Which brings us to **package tours.** Unlike escorted tours, these generally package costs rather than people. Some companies bundle every aspect of your trip, including tours to various sights, but most deal just with selected aspects, allowing you to get good deals by putting together an airfare and hotel arrangement, say, or an airfare and greens fee package. Most packages tend to leave you a lot of leeway, while saving you a lot of money.

How do you find these deals? Well, we suggest some strategies in the two following sections, but every city is different; the tour operators we mention may not offer deals convenient from your city. If that's the case, check with local travel agents: They generally know the most options close to home and know how best to put together escorted tours and airline packages.

Joining an escorted tour

You may be one of the many people who loves escorted tours. The tour company takes care of all the details and tells you what to expect at each leg of your journey. You know your costs up front and, in the case of the tamer tours, you don't get many surprises. Escorted tours can take you to the maximum number of sights in the minimum amount of time with the least amount of hassle. Many escorted tours to Montréal and Québec City also include other Canadian cities, like Toronto and Ottawa, or other regions, like Eastern Canada.

If you decide to go with an escorted tour, we strongly recommend purchasing travel insurance, especially if the tour operator asks to you pay up front. But don't buy insurance from the tour operator! If the tour operator doesn't fulfill its obligation to provide you with the vacation you paid for, you have no reason to believe that the operator will fulfill its insurance obligations, either. Get travel insurance through an independent agency. (We tell you more about the ins and outs of travel insurance in Chapter 7.)

When choosing an escorted tour, along with finding out whether you have to put down a deposit and when final payment is due, ask a few simple questions before you buy:

- ✔ **What is the cancellation policy?** Can the tour company cancel the trip if it doesn't get enough people? How late can you cancel if you're unable to go? Do you get a refund if you cancel? What if the tour group cancels?

- ✔ **How jam-packed is the schedule?** Does the tour schedule try to fit 25 hours into a 24-hour day, or does it give you ample time to relax by the pool or shop? If getting up at 7 a.m. every day and not returning to your hotel until 6 or 7 at night sounds like a grind, certain escorted tours may not be for you.

- ✔ **How large is the group?** The smaller the group, the less time you spend waiting for people to get on and off the bus. Tour operators may be evasive about this, because they may not know the exact size of the group until everybody has made reservations, but they should be able to give you a rough estimate.

✔ **Is there a minimum group size?** Some tours have a minimum group size and may cancel the tour if it doesn't book enough people. If a quota exists, find out what it is and how close the tour company is to reaching it. Again, tour operators may be evasive in their answers, but the information may help you select a tour that's sure to happen.

✔ **What exactly is included?** Don't assume anything. You may have to pay to get yourself to and from the airport. A box lunch may be included in an excursion, but drinks may be extra. Beer may be included but not wine. How much flexibility do you have? Can you opt out of certain activities, or does the bus leave once a day, with no exceptions? Are all your meals planned in advance? Can you choose your entree at dinner, or does everybody get the same chicken cutlet?

Finding escorted and package tours

The travel section of your local Sunday paper lists many of the deals available. Check ads in national travel magazines like *Travel & Leisure, National Geographic Traveler,* and *Condé Nast Traveler.* Big hotel chains and airlines also offer packages.

Some of the following companies offer both package and escorted tours. Normally, a travel agent books these packages, but you can call or visit the company Web sites on your own, too. Remember that some agencies have better reputations than others; your travel agent, if you have one, can guide you. Transportation to and from airports is often included but is sometimes optional.

✔ **Air Canada Vacations (☎ 800-254-1000;** www.aircanada.ca/vacations/canada) is the largest carrier flying into Montréal. It offers lots of options for visiting both cities, separately or together, including escorted tours, independent packages, fly/drive tours, ski holidays, and more. This is a great place to start.

✔ **Colette Tours (☎ 800-340-5158;** www.colettetours.com) offers three-, four-, and five-day getaways to Québec City, Montréal, or both cities, including accommodations, dinner at local restaurants, and city tours. Longer city tours of Eastern Canada also offer stops in Montréal and Québec City.

✔ **Continental Airlines Vacations (☎ 800-301-3800;** www.covacations.com) offers separate packages to Montréal and Québec City, with hotel and airfare included and car rental optional. This is a good option if you like fancy hotels, because its packages include accommodations in upscale hotels.

Cruising into Québec City

Some Eastern seaboard cruises now offer stops in Québec City, which is one of the only cities in North America where the most interesting neighborhood — the Old City — is right beside the port, although you have to walk a little ways to reach it. Trouble is, you won't get to stay long. The cruise liners dock right at the foot of Québec City's cliff. When you get out of the ship yards, you're in the heart of Basse-Ville (Lower City). See Part IV for details on what you can do when you get off the ship.

✔ **Gogo Worldwide Vacations** (☎ **800-299-2999** or 702-457-1615; www.vacations.gofox.com) offers two- or three-night stays in Montréal and Québec City and cruises that pass through one or both ports. The short-stay packages do not include airfare, but they offer a good choice of hotels. Most of the packages are targeted to specific tastes and preferences, including casino admission, sightseeing, and admission to historical and cultural attractions, depending on what you're into. This company accepts reservation from U.S. and Canadian travel agents only.

✔ **Yankee Holidays** (☎ 800-225-2550 or 978-922-4819; www.yankee-holidays.com) offers vacation packages of mainly of the two-day, three-night variety to both cities. Packages are targeted toward specific interests and can include museum passes, show tickets, gourmet meals, sightseeing tours, and festival admissions. The activity options are more limited in Québec City. Airfare is not included.

Making Your Own Arrangements

The biggest plus to making your own travel arrangements is flexibility. Your trip feels more like an adventure. You can be spontaneous. You can have more contact with the locals. Some people like that, some people don't. We encourage it, not only because we *are* locals, but because the rest of the locals are so vivacious and charming, that you'll enjoy the experience. There's no real need to worry about language. Almost everyone who works in tourism in Québec speaks some English. Our only advice? Pump a little iron before your trip so you can gesticulate to the max. You may need to use your arms to make yourself understood.

If you want to go it on your own, the following sections help you with the basics.

Flying into town

Montréal's recently renamed **Pierre Elliott Trudeau International Airport** (☎ 800-465-1213 or 514-394-7377) is your likely point of entry. A 20-minute drive from downtown, it's served by most of the world's major airlines, including Air Canada (☎ 888-247-2262), American (☎ 800-433-7300), Continental (☎ 800-231-0856), Delta (☎ 800-221-1212), and US Airways (☎ 800-432-9768). For a complete list of airlines flying into Montréal, see the Appendix. If you're flying with a charter company, you may arrive at **Mirabel Airport,** a 45-minute drive from Montréal. Taxis shuttle services are available from both airports to downtown Montréal.

Québec City's **Jean-Lesage International Airport** (☎ 418-640-2700) is served by a number of major airlines, including Air Canada, but most of the traffic passes through Montréal first. Only Air Canada and Continental offer direct flights from other airports.

Getting the cheapest airfare

Competition among the major U.S. airlines is unlike that of any other industry. Every airline offers virtually the same product (basically, a coach seat is a coach seat is a coach seat), yet prices can vary by hundreds of dollars.

Business travelers pay the premium rate for airfare because they need to leave on precise days and precise times, and because they make last-minute changes as often as they change their clothes. Everyone else can save money by planning far in advance, committing to your departure date and following these tips:

- ✔ **Buy your ticket early.** Purchase your ticket 14 to 21 days in advance, and you only pay a fraction of the full fare.

- ✔ **Fly midweek.** Rates are lower if you leave on Tuesdays, Wednesdays, or Thursdays and stay over a Saturday night.

- ✔ **Look for seat sales.** All major airlines have promotions when the rates on their most popular routes plummet. It's all happens rather randomly, so it can be hard to plan your trip months in advance if you're counting on a seat sale. But you never know. Seat sales are advertised in the travel section of your paper. Travel agents know about them and you can call airlines directly and ask. Watch out for catches, like non-refundable tickets and penalties for changing dates.

- ✔ **Try a consolidator.** These companies (also called *bucket shops*) advertise in the travel section of major newspapers. They buy seats in bulk and resell them at discounted rates. The tickets are usually non-refundable. Always ask for a confirmation number and call the airline to confirm your seat.

Some of the better known consolidators are:

- **Council Travel** (☎ **800-226-8642**; www.counciltravel.com)
- **FLY-CHEAP** (☎ **800-359-2432**; www.1800flycheap.com)
- **Travel Bargains** (☎ **800-247-3273**; www.1800airfare.com)

Consolidator tickets are usually nonrefundable or rigged with stiff cancellation penalties, often as high as 50% to 75% of the ticket price, and some put you on charter airlines with questionable safety records.

Finding deals on the Web

Booking tickets online has definitely gone mainstream, and you can surf oodles of sites to find tickets. Among the best known ones are **Arthur Frommer's Budget Travel Online** (www.frommers.com), **Travelocity** (www.travelocity.com), **Orbitz** (www.orbitz.com) **Lowestfare** (www.lowestfare.com), **Smarter Living** (www.smarterliving.com), and **Travel One** (www.travelone.com). For Canadian departures, there's **Expedia** (www.expedia.ca).

Somehow, the do-it-yourself method of booking tickets online makes you feel as though you're getting a deal. In reality, the Web is not always a deal. In our experience, very few Web prices are lower than what an experienced travel agent can find.

Arriving by train

If flying isn't an option, or if you're in the mood to see some countryside, you can always take the train. It's slower, but it's more romantic than air travel and not terribly stressful. Take a book along (we recommend the one you are reading now), spend hours talking to perfect strangers, or stare out the window like a six-year-old on a car trip with his parents. Montréal's **Central Station** is located at 895 rue de la Gauchetière Ouest (☎ **514-989-2626**). Québec's **Gare du Palais** is located at 450 rue de la Gare-du-Palais (☎ **418-692-3940**).

VIA Rail (☎ **888-842-7245**; www.viarail.ca), Canada's national passenger rail network, offers three-day cross-country trips departing several days a week. Prices vary depending on whether you take a sleeping compartment and/or meal package.

Amtrak (☎ **888-872-7245**; www.amtrak.com) offers daily departures to Montréal from New York City, departing in the morning and arriving in the early evening.

Traveling between Montréal and Québec City

Montréal and Québec City are about three hours apart by bus or car.

By bus

Travel by bus is definitely the handiest way to travel between the cities. Express buses leave Montréal and Québec City on the hour, and both bus stations are central. Montréal's **Central Station** (☎ **888-999-3977** or 514-842-2281) is located at 505 bd. de Maisonneuve. Québec City's **Bus Terminal** is located at 320 rue Abraham-Martin ☎ **418-525-3000**. Get to the stations a half-hour before departure, but don't worry, because the buses never sell out — they just get another bus. Round-trip bus fare is C$57 (US$43) for adults; C$50 (US$38) seniors and students, C$35 (US$26) children ages 5 to 12; and free for kids 4 and under.

By car

The highway between Montréal and Québec is not exactly what you'd call a scenic route — the scenery is pretty dull, actually — but if you want to drive, no one's going to stop you. Speaking of which, remember that the speed limit is in kilometers, not miles. The posted limit of 100 kilometers per hour is about 62 miles per hour. The two best-known car rental agencies are **Avis Rent a Car** (☎ **800-321-3652**) and **Hertz Canada** (☎ **800-263-0678**).

By ferry

Québeckers themselves sometimes forget that the St. Lawrence River joins Montréal and Québec City. Since 1999, a high-speed ferry makes the trip up (and down) the river in four hours. If you have some time to kill — only an extra hour, actually — this is a great way to see the river and the life around it, including farms, villages and, okay, some factories, too. Contact **Les Dauphins du Saint-Laurent** (☎ **877-648-4499** or ☎ 514-281-8000). Roundtrip ferry fare is C$109 (US$82) for adults, C$79 (US$59) for kids under 12; a one-way ticket costs a little more than half that much.

Chapter 6

Deciding Where to Stay

Accommodation options in Montréal and Québec City run the full gamut, giving you loads of choices for your stay. You can opt for the cinder-block austerity of a college dorm room, the opulent luxury of a penthouse suite, and anything in between. With more than 25,000 rooms, Montréal has the highest proportion of hotel rooms per capita in North America. Québec City has fewer total rooms, but still offers enticing options at every price level.

Wherever you decide to hang your hat, the comfort of your room inevitably colors your stay. Unless you possess unlimited resources, though, spending more on accommodations usually means spending less elsewhere — like on shopping — during your vacation.

Prices for double rooms at the most lavish hotels begin around C$250 (US$190) a night. That may sound steep, but compared to elsewhere in the world, it's a steal. The weak Canadian dollar sweetens the deal, so Montréal or Québec City may be the place to splurge on lap-of-luxury accommodations if that's what you're into.

If that's not what you want, both cities offer loads of affordable options, too. To decide where you fit in, ask yourself how much time you plan to spend in your hotel room. Is it just a place to stash your belongings during the day and crash at night, or is your room a sort of destination of its own?

Your accommodations will probably take the biggest bite out of your travel budget. If you've started planning the financial aspect of your trip to Montréal and Québec City, you probably have an idea of how much you want to spend per night.

Choosing a Place That Suits Your Style

Montréal and Québec City offer a variety of hotel styles; one of them is sure to suit your mood and budget. In this section, we briefly discuss the different types of accommodations available in the most centrally located neighborhoods of both cities.

Boutique hotels

Step into a world of design-forward surroundings and attentive care. Because boutique hotels usually offer fewer than 100 rooms, you receive the conscientious hospitality that has long since disappeared from the hustle and bustle of larger hotel operations. The good feng shui and the Zen-like service make you feel like you've stumbled into a futuristic utopia.

Luxury hotels

The classic elegance and grandeur of these hotels make them the pinnacle of luxury accommodations. The committed staff in dapper uniforms buzz about seeing to the guests' every desire (well, almost). The rooms are top-notch, and the amenities usually include a pool, a spa, and a gym.

Chain hotels

A familiar name can be comforting when you're away from home. International hotel chains, such as Hilton, Holiday Inn, Marriott, Novotel, and Sheraton, offer guests a similar product the world over, so you know more or less what to expect. Most of these large, somewhat anonymous hotels are downtown and cater to business travelers and convention-goers. The rooms are well kept, and the decor is usually subdued and inoffensive.

Independent hotels

The rooms and services can vary greatly among independently owned and operated establishments. They tend to be smaller, offer more personalized service, and exude greater amounts of local character and flair than large chain hotels.

Bed and breakfasts (B&Bs)

B&Bs can be anything from one to half a dozen rooms in a private house. The home usually has a separate bathroom for guests, but you may have to share it if other guests are at the B&B. In-room bathrooms are available at some B&Bs but usually at a premium. As the name indicates, the deal includes breakfast — either continental or full. The proprietors are usually welcoming, helpful types, brimming with interesting perspectives and insider recommendations. Although they don't offer the amenities of a large hotel, these places can sometimes be a surprisingly inexpensive way to travel.

In Montréal, several agencies broker the available rooms at the bed and breakfasts in the city:

- ✔ **B&B Downtown Network, ☎ 800-267-5180**
- ✔ **Montréal Oasis, ☎ 514-935-2312**
- ✔ **Bienvenue B&B, ☎ 800-363-9635** or 514-844-5897

For Québec City B&Bs, click on www.bedsandbreakfasts.ca/quebec-city-bed-breakfasts.htm.

Location, Location, Location

After price (see the "Price, Price, Price" section later in this chapter), location may be your most important consideration when deciding where to stay. If your hotel is well situated, you can see and do more because you spend less of your time commuting. Sure, the same room near the airport is cheaper, but you may spend all your savings getting back and forth.

Thankfully, you'll find no lack of choice in terms of budget and style in the neighborhoods of both Montréal and Québec City. After you're in the heart of either city, many of the best attractions, restaurants, shopping districts, and nightlife are within a surprisingly short distance from your hotel room.

Montréal's neighborhoods

Montréal's municipal slogan of "one island, one city" is somewhat deceiving, because the Island of Montréal actually consists of 27 boroughs. We focus on the downtown core, because that's where all the action is. That said, you don't have to worry about the bright lights of the big city getting in the way of a good night's sleep. Most hotels do their best to ensure their guests get plenty of peace and quiet.

In this section, we limit the discussion about Montréal's downtown neighborhoods to the ones where most of the hotels are — see Chapter 10 for a selection of our favorites. In Chapter 9, we describe all of Montréal's neighborhoods in more detail.

Downtown

Luxury and chain hotels dominate among the businesses, galleries, shops, and high-rise buildings Downtown. Many are scattered along rue Sherbrooke and just off of rue Ste-Catherine to the north and south. The downtown area also offers a cluster of hotels on the slope, south of boulevard René-Levesque, going toward Vieux-Montréal.

Staying downtown puts you within striking distance of several appealing neighborhoods and attractions. Chinatown, the Quartier Latin, Vieux-Montréal, McGill University, and Parc Mont-Royal all surround the central core.

Rue Ste-Catherine, Montréal's main drag, bustles with foot and car traffic well into the wee hours of the morning, but the surrounding streets empty of people shortly after the end of the business day and can seem desolate at night. That said, compared to other North American cities, Montréal's Downtown is very safe — even at night.

In a nutshell, you get:

✔ An ideal location that provides quick access to surrounding neighborhoods

✔ Upscale accommodations surrounded by shopping, theaters, and cafes

✔ Nearby rue Crescent, a popular nightlife destination for tourists

But . . .

✔ You pay a premium for being Downtown.

✔ The noise starts early and ends late.

Vieux-Montréal

Staying in Vieux-Montréal definitely adds a certain *je ne sais quoi* to your visit. The centuries-old architecture stacked along crooked cobblestone streets is romantic and magical, day or night. In the evening, you feel completely removed from the hubbub and honking of Downtown. However, on weekday mornings, Vieux-Montréal becomes the city's financial district, swarming with rushing office workers, lurching delivery trucks, and whistling bike couriers.

Vieux-Montréal has seen a recent rash of boutique hotel openings in several its 19th-century office buildings. Although the ornate and imposing exteriors remain the same, Montréal's best architects and designers gut and fill the interiors with a select number of spacious hotel rooms that offer high ceilings and ultra-modern decor. The results are breathtaking. These boutique hotels are increasingly the destination of choice among visiting A-list celebrities, but they are very pricey.

Otherwise, independent hotels and B&Bs round out the accommodation offerings in this part of town. Many try to cash in on their buildings' locations and roles in the founding of the French colony, but that history is half the fun of Montréal's most historic district, where you're likely to be swept away by its Old World charm.

In a nutshell, you get:

- A beautiful yesteryear setting, sure to inspire
- A neighborhood that's wonderfully desolate by evening — the perfect place to get away from it all, except for the echoing hooves of horse-drawn carriages
- Hotels near the waterfront and historic attractions

But . . .

- This area is somewhat isolated from downtown and the other neighborhoods.
- Walking home at night, although not dangerous, is a bit of a hike.

Quartier Latin

Nights in the Quartier Latin (the Latin Quarter) are always hopping. In mid-July, the neighborhood becomes downright outlandish as the Just For Laughs comedy festival takes over and turns it into a hilarious human zoo. During the rest of the summer, beer- and sangria-drenched patrons lounge on the sidewalk terraces late into the night.

The independent, European-style hotels in this neighborhood offer some of the city's more reasonable accommodation options, although the hotels start getting seedy if you go south of rue Ste-Catherine or east of rue St-Hubert. One or two chain hotels sit along rue Sherbrooke, and plenty of B&Bs are options in the townhouse-lined streets to the north surrounding the swank Carré St-Louis. The Quartier Latin is also a great starting point for visiting other Montréal neighborhoods — it's crammed between Vieux-Montréal, Downtown, the Plateau, and the Gay Village.

In a nutshell, you get:

- A colorful neighborhood with lots of bars and cafes frequented by a largely French-speaking clientele
- Proximity to boulevard St-Laurent and boulevard St-Denis, both of which have excellent shopping, restaurants, and nightlife

✔ A high concentration of BYOB restaurants, particularly on rue Prince Arthur and avenue Duluth, where patrons can bring their own wine (see Chapter 10 for more dining details)

But . . .

✔ The neighborhood can be noisy.

✔ If you go beyond the quarter's boundaries, the accommodations quickly become seedy.

Plateau

By staying here, you've invaded the turf of the city's trendiest inhabitants. You, too, can be a *Plateau-zard* for the duration of your stay. During the afternoons, you can swagger down avenue Mont-Royal, looking for just the right accessory for a party later on that night or just for fun — *pour le fun,* as they say around these parts. When you're done shopping, you can brood over a coffee and watch the world go by from an establishment's window-side table; or, if the weather is warm enough, retreat to a terrace for more libations. Note that claiming to be an artist of some sort will help you acclimatize to your new surroundings.

Apart from the main commercial streets, rue St. Denis and avenue Mont-Royal, much of this neighborhood remains residential. This means that much of the accommodations offered are of the bed-and-breakfast variety. But in recent years, some small, independent hotels have set up shop, as well.

In a nutshell, you get:

✔ Great shopping and dining along the commercial streets

✔ The reassurance that you are among a select few, and you're the envy of other Montréalers at large

✔ Lots of parks and tree-lined streets with townhouses; ideal for strolling

But . . .

✔ You may feel somewhat removed from the hustle and bustle downtown.

✔ If you don't like bed and breakfasts, your choice of accommodations is somewhat limited in this area.

Québec City's neighborhoods

Québec City's smaller size, compared to that of Montréal, makes location less crucial in choosing where to stay. However, you have a steep cliff to contend with and at some point, you may find yourself wondering about the best way to get up and down it. The old city, atop the cliff and within the fortifications, feels magical and romantic. The area at the bottom of the cliff and by the water has a gloomy appeal. Outside the historic districts, everything feels less touristy and more contemporary.

Inside the walls (Haute-Ville and Basse-Ville)

Besides the first-class, luxury accommodations of the Fairmount Château Frontenac, many of your accommodation options inside the wall of the Old City are small, family-run, European-style, independent hotels and B&Bs. This has its pros and cons. Comfort and service standards vary greatly, and rooms can be hard to get. Also, elevators are rare in these places, so if you stay in the Old City, you almost certainly have to climb stairs. And if you stay in the **Basse-Ville** (Lower City), you have to either climb a foreboding set of stairs to see the **Haute-Ville** (Upper City) every day, or wait for the *funiculaire* (elevator).

In a nutshell, you get:

- ✔ A neighborhood
- ✔ Easy walking distance to almost all the attractions you want to see

But . . .

- ✔ Prices and standards of hotels can vary widely from hotel to hotel.
- ✔ Some streets can be pretty noisy with tourists coming and going.

Outside the walls

If the idea of staying in the Old City makes you claustrophobic, you can find plenty of accommodations just beyond its gates. These spots are still an easy walk from the Old City, but they give you a little breathing room, especially during peak season, when the Old City has a distinct bee's nest feel to it. The best areas outside of the walls are in the vicinity of **Grande-Allée** and **boulevard René-Levesque,** two long streets that run west of the Old City gates. The Grande-Allée is reputed for its nightlife. Packed with bars, restaurants, and terraces, it's almost a destination in itself. Avenue Cartier, a lively shopping street just off Grande-Allée has a number of B&Bs. Québec City's two big chain hotels are on boulevard René-Levesque, a bland throughway with no more than proximity to the Old City to recommend it.

In a nutshell, you get:

- ✔ A little more peace and quiet
- ✔ The possibility of staying in a chain hotel
- ✔ Slightly cheaper accommodations

But . . .

> ✔ Atmosphere may be lacking.
>
> ✔ You have to walk from 5 to 15 minutes to the Old City.

Price, Price, Price

In keeping with the dollar sign categories that we use to rate the hotel listings in Chapters 9 and 16, this section tells you what you can expect in terms of the rooms and the service at each price level. These are only the most general guidelines. The best way to know what you're actually going to get — and for what price — is to call hotels and ask specific questions about the available rooms.

$ (under $100)

Simple and inexpensive, these accommodations should offer all the basics: a room with a lock, a firm bed, and clean towels and sheets. A light continental breakfast may be included. Hotels offering rooms at these prices probably don't have an extensive catalog of services to cater to your every whim, but the front desk clerks are usually delighted to point you in the right direction for whatever you want.

$$ ($100–$200)

Many of the rates offered by the chain hotels fall into this price range, as do the rates of the fancier independents. You can already expect the amenities to be better, like bathrooms with hair dryers, coffee makers with complimentary coffee, and Internet access. Some hotels in this category may have kitchens that provide late-night room service or a breakfast cart. Some even have swimming pools.

$$$ ($200–$300)

Along with the upper-end of the chain hotels, boutique hotels and luxury hotels begin competing in this price bracket, with fine bed linens, feathery pillows, fluffy towels, and bathtubs built for two. The first-class hotels seem to differentiate themselves by striving for regal scale and elegance, while boutique hotels are strikingly modern. Expect high-speed Internet access in your room.

$$$$ ($300 and up)

At this price, you should want for nothing in terms of your stay. Expect a great view, an in-room hot tub, a CD player, thick terrycloth bathrobes, and even flowers. And highly deferential, personalized service is included, as well.

Booking Your Accommodations

If you walk into a hotel lobby late at night carrying your bags and ask for a room, you end up paying top dollar. Like seats on a commercial airline flight, the same hotel room can go for a variety of prices. What you pay largely depends on how you book it. So, with a little time and gumption, you may save enough to stay an extra night.

Uncovering the truth about rack rates

In the hotel business, as in life, you don't get the room you deserve. You get the one you negotiate. To make your stay in Montréal or Québec City all the more fabulous, invest some time beforehand and get the right room at the right price.

The prices that hotels advertise are not always their actual prices, but are their *rack rates,* or in other words, the suggested retail price of their rooms. When the savvy guest hears this rate, he or she responds with a knowing chuckle and orients the discussion toward a lower price. You should, too. It's as simple as asking whether you're eligible for any discounts or upgrades.

Getting the best room and rate

In advance of your departure, you can turn to a variety of sources to ensure the best rate for your hotel room. If you're not satisfied with the quote at the toll-free call center that's handling the reservations, ring the front desk of the hotel, instead. Also check the hotel's Web site, because some hotels may offer a bargain when you book online. Reserving through a travel agent may also yield a better price.

In order to make a meaningful price comparison between room rates, always ask whether the quoted price includes sales tax. If it doesn't, count on paying 15% more at checkout. Ask about any other hidden charges that you may encounter during your stay, like parking.

The timing of your trip dictates how much you end up spending on accommodations. Hotel room prices are higher during the tourist season, which is from early May through September. During the summer, Montréal hosts a variety of festivals and special events, and rooms can be scarce during the festival season. Check what's going on during your stay, and then book well in advance if you plan to arrive during a major event. (See Chapter 2 for Montréal's and Québec City's festival and events schedules.)

During the rest of the year, expect to pay between 10 and 15% less than during the summer peak. If you're staying only for a couple days in the middle of the week, be sure to ask for the mid-week rate.

Membership has its privileges, and now's the time to cash in on any you have. When making your reservation, remember to mention any corporate reward packages, frequent flyer programs, or travel insurance you may have. If you belong to a union or professional association, mention it. You never know what rewards await you.

To ensure you get peace and quiet in your room, request one on an upper floor, away from the hotel's meeting areas, dining rooms, and other noisy amenities like the pool. Also ask that your room be away from any scheduled renovations. In addition, more and more hotels distinguish between smoking and non-smoking rooms. If you feel adamant about getting one room or the other, be sure to tell every person handling your reservation about your preference.

Corner rooms are often big and bright, and sometimes one is available at the same rate as a standard room. If you're traveling as a family or small group, consider asking about a suite, which may sleep as many people, but usually costs less than two separate rooms. If you're not happy with your room, tell the front desk immediately. Most hotels exchange your room if another is unoccupied.

Avoid racking up a huge bill by not using the room's phone and resisting the temptation to raid the minibar. None of this is free. Most hotels even charge a fee to connect local calls. If you need to make dinner reservations, ask the concierge to book them. Otherwise, leave the hotel, pick up snacks and a long-distance calling card, and then use a payphone on the streets surrounding your hotel. Ask the concierge or the front desk clerk for the whereabouts of the closest *dépanneur,* the universally understood term for a convenience store.

Surfing the Web for hotel deals

Gleaning impressions from the Internet can be helpful when you're choosing accommodations. Through the pictures on a hotel's Web site, you can get a feel for its lobby, facilities, rooms, and neighborhood location — invaluable information.

Remember that unless you see an advertised discount for booking online, the prices on the Web are the rack rates. So much for trying the back door. At best, you get a ballpark figure that you can use to haggle for a better price.

However, you can use the Web in other ways to hunt for discounted rooms. Check out one of the Web's "big three" mega-portals for travel information and bookings: Expedia.ca, Travelocity.ca, and Orbitz.com. Expedia is probably the best for sourcing discounted hotel rooms, because of its long list of special deals. Travelocity runs a close second.

Hotel specialist sites www.Hotels.com and www.HotelDiscounts.com are also reliable. **TravelAxe** is an excellent site (www.travelaxe.net) that can help you search multiple hotel sites at one time, even ones you may never have heard of.

If Russian Roulette's your game at the casino, you can get a real kick out of looking for accommodations via www.Priceline.com and www.Hotwire.com. At either site, you bid on the neighborhood, quality level, and price of your hotel before the site comes back with a match. While Hotwire tells you the prices before you buy, Priceline plays its cards close to its chest. A spoiler site, www.BiddingForTravel.com, tells you what hotel prices on Priceline are going for.

Note: Hotwire overrates its hotels by one star — what Hotwire calls a four-star is a three-star anywhere else.

Wherever you may wander in cyberspace in search of a hotel room, use online research only to get ideas. Calling the hotel directly remains the best way to negotiate price and make reservations. With the same phone call, you can clear up other details about your accommodations, finding out where to park, what the neighborhood is like, and so on. Either way, nail down your lodgings before you leave, so that you don't waste precious vacation time haggling.

Getting by without a reservation

If you're trundling around at dusk with no place to stay, call one of Tourism Québec's **Infotouriste Centres, ☎ 877-266-5687.** The staff there can get you situated for one night or for the duration of your stay.

Or, stop in. The centers are open from 8 a.m. to 7:30 p.m. Monday through Friday and from 9 a.m. to 5 p.m. on weekends. In Montréal, the office is located downtown at 1001 Square Dorchester, near the corner of rue Peel and rue Ste-Catherine. Québec City's Infotouriste Centre is right across the square from the Château Frontenac at 12 rue Ste-Anne. Look for the blue and white question-mark sign.

Tourisme Québec's member hotels set aside rooms for a proprietary database spanning every price range and star-rating. Friendly bilingual representatives tell you whether any are available in places that may otherwise claim to be sold out. They can also book B&Bs, condos, chalets, and university dormitories. The latter are available only during the summer season.

Chapter 7

Taking Care of the Remaining Details

*T*ime is especially precious when you're traveling, so you don't want to learn on the job. This chapter explains all the things you need to know *before* your vacation, so that you don't waste time during your trip worrying about what you should have done before you left. We cover stuff like what to expect at customs, what kind of travel insurance you need, how to rent a car, which reservations to make before your departure, and, of course, what to bring with you.

Getting through Customs

Canadians are well known for being particularly nice, saying sorry all the time, and not wanting to offend. Our customs officers, however, are more serious individuals and of firmer constitution (which is why they are protecting our borders). The drill here, as at any border crossing, is to answer the customs officers' questions: no more, no less. The vacation interview is like the opposite of a job interview, but you should treat it seriously just the same.

Customs officers usually ask where you're from, how long you plan to stay, and maybe, whether you have anything to declare. Your answer to this last question is "no," unless you are importing goods or an incredibly large sum of cash. Just answer politely (Canadians really like that) and don't take the interrogation personally.

U.S. citizens and permanent residents don't require visas or passports to enter Canada, but you must provide proof of citizenship in the form of a photo ID (a certificate of citizenship or naturalization, or a birth certificate presented with valid photo identification, such as a driver's license). If you're not a U.S. citizen but are a permanent resident of the United States, also bring your green card.

All other foreign travelers visiting Canada need at least a passport — and maybe a visa. Before you go, find out what you need to enter Canada by visiting the **Canadian Customs and Revenue Agency** Web site at www.ccra.gc.ca. You can also call ☎ **800-461-9999** or 204-983-3500. **Citizenship and Immigrations Canada** (www.cic.gc.ca) also provides information on entry requirements and a list of visa offices abroad. You can try the office by phone at ☎ **819-994-2424.** If you book your trip through a travel agency, your agent should be able to provide you with this information. Sometimes, they even have the necessary visa application forms.

For automated information on how to get a U.S. passport, contact the **National Passport Information Center ☎ 900-225-7778** or visit the U.S. State Department's travel information Web site at http://travel.state.gov.

What you can bring in, and what you can bring back — those are the questions. The following sections have the answers:

What you can take in

Your airline can tell you how much baggage you can bring. Canadian customs limits how many cigars (50), cigarettes (200), and how much loose tobacco (8 ounces/400 grams) you can bring in. Customs also sets limits on alcohol. You can bring 40 ounces of liquor or wine, or 288 ounces (one case of 24 12-ounce bottles) of beer.

Pets with proper vaccination records may be admitted, but check with **Canada Customs** first (see the preceding section for contact information). Need we mention that you can't bring any revolvers, pistols, or fully automatic firearms into Canada? So, you have to forego your right to bear arms for the duration of your stay. Fishing gear is okay, but you need a nonresident license.

What you can bring back

U.S. citizens who have been out of the country for at least 48 hours can bring back US$400 in goods, duty-free. This includes 200 cigarettes, 100 cigars, and one liter of an alcoholic beverage. In addition, you can mail US$200 worth of goods to yourself and US$100 to someone else. Note that you can only do this once every 30 days. You may bring back tinned goods, but no fresh foods. For a complete list of items you cannot bring into the United States, look in your phone book under **U.S. Government, Department of the Treasury, U.S. Customs Service** or visit the Customs Service Web site at www.customs.ustreas.gov/travel/travel.htm.

If you're a citizen of the United Kingdom, Australia, or New Zealand, check out the regulations on what you can bring back by contacting the following agencies:

- ✔ **HM Customs and Excise** (UK), ☎ **0181-910-3744,** www.hmce.gov.uk

- ✔ **Australian Customs Services,** ☎ **02-9213-2000,** www.customs.gov.au

- ✔ **New Zealand Custom Services,** ☎ **09-4-359-6655,** www.customs.govt.nz

Considering Travel and Medical Insurance

Before you opt for additional travel insurance, figure out what insurance you already have. Then think about what you may still need. Here are your options:

- ✔ **Trip cancellation insurance:** This means you get your money back if you have to back out of the trip, if you have to return home early, or if your supplier goes bankrupt. This type of insurance makes sense if you buy well in advance (because you can't foresee what may happen months down the road) or pay for a lot of your trip up front (as in the case of a cruise or a package tour).

- ✔ **Medical** and **lost luggage insurance:** If you have medical insurance at home, your plan probably covers you abroad. Check with your provider. If you're only partially covered, you can buy supplementary insurance.

  If you get sick when you're in another country, you probably have to pay the expenses up front and get reimbursed when you get home. Find out how payment works with your specific type of coverage.

  Your homeowner's insurance may cover stolen luggage. Again, check your policy. Otherwise, if the airline loses your luggage, it is responsible for US$2500 on domestic flights and US$9.07 per pound on international flights. Remember to pack valuables in your carry-on.

Some credit card companies (American Express and certain gold and platinum Visas and MasterCards) offer limited travel insurance coverage if you purchase your ticket with the card. To find out more, check with your credit card company (see the Appendix for contact information).

If you decide to buy travel insurance, consider the four following companies:

- **Access America,** 6600 W. Broad St., Richmond, VA 23230 (☎ **800-284-8300;** Fax: 800-346-9265; www.accessamerica.com)

- **Travelex Insurance Services,** 11717 Burt St., Ste. 202, Omaha, NE 68154 (☎ **800-228-9792;** www.travelex-insurance.com)

- **Travel Guard International,** 1145 Clark St., Stevens Point, WI 54481 (☎ **800-826-1300;** www.travel-guard.com)

- **Travel Insured International, Inc.,** P.O. Box 280568, 52-S Oakland Ave., East Hartford, CT 06128-0568 (☎ **800-243-3174;** www.travelinsured.com)

Dealing with Illness Away from Home

Getting sick while you're on vacation can be exasperating, but following the tips in this section helps you avoid emergencies and cope with common medical situations:

- If you suffer from a common illness, consult your doctor before you leave. If you suffer from chronic condition like epilepsy, diabetes, or heart problems, wear a **Medic Alert Identification Tag** (☎ **800-825-3785;** www.medicalert.org), which alerts doctors in Montréal or Québec City to your condition and gives them access to your records through a 24-hour hotline.

- Carry your medical or travel insurance identification card in your wallet. The card has an emergency number that you need to call if your insurer requires pre-treatment authorization. Before you leave, ask your insurer about the procedure for coverage in medical emergencies.

- Pack prescription medication in your carry-on luggage and keep them in their original containers, with pharmacy labels — otherwise airport security may seize them. Bring along copies of your prescription in case you lose your pills on the road.

✔ Pack an extra pair of contact lenses or glasses in case you lose them.

✔ Bring along any over-the-counter remedies you may need for common ailments, such as diarrhea or upset stomach. Bringing your own is quicker and easier than trying to find the Canadian equivalent.

If you need a doctor, ask at your hotel's front desk, which can direct you to the nearest hospital or walk-in clinic for medical treatment in English (which is most places). The province of Québec has a large system of community health centers called **CLSCs**, which usually accept walk-ins. See the Appendix for locations of healthcare facilities.

Renting a Car (and Understanding Why Not To)

If you plan to spend most of your time visiting Montréal within city limits, a car is probably more trouble than its worth. In Québec City, driving is even less advisable. And Vieux-Québec is so small that you can walk anywhere you want to go.

Parking in either city can be tough. Although you find lots of metered parking in downtown areas, competition for those spaces is fierce. In Montréal's residential neighborhoods, a system of reserved parking zones still has many locals baffled; you get the added handicap of trying to figure out the signs in French. To get out of the downtown core of Montréal, take the subway (known as the **Métro**) or any number of bus lines. Ask for a public transportation map at your hotel or at the ticket booth of any Métro station. You can also easily flag taxis in both cities.

Still want to drive? Well, the truth is, finding your way around Montréal is easy in a car, and renting one is a snap (see the Appendix for agencies in both cities). Just remember that traffic signs are in French. Some other peculiarities to keep in mind are a follows:

✔ It's legal to turn right on a red light everywhere in Québec except in Montréal.

✔ At many lights in both cities, the greens start out as green point-ing arrows. For their duration, you can travel through the intersection only in the directions they are pointing.

✔ Gas is more expensive in Canada than the U.S. You'll pay around C$30 (US$22) to fill the tank of a mid-size car.

Cutting the cost of car rental

The rates at most major car rental companies are about the same in both cities, but the following tips help you save money:

- ✔ **Weekend rates are cheaper.** This may mean picking the car up Thursday afternoon or Friday morning and returning it Monday morning. If you rent for 5 days or more, the daily rate is cheaper.

- ✔ **Check your car insurance policy at home.** You're probably insured for rental cars, so you don't need to buy extra insurance when you rent — just make sure you take your policy number with you.

- ✔ **Shop around.** Even within one company, rates vary between agencies. Rates are higher during the tourist season (May to September). Local rental agencies may offer better rates than national chains. Ask at the front desk of your hotel.

- ✔ **Estimate your driving distance.** When you rent, the rates for unlimited mileage are higher. Plan where you're going — if your mileage will be low, don't pay any extra for unlimited mileage.

Preparing for additional charges

In addition to the standard rental prices (C$30–C$50/ US$22–US$36 a day in Montréal and Québec City), other optional charges, discussed in the two following sections, can add up.

Understanding general charges

The **Collision Damage Waiver (CDW),** which requires you to pay for damage to the car in a collision, costs up to US$15 a day. Many credit card companies cover this fee; ask your company before you sign up.

Car rental companies also offer **liability insurance** (if you harm others in an accident), **personal accident insurance** (if you harm yourself or your passengers), and **personal effects insurance** (if possessions are stolen from the car). Your car insurance policy at home probably covers these situations as well, so check before you leave. You can probably safely skip the personal effects insurance (unless you're driving around with a stack of CDs, which petty thieves in Montréal love to steal), but you should definitely be covered for harm to yourself and others.

Reviewing Québec's extra charges

Taxes on purchases are steep in Québec. The General Sales Tax (on your bill, in French, this shows up as the TPS) is 7%. Then, the Provincial Sales Tax (TVQ) is 7.5%. Québec squeezes an extra bit of provincial sales tax out of each purchase by calculating the TVQ on the total of the original price *plus* the TPS. We're not sure how they get away with it, but no one seems to complain.

Making Dinner Reservations in Advance

If you're counting on attending any of the big shows at festivals — particularly the **Jazz Festival** or **Just for Laughs Festival** — purchase your tickets in advance. In the summer, try to book your room at least several weeks in advance — on the weekend of Montréal's Gay Pride Parade (early August), for example, there isn't a room to be had in town. The following sections give you some tips for advance planning.

Surfing ahead of time

The Web is the best and cheapest way to find out what's going on in Montréal and Québec City, make reservations, and buy tickets before you leave home. Here are our favorite sources for Montréal:

- **Events:** To find out what's going on in Montréal, visit the Montréal Plus Web site at www.montreal-plus.com or Tourism Montréal at www.tourism-montreal.org.

- **Sports:** Get schedules and reserve tickets for Montréal Allouettes, Canadiens, Expos, or Impact, through the Admission Network, www.admission.com.

- **Entertainment:** The best sources are the sites of Montréal's weekly cultural magazines, the Montréal *Mirror* (www.montrealmirror.com) and *Hour* (www.hour.ca), and Montréal's English-language daily paper, *The Gazette* (www.montrealgazette.com).

And for Québec City:

- **Culture:** *Voir* (voir.ca) is a free weekly cultural magazine, with a Québec City edition. The site covers special events and concerts, as well as film and dining.

- **A little bit of everything: Québec Plus,** www.quebecplus.ca, operated by the phone company's Internet arm, has directories of entertainment, accommodations, shopping, dining, and nightlife, bolstered with profiles and seasonal features.

  Bonjour Québec (www.bonjourquebec.com), operated by the Province's Ministry of Tourism, contains pages on all of the province but has a section devoted to Québec City and the surrounding area.

  Québec City's city's official site, www.quebecregion.com, is run by the Québec City and Area Tourism and Convention Bureau.

Reserving a table for dinner

Québeckers eat late. In the summer, restaurants in Montréal and Québec City fill up at 9 p.m. and serve until 11 p.m. or later. If you want to be in the thick of the eating action, don't make dinner reservations before 7:30 p.m. On the flip side, if you want to get a table at a popular restaurant at the last minute, tables are almost always available at 6 p.m. or earlier.

Weekends are the only time you have trouble making same-day reservations at most restaurants. In Chapters 10 and 17, we tell you which restaurants require reservations. If all our suggestions are booked, don't despair. Ask for alternatives at the front desk of your hotel. Neither city suffers from a shortage of culinary choices.

Québeckers have not succumbed the global trend of banning smoking in bars and restaurants — not yet, anyway — so Québec is still a smoker's haven. While restrictions exist, restaurants almost always have a smoking section and smoking-friendly bar. Club-hoppers tend to indulge heartily. Consider yourself warned.

Getting a Few Packing Tips

Think you can visit Montréal and Québec City in a sweat suit and sneakers? Think again. Both cities are slightly more stylish and formal than the North American norm; you really won't feel comfortable walking around in a jogging suit. Make sure you have at least a decent pair of slacks, a nice shirt, and clean shoes.

After you set your style standards, think practically. The weather is always unpredictable, so make sure you have at least one warm sweater, plus sunscreen, a sun hat, and an umbrella. For winter, bring a warm coat, mitts, hats, gloves, and boots — sorry, there's no way around it.

Travel lightly. We know we just told you to be stylish and prepare for rain or shine, but don't break your back over it. One large, preferably wheeled, suitcase and a carry-on bag is the way to go.

What not to bring

You probably don't need formal wear, so don't bog down your bags with fancy suits or satin pumps. For women, one dressy — preferably a knit — outfit will do. For men, one jacket and tie combo will suffice. The best idea is always to have something versatile.

What to bring

Your airline can tell you how much luggage you can bring. Usually you are allowed to check two pieces and carry one small bag with you, but many charter airlines allow only one checked piece of luggage and a carry-on bag. Airlines have become fairly strict about baggage limitations in the last couple of years, so if you plan to take a lot with you, call the airline for specific weight and size limitations. You don't want any unpleasant surprises at check-in.

Your carry-on bag should contain whatever you can't afford to lose, and whatever you need to get by for a day in case your luggage gets lost (if they lose your bag, most airlines locate it quickly). Return tickets, vital documents, toiletries, an extra pair of underwear, something to read, a small bottle of water, and a light sweater or jacket does the trick.

Don't pack any sharp objects (scissors, tweezers, etc.) in your carry-on bag. These items are strictly prohibited. Pack them in your checked luggage, instead, or leave them at home.

In addition, think about the following when packing:

- ✔ **Leave your new shoes at home.** Even if your old ones are a little scuffed, you'll be far happier walking around in them instead of nursing bruises and blisters.

- ✔ **Find a color scheme.** When packing, choose colors that complement each other. Black, white, grey, and navy work wonders, as do beige and brown. Remember, most of the people who see you while traveling will probably never see you again.

- ✔ **Stick to knits.** They don't wrinkle. Leave your linen shirts at home. They're not worth it.

- ✔ **Bring along a little laundry soap.** A small bottle of laundry detergent weighs a lot less than those three extra shirts you were going to bring along just in case you dribble truffle juice down your collar. Do a little hand washing in the hotel sink.

- ✔ **Save up small bottles.** Pour into them only as much shampoo or shower gel as you need for your stay. You won't believe how much space and weight you save. Pharmacies also sell miniature travel versions of everything from toothpaste to hand cream.

- ✔ **Find an itsy-bitsy, teeny weeny, yellow polka-dot . . . umbrella.** They make umbrellas these days that practically fit into your fist. An umbrella is a must for any trip to Montréal or Québec City; a compact version takes some weight off your shoulders.

Part III
Exploring Montréal

The 5th Wave   By Rich Tennant

© RICHTENNANT

"Montréal is wonderful. We spent the morning at Vieux Port, the afternoon at Vieux Mont-Royal, and right now we're at Vieux hotel room."

In this part . . .

Now comes the fun part. Here's where we tell you about the city and guide your through its highlights, its best hotels and restaurants, and its hottest attractions. You can follow one of our itineraries for visiting Montréal on foot. And in case you want to swap urban landscapes for mountains, lakes, and rivers, we finish with a few recommended day drips around Montréal.

Chapter 8

Arriving and Orienting Yourself in Montréal

Montréal is an island with a mountain in the middle. Well, sort of. Mont Royal is a 761-foot-high hill, topped by a crucifix, that everyone calls the "the Mountain." It looms large over several Montréal neighborhoods. And unless you're near the water, like in Vieux-Montréal, it's not obvious that you're on an island in the mighty St. Lawrence River. Suburban Montréalers who creep over the bridges on their daily commutes never forget it, though.

In this chapter, we help you get to your downtown accommodations, whether you arrive by air, land, or river. We also familiarize you with your new surroundings — Montréal's delightfully distinct and colorful neighborhoods — and tell you how best to travel between them.

Arriving in Montréal

If you arrive at one of Montréal's two airports from outside of Canada, you must go through Canadian Customs and Immigration. See Chapter 7 for what to expect.

Flying into the airport and getting to your hotel

You will probably arrive at Montréal's recently renamed **Pierre Elliott Trudeau International Airport** (☎ **800-465-1213** or 514-394-7377; www.admtl.com), formerly known as Dorval. After clearing customs

Greater Montréal

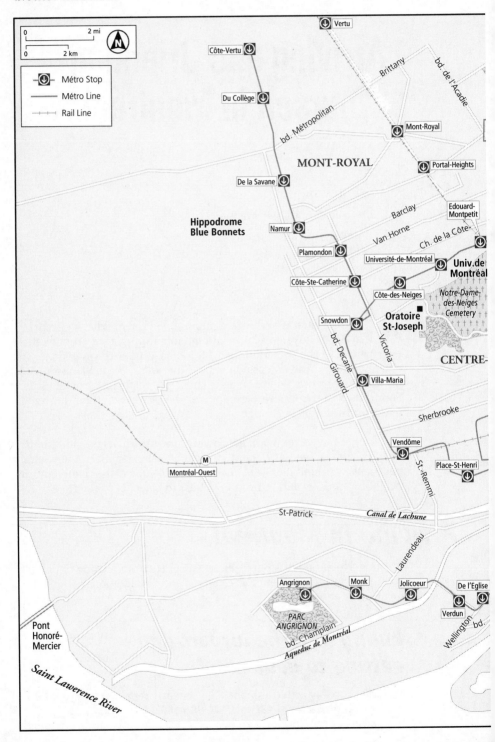

0 2 mi
0 2 km

Métro Stop
Métro Line
Rail Line

Vertu
Côte-Vertu
Brittany
bd. de l'Acadie
Du Collège
bd. Métropolitan
Mont-Royal
MONT-ROYAL
Portal-Heights
De la Savane
Barclay
Edouard-Montpetit
Hippodrome Blue Bonnets
Namur
Van Horne
Ch. de la Côte-
Plamondon
Université-de-Montréal
Univ.de Montréal
Côte-Ste-Catherine
Côte-des-Neiges
Notre-Dame-des-Neiges Cemetery
Snowdon
Oratoire St-Joseph
Victoria
bd. Décarie
CENTRE-
Girouard
Villa-Maria
Sherbrooke
Vendôme
St-Remmi
Place-St-Henri
Montréal-Ouest
St-Patrick
Canal de Lachune
Laurendeau
Angrignon
Monk
Jolicoeur
De l'Eglise
PARC ANGRIGNON
Verdun
Pont Honoré-Mercier
bd. Champlain
Aqueduc de Montréal
Wellington bd.
Saint Lawerence River

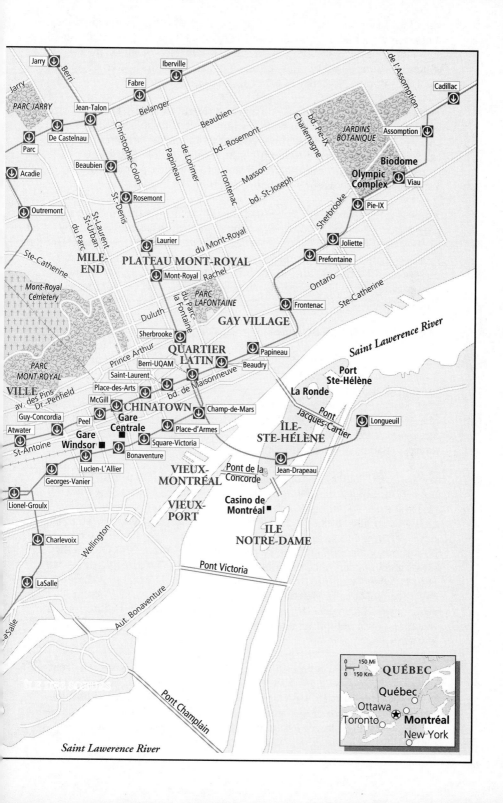

Jarry · Jarry · Berri · Iberville · Fabre · Cadillac
PARC JARRY · Jean-Talon · Belanger · Beaubien · bd. Pie-IX · JARDINS BOTANIQUE · Assomption · de l'Assomption
De Castelnau · Beaubien · bd. Rosemont · Charlemagne · Charlemagne
Parc · Papineau · de Lorimer · Frontenac · Masson · bd. St-Joseph · Biodome
Acadie · Christophe-Colon · St-Denis · Rosemont · Olympic Complex · Viau
Outremont · St-Laurent · St-Urban · du Parc · Pie-IX
Ste-Catherine · MILE-END · Laurier · du Mont-Royal · Sherbrooke · Joliette
Mont-Royal Cemetery · PLATEAU MONT-ROYAL · Mont-Royal · Rachel · Prefontaine
PARC LAFONTAINE · Ontario · Saint Lawerence River
Duluth · du Parc; la Fontaine · Ste-Catherine
PARC MONT-ROYAL · Sherbrooke · GAY VILLAGE · Frontenac
VILLE · Prince Arthur · QUARTIER LATIN · Papineau · Port Ste-Hélène
av. des Pins · Saint-Laurent · Berri-UQAM · Beaudry · La Ronde
Dr.-Penfield · Place-des-Arts · bd. de Maisonneuve
Guy-Concordia · McGill · CHINATOWN · Champ-de-Mars · Pont Jacques-Cartier · ÎLE-STE-HÉLÈNE · Longueuil
Atwater · Peel · Gare Centrale · Place-d'Armes
St-Antoine · Gare Windsor · Square-Victoria
Bonaventure · VIEUX-MONTRÉAL · Pont de la Concorde · Jean-Drapeau
Lucien-L'Allier · Georges-Vanier · VIEUX-PORT · Casino de Montréal · ÎLE NOTRE-DAME
Lionel-Groulx · Charlevoix · Wellington · Pont Victoria
LaSalle · Aut. Bonaventure
Pont Champlain
Saint Lawerence River

QUÉBEC
0 150 Mi
0 150 Km
Québec
Ottawa
Toronto
Montréal
New York

and claiming your checked baggage, you may want to exchange money.
A currency exchange counter, open between 4:30 p.m. and 12:30 a.m.,
and a 24-hour ATM are located on the Arrivals level of the airport —
which is where you'll be. Car rental agencies are also located at this
level, but you have plenty of other ways to get downtown.

There's a slim chance that you'll arrive at **Mirabel Airport,** about
34 miles away. Mirabel's air traffic is now limited to charter flights
and freight. Because of the reduced foot traffic in the terminal, the
car rental agencies have closed up shop, but fear not: Taxis, limousines, and an airport shuttle are all there to get to you downtown.
You'll also find a currency exchange counter at Mirabel.

Taxis and limousines are available from either airport (see the preceding section). Airport limousines are not the stretch brand favored by
Britney Spears, but black, tinted-window, leather-interior sedans of the
type used for whisking around international dignitaries. The cabs are
metered, and a trip downtown costs about C$30 (US$23); limousines
charge a flat fee of C$70 (US$53) plus tip from Trudeau. From Mirabel, it's
an estimated C$45 (US$34) for a taxi and C$85 (US$64) for a limousine.

The Aérobus (☎ **514-399-9877**) is a **shuttle bus** that runs frequently
between each airport and downtown. This is the best value for getting
downtown at C$12 (US$9) from Trudeau, and C$33 (US$25) from Mirabel.
It makes two stops, first downtown at 777 rue de la Gauchetière, behind
the Fairmount Queen Elizabeth Hotel, and then at Montréal's bus station, **Station Central,** in the Quartier Latin, adjacent to the Berri-UQAM
Métro stop. From de la Gauchetière, a free minivan takes travelers to
any hotel. If you're not staying in a hotel, you may try asking for a lift,
anyway. You're bending the rules, but it's worth a try.

For a mere C$2.50 (US$1.80) you can get downtown by **public transportation,** but it's a bit of a schlep, requiring two buses and a subway
(Métro) ride. To us, it's worth the extra bucks for the shuttle, especially if you have lots of luggage. If you arrive with only a carry-on bag,
however, you can save some money going this route. Catch the city-
bound buses No. 204 on the island across the first lane of traffic on the
lower level in front of the terminal. It takes you on a short ride to Dorval
Station, where you transfer to a second bus, No. 211, that goes directly
to the Lionel-Groulx Métro (Orange Line). Hold onto your transfer
stub — which the first driver extends in exchange for your fare —
because you'll need it to get on the second bus and then onto the
subway.

We discourage **renting a car,** mainly because Montréal is such a great
walking city and because its traffic, one way streets, and scarce parking are maddening. However, at Trudeau airport, a gauntlet of booths
belonging to the usual suspects of car rental agencies are near domes-
tic arrivals on the lower level. After you have your keys in hand, you
can drive into town.

Cruising into town

From the airport, follow the signs for Autoroute 20 Est (Highway 20 East). You encounter many sharp turns exiting the airport, so be careful. Eventually, you come to a light and a traffic circle going through an overpass. Follow it around and get on the highway ramp on the other side — going eastbound. Follow the signs for Montréal, and **Centre-Ville,** and this highway takes you right into the heart of the city.

From the Canada–U.S. border, allow an hour to get to Montréal. Depending on where you crossed, you approach Montréal's South Shore on either Autoroute 15 or Autoroute 10. To get to Montréal proper, you must traverse the river onto the island via one of the bridges; look for the Pont Jacques-Cartier.

From Ontario, you're about an hour away after you cross into the province of Québec going east along the Trans-Canada Highway. To remind you that you're no longer in Ontario, an extravagant, three-dimensional, illuminated sign, cum monument, stands on the border. You'll find an **Infotouriste Centre** at the first rest area, but you can always wait until you get to town. Eventually, the highway splits, so take Autoroute 20 and follow it straight into downtown, or *centre-ville,* in French. At one point, Autoroute 20 breaks down into a slower road with a series of traffic lights, but do not despair, the highway starts again, after a mile or two.

From Québec City, travel west along Autoroute 20 or 40; either takes you through Montréal. Autoroute 40 runs along the top of the island, and Autoroute 20 along the bottom.

Rolling into the station

In these ultra-fast times, rail travel has an undeniable romance. All trains bound for Montréal arrive at the downtown **Gare Centrale,** 895 rue de la Gauchetière Ouest (☎ **514-989-2626**). After you disembark and claim your luggage, you have several options. The Gare Centrale connects to the Bonaventure Métro station through a twisting network of store-lined corridors; follow the signs. Closer at hand, you'll find a taxi stand on the same level as the main hall. In addition, several excellent, though pricey, hotels are within walking distance. The Infotouriste Centre, a good place to begin your visit, is at the north end of nearby Square Dorchester. See the "Information, Please" section for hours.

If you've ever wanted to know the words to Canada's national anthem, they are inscribed along the bottom of the bas-relief sculpture on the upper walls around Gare Centrale's main hall.

Docking at a pier

Les Dauphins du Saint-Laurent (☎ **514-288-4499;** www.dauphins.ca) are high-speed hydrofoils that ferry passengers between Montréal and Québec City. In Montréal, they dock at the Quai Jacques-Cartier in Vieux-Montréal.

Cruise ships dock at the **Iberville Terminal** of the St. Lawrence Seaway, Montréal's commercial port. It's a five-to-ten minute taxi ride from downtown.

Information, Please

Québec's Ministry of Tourism runs Montréal's **Infotouriste Centre,** 1001 Square Dorchester (www.bonjourquebec.com), a block south of rue Ste-Catherine, between rue Peel and rue Metcalf, and at the north end of Square Dorchester. It's the city's main resource for travel information on Montréal and the surrounding regions, and it's chock full of free flyers and booklets. The keen and knowledgeable staff can answer almost any query you can muster. During the high tourist season, from the beginning of June through early-September, the center is open daily from 8:30 a.m. to 7:30 p.m. After Labour Day until the end of May, it operates daily from 9 a.m. to 6 p.m. You can also reach the center by phone, ☎ **877-266-5687** or 514-873-2015, should you need some roadside assistance while out and about. With different hours than the actual information center, lines are open Thursday to Tuesday from 8 a.m. to 10 p.m. and Wednesday from 10 a.m. to 10 p.m. during the high tourist season, and Thursday to Tuesday from 9 a.m. to 7 p.m. and Wednesday from 10 a.m. to 7 p.m. the rest of the year. On weekends, all year around, you can reach the center from 9 a.m. to 5 p.m.

The **Tourist Information Centre of Vieux-Montréal** (www.tourism-montreal.org) is at 174 rue Notre-Dame Est, at the northwest corner of Place Jacques-Cartier, an immense sloping square in honor of the city's founder. This is an excellent resource with a helpful staff, maps, and brochures.

Figuring Out the Neighborhoods

Although a map comes in handy, Montréal's central neighborhoods are so different from each other that you can orient yourself just by looking around. You can walk them all in a single day, if you're an athlete. If you're a normal person, take your time. Depending on your interests, you can walk through each neighborhood in a matter of minutes, spend an afternoon visiting, or take the whole day exploring its different parts.

Vieux-Montréal

This is the oldest part of the city and the crown jewel of Montréal's neighborhoods. Travelers flock here to soak up the European flavor from the well-preserved remains of the French and English colonial periods. Just exploring the neighborhood's nooks and crannies is a treat. Walk down an interesting-looking street and then another; find a secret courtyard, fountain, or square; ride in a horse-drawn carriage; or stop for drinks in the heart of it all: at an outdoor terrace along Place Jacques-Cartier.

Montréal boasts plenty of historic sites, museums, tours, shops, galleries, cafes, and other attractions, but just being here is the real trip. You can fancy yourself in a European capital or on the back lot of a Hollywood studio. In fact, Vieux-Montréal often passes as Paris in television and film productions shooting on location.

Downtown

Rue Ste-Catherine is downtown main commercial artery. It is crowded all day long with business people, tourists, shoppers, and all varieties of Montréal street creatures. In the morning, office types wielding aluminum mugs of caffeine dodge delivery trucks. After lunch, the shoppers are out in full force, hitting the street's boutiques, department stores, and shops. The foot traffic is especially heavy after work as the two crowds mingle. By dark, the mobs thin, leaving behind couples rushing to catch a movie or packs of friends carrying on into the night.

There's plenty more to downtown than the bright lights of rue Ste-Catherine. If you're a culture vulture, you can get your fix at the **Centre Canadien de L'architecture** (Canadian Center for Architecture), the **Musée des Beaux Arts** (Fine Arts Museum), and **McGill University's** gated campus.

Chinatown

Dim sum, dragon-beard candy, bubble tea, exotic fruits, herbal remedies, and curio shops — Montréal's Chinatown reveals many treasures to the adventurous traveler. The red, imperial arches along boulevard St-Laurent mark the neighborhood's northern and southern borders. Halfway in between and to the west, you can stroll along rue de la Gauchetière, which is closed to cars and has a good concentration of Chinese shops and restaurants.

Quartier Latin

Rue St-Denis, south of rue Sherbrooke, spills into Montréal's lively Latin Quarter. Serviced by the city's largest Métro station, Berri-UQAM, and squeezed between downtown, the Plateau, the Gay Village, and Chinatown, this neighborhood's central location makes it a crossroads of sorts. By evening, it fills with friends looking for a spot to rendezvous over drinks. During the warmer months, the same friends are hanging out on the numerous terraces that run the length of the street. The **Bar St-Sulpice** is a choice destination for such occasions, with its huge beer garden that's extremely popular among university students.

Gay Village

Happily, Montréal is an extremely gay-positive city. The stretch of rue Ste-Catherine, east of rue Amherst and as far east as avenue Papineau, is the epicenter of Montréal's vibrant and colorful gay community. Gay couples wander along the restaurant- and boutique-lined street hand-in-hand, and life goes on in a perfectly banal way.

Plateau

For a long time, this has been Montréal's trendiest neighborhood. In the early '90s, the low rents of this former working-class neighborhood attracted artists and other creative types, and hip boutiques, restaurants, bars, and cafes soon followed. Now the very people who made the Plateau what it is are fighting tooth and nail to keep their rent-controlled apartments, as Plateau's absentee landlords look to cash in with the condo crowd.

Despite the recent gentrification, everyone here still has their look and plenty of swagger. It's a great neighborhood for people watching, shopping, and eating. The main streets with all the action include avenue Mont-Royal, boulevard St-Laurent, and rue St-Denis.

Mile End

Mainly a residential area, a mix of artists, writers, students, young couples, and immigrant families — predominantly Greek, Orthodox Jew, and Italian — inhabit this idyllic neighborhood. The shops along rue St-Viateur reflect the community's varied tastes and backgrounds. For several blocks, between avenue du Parc and boulevard St-Laurent, rue St-Viateur is full of appealing, yet quaint, health food stores, cafes, restaurants, booksellers, gourmet shops, and the like. **Café Olympico** is the neighborhood hangout, with some of the best coffee in town.

One block north, on rue Bernard, you find a similar scene, but everything becomes decidedly more upscale west of avenue du Parc, which is the neighborhood of **Outremont.** Although only open seasonally, **Bilboquet,** at the westernmost point on this commercial strip, serves up scoops of homemade ice cream in a wide variety of interesting flavors, including maple taffy, or *tire* (pronounced TEER), which is available only for a few fleeting days in the spring.

Mile End is also bagel country. Montréal's bagels are even better than those in New York City; some say that they're the best in the world! Scrawnier and chewier than their Big Apple cousins, the dough of a Montréal bagel is thinner, so the inner circle is much bigger, making it more difficult to schmear with your favorite topping. **St-Viateur Bagel** and **Fairmout Bagel,** a block south on rue Fairmount, are the city's two most famous factories, churning out the bagels 24/7, and Montréalers keep up a perennial debate as to which bagel is best.

Little Italy

Boulevard St-Laurent north, way north, is the heart of Montréal's Italian community. This is where to go to catch up on European soccer league scores, challenge elderly men to bocce ball games in **Parc Martel,** or sip cappuccino and munch on biscotti at a sidewalk cafe. The loyal patrons of the '50s-style **Café Italia** claim that the coffee here is the best in Montréal.

At the strip's northern end, and a couple of blocks east of the intersection of boulevard St-Laurent and avenue Jean Talon, the immense Marché Jean Talon (Jean Talon Market) is at the geographical center of the city. It's packed on weekends. Formerly filled with new Canadians foraging for deals on produce, the crowd these days consists also of culinary highbrows searching for *terroir* items — quality local ingredients — and frugal gourmets of all stripes shopping for produce, cheeses, meats, and specialty items from Québec's bountiful regions, like ostrich meat from Salaberry de Valleyfield.

Getting Around Montréal

However you choose to get around Montréal, keep in mind that it's a large city with all the modern conveniences and headaches caused by the sheer volume of people on the move. In other words, getting around the city has its pros and cons.

On the plus side:

- ✔ The city's central neighborhoods are compact and well served by bike paths and an extensive public transport system that includes four subway lines and a network of buses.
- ✔ Taxis are plentiful and reasonably priced.

On the minus side:

✔ Driving in the city can be a hassle, because of an inordinate number of narrow, one-way streets. Chances are, you'll spend some of your time in a taxi stuck behind a garbage or recycling truck, with only Montréal's mediocre English-language radio programming to help you pass the time.

✔ Parking and rush hours are the same nightmares you get in any big city.

By foot

Walking is one of the best ways to travel in Montréal (see Chapter 11 for suggested walking itineraries). With the occasional support of public transportation and taxis, you can get everywhere you need to go on foot. Along the way, you experience much more of what Montréal has to offer. Even in the cold weather, a couple layers of clothing and a brisk pace go a long way toward combating the elements. So, don gloves, a warm hat, and a scarf.

Compared to most of the continent, where suburban attitudes are the rule, Montréal *feels* urban. Montréal's spirit is on the sidewalks of the neighborhoods, not in malls in the outlying areas. The sights and smells of the rapidly changing streetscapes are a feast for the senses.

The city's streets are inordinately safe by North American standards. While a modicum of street smarts is a must, there's no mood of fear and imminent danger on Montréal's streets. In fact, it's quite the contrary. The general population of stylish pedestrians is laid back, friendly, and usually glad to offer directions.

By public transportation (Métro and bus)

Completed for Expo '67, Montréal's Métro stations were built with a futuristic vision that has yet to materialize above ground. Today, the look is retro, maybe a little kitschy. Even the orange interiors of the trains are reminiscent of something out of Stanley Kubrick's film *2001: A Space Odyssey.*

Run by the *Sociéte de Transport de Montréal,* or STM (☎ **514-288-6287;** www.stm.qc.ca), the Métro has 65 stops. The lines extend to the farthest reaches of the city. The downtown core is serviced by the Green and Orange lines, between Lionel-Groulx in the west and Berri-UQAM in the east. The trains run from 5:30 in the morning until about 12:30 a.m. See the Cheat Sheet in the front of this book for a tear-out map.

Ask the ticket collector at any Métro station for a free map of the Island of Montréal's entire transit system, which includes all the bus routes. (The map is very handy, even if you never board public transport during your stay.) Near the ticket booths, schedules and routes of individual buses departing from that station are available. Most bus stops around the city have a departure schedule. The buses on some of the city's major arteries run 24 hours a day; other schedules vary. During the day, the service, both above and below ground, is regular, so you won't need to plan around it, but just in case, you can also get transit schedules by calling the STM or visiting its Web site. (See Chapter 4 for information on public transportation for the disabled.)

A single fare is good for one transfer, or *correspondence,* between the Métro and the buses. The rule is that you have to take a transfer at your point of origin, not ask for one later. In the Métro stations, silver mechanized dispensers just beyond the turnstiles spit transfers out at the press of a button. Bus drivers automatically extend one to you when you pay the fare, and they're valid for an hour and a half. Should you forget to grab one before getting on the subway, you can get it on your way out, and buses usually accept them. If the driver questions you, tell him you're a tourist and he'll probably let you on. You must also produce a valid transfer when switching between buses.

The STM charges C$2.50 (US$1.90) for a single ride, but if you plan to use public transit several times while in Montréal, buying in bulk may prove more economical. A strip of six tickets costs C$10 (US$7.50), a single-day pass is C$7 (US$5), a three-day pass is C$14 (US$10.50), and a weekly pass (from Monday to Sunday) runs you C$16 (US$12). Monthly passes are also available for C$54 (US$41). You can buy any of these at a Métro station's ticket booth and at some *dépanneurs* (convenience stores) and drug stores throughout the city.

By bicycle

Montréal is North America's bicycling capital. Despite the harsh winter climate that sends most cyclists into hibernation for four months, *Bicycling Magazine* rated Montréal tops in North America for its cycling infrastructure and culture.

A bike is great way to get around Montréal when the weather's not too nasty, although doing battle in traffic with aggressive drivers can be a hair-raising experience. Luckily, the city has an extensive network of bike paths, 240 miles in all, that provides a less harrowing ride through much of the city, including stretches through parks and along the waterfront.

You can rent a bicycle at several places in Montréal. These are the best:

- ✔ **Montréal on Wheels,** 27 rue de la Commune Est; ☎ **514-866-0633;** www.caroulemontreal.com

- ✔ **La Cordee Plein-Air,** 2159 rue Ste-Catherine Est; ☎ **800-567-1106** or 514-524-1106; www.lacordee.com

- ✔ **Cycle Pop et Pop Tours,** 1000 rue Rachel Est; ☎ **514-526-2525;** www.cyclepop.ca

By car

If there were no cars in the streets, Montréal would be an easy city to navigate. Unfortunately, the driving culture here is somewhat distinct from the rest of Canada. Drivers don't ask; they take. For example, in other cities, drivers request a lane change by using their turn signals, Montréalers don't really wait for an answer, they just signal and squeeze right in, often simultaneously — that is, if they bother to signal at all.

There's more. You can't turn right on a red light in Montréal (a fine rule when you consider that many drivers here are still learning to associate red lights with full stops). A green arrow means you can turn only in that direction; a solid green means you can go in any direction. Advanced (flashing) green lights can occur either at the beginning or at the end of a green light's phase. On a flashing green, the oncoming traffic has a red light, pedestrians are supposed to stay put, and drivers with the light can turn right and left at will.

And then there are the turning signs. Rather than say where you can't go at an intersection, Québec's traffic signs tell drivers where they *can* go. Most intersections have a white sign with a green circle around a set of black arrows. These black arrows indicate the directions a car can legally turn at that intersection. A sign with an arrow pointing straight ahead and an arrow pointing to the right means you *can't* turn left. Go figure. If you don't see a sign with green arrows, you can turn in any direction.

Filling up

In Canada, car owners buy their gasoline or diesel fuel by the liter, which is roughly equivalent to a quart. Canadian gas prices are somewhat more expensive than in the United States but are still considerably cheaper than European fuel. Multiply the per liter price by four for an approximate gallon comparison.

Parking tips for the brazen

Like any big city, parking in Montréal is a hassle. Deciphering the parking signs is probably the most difficult part. You need not only a keen eye but a firm grasp of the days of the week in French. (Beginning with

Monday, they are: *lundi, mardi, mercredi, jeudi, vendredi, samedi,* and *dimanche.*) Most of the time, these words appear in their abbreviated form on the signs, which is just the first three letters of each. You also need to familiarize yourself with 24-hour (military) clock times.

One plus to driving is that Montréal has lots of metered parking downtown and in the commercial areas of the city. You can also find free parking on the residential neighborhoods just north of rue Sherbrooke, though to be honest, you may spend half the evening looking for a spot.

Montréal residents with parking permits add to the confusion, hogging much of the residential curbsides. Arrows delimit the extent of their permit parking zones. If you see two empty spots in a row, chances are, you're staring at a restricted zone.

The downtown area has plenty of parking lots. They hit you up for C$12 to C$15 per day (US$9–US$12) — not bad compared to other large cities, but it still hurts.

By taxi

Montréal taxis don't sport bold color-schemes or patterns like cabs in other cities. A white light mounted on its roof is the only indication that a vehicle is a taxicab. When the light is on, the cab is available. Getting around in one of them is a reasonable proposition as long as you don't get snarled in traffic. At that point, you ride can begin to get expensive. The meter starts at C$2.50 (US$1.90) and climbs at a rate of roughly C$1.80 (US$1.25) per mile of driving or C45¢(US10¢) per minute of waiting in traffic. Trips across the downtown core, usually range between C$5 (US$3.75) and C$12 (US$9). The city's chauffeurs are a mixed bag, from career cabbies, who can tell you that boulevard René-Levesque used to be called rue Dorchester, to recently arrived immigrants, sometimes sitting on their Ph.D.s in chemistry.

Hailing a cab is easy. Just stick out you hand, and cabs swarm you like gadflies. Late at night, the more enterprising chauffeurs sometimes honk gently at pedestrians to remind you of their presence.

If you aren't near a main artery or don't feel like waiting for a taxi to pass, you can call for one. These are the two big local cab companies:

- ✔ **Taxi Diamond, ☎ 514-273-6331**
- ✔ **Taxi Co-op, ☎ 514-725-9885**

Chapter 9

Montréal's Best Hotels

. . . .

In This Chapter

▶ Checking into Montréal's best hotels

▶ Choosing small inns as alternatives

▶ Reviewing handy lists of accommodations by neighborhood and price

. . . .

*M*ontréal offers an incredible array of hotel rooms at a full range of prices. However, booking a room on short notice can be a problem, especially during weekends or anytime during the high tourist season (May through September). To get the room you want, plan ahead. Making your reservations well in advance can save you money, too.

The hotels in this chapter are our picks of the city's best, based on value, comfort, and convenience. Each listing includes $ symbols, indicating the price range of the hotel's rack rates for one night. These provide a rough guideline, so don't be afraid to investigate an interesting choice if it seems pricey. Most of the time, a better rate is available, so make sure you ask. After you have an idea of what's out there, see Chapter 6 for all our tips on wrangling the best deal. At the end of this chapter, we include an index of the hotel listings, organized by neighborhood and by price.

Each listing includes a $ symbol indicating the price range of the rooms. Prices are the rack rates, the standard rate for a double room for one night, before taxes. The $ signs represent the following prices ranges:

$	Less than C$100 (US$75)
$$	C$100–C$200 (US$75–US$150)
$$$	C$200–C$300 (US$150–US$225)
$$$$	More than C$300 (US$225)

Montréal's Hotels from A to Z

Auberge de La Fontaine
$$–$$$ **Plateau**

Staying at this inn on Montréal's third largest park lets you be a temporary resident of the uber-trendy Plateau neighborhood. Two attached, renovated townhouses contain 21 rooms. An elaborate and healthy continental breakfast is served in the lobby, which has large windows for gazing at lovely La Fontaine Park, across the street. Two suites with hot tubs that overlook the park are extremely popular among guests. Stroll along nearby avenue Mont-Royal and rue St-Denis to your heart's content.

1301 rue Rachel Est. ☎ *800-597-0597 or 514-597-0166. Fax: 514-597-0496. Internet: www.aubergedelafontaine.com. Parking: Three free spaces behind the hotel and on the surrounding streets. Rates: C$120–C$253 (US$90–US$190). Rates include continental breakfast. AE, DC, DISC, MC, V. Métro: Champs-de-Mars.*

Best Western Hotel Europa
$–$$ **Downtown**

Although the lobby resembles the far off land of Atlantis, the Europa provides the familiar comforts of the Best Western hotel brand. Located just south of rue Ste-Catherine, the Europa has 180 rooms, on six floors. Each room contains a king, queen, or two double beds; contemporary, European wood furnishings finish the room. The white bathrooms are no frills but seem particularly clean. You find plenty of English-language service in this part of the city.

1240 rue Drummond. ☎ *800-361-3000 or 514-866-6492. Fax: 514-908-2879. Internet: www.europahotelmtl.com. Parking: C$15 (US$11). Rates: C$79–C$239 (US$55–US$179). AE, MC, DC, V. Métro: Peel.*

Château Royal Hotel & Suites
$$–$$$ **Downtown**

This hotel on rue Crescent used to have a reputation for rocking as hard as the nightlife strip it's on, but since 2001, a new management team with a strict, and explicit no-party policy has turned this 113-suite establishment around. A former apartment building, the Château Royal is a great value for families, small groups of travelers, individuals on extended stays, and people who enjoy having their very own downtown apartment with a balcony while on vacation. The bachelor, one-, and two- bedroom suites come with a full kitchen, stocked with pots, pans, and dishes. The marble bathrooms include a bath and shower.

1420 rue Crescent. ☎ *800-363-0335 or 514-848-0999. Fax: 514-848-9403. Internet: www.chateauroyal.com. Parking: Valet C$17 (US$12). Rates: C$190–C$290 (US$142–US$217). AE, DC, DISC, MC, V. Métro: Guy-Concordia.*

Crowne Plaza

$$$–$$$$ Plateau

Well located near the Plateau, Quartier Latin, and the Gay Village, this 24-story, converted apartment building has spacious rooms and excellent views and is a good foothold for exploring the trendy neighborhoods east of boulevard St-Laurent. It is also adjacent to the Sherbrooke Métro station. Painted vines climb along the low archways of the marble-floored lobby. Stark landscape murals, plants, and flower arrangements give it a winter garden feel. The rooms are quite large and include a sitting area and a large desk, but come with a standard-size bathroom.

505 rue Sherbrooke Est. ☎ *800-477-3365 or 514-842-8581. Fax: 514-842-8910. Internet:* www.cpmontreal.com. *Parking: C$16 (US$12). Rates: C$209–C$309 (US$157–US$232). AE, DC, MC, V. Métro: Sherbrooke.*

Delta Centre Ville

$$$–$$$$ Downtown

This 28-story glass tower is part of a Canadian chain of corporate hotels and is of no relation to the airline. Its spacious rooms offer great skyline and river views and all the amenities that today's weary business travelers demand. When it opened in 1977, this hotel was state-of-the-art. Today, the Delta still has the city's only revolving restaurant on its top floor, amusingly named, *Tour de Ville.*

777 rue Université. ☎ *800-268-1133 or 514-879-1370. Fax: 514-879-1761. Internet:* www.deltahotels.com. *Parking: C$18 (US$13). Rates: C$179–C$350 (US$134–US$262). AE, DC, DISC, MC, V. Métro: Square-Victoria.*

Fairmont The Queen Elizabeth

$$–$$$ Downtown

Built atop the Gare Centrale, the Queen E is the *grande dame* of Montréal's hotels. It's also where John and Yoko did their nude rendition of "Give Peace a Chance" in 1969, while the couple was on their honeymoon. Now a Fairmont property, the Queen was cited on *Condé Nast Traveler*'s 2002 Gold List. The hotel's Beaver Club restaurant is one of the best places for fine Continental cuisine in Montréal. You'll find several grades of accommodation, but even the so-called moderate rooms are pretty lavish. The downtown location is convenient, but there's lots of traffic.

900 bd. René-Levesque Ouest. ☎ *800-441-1212 or 514-861-3511. Fax: 514-954-2256. Internet:* www.fairmont.com. *Parking: Valet C$22 (US$16). Rates: C$189–C$269 (US$141–US$201). AE, DC, DISC, MC, V. Métro: Bonaventure.*

Downtown Montréal Accommodations

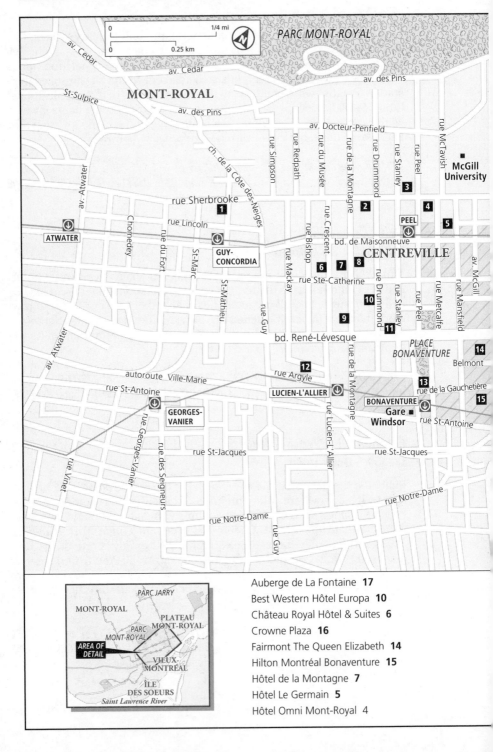

Auberge de La Fontaine **17**
Best Western Hôtel Europa **10**
Château Royal Hôtel & Suites **6**
Crowne Plaza **16**
Fairmont The Queen Elizabeth **14**
Hilton Montréal Bonaventure **15**
Hôtel de la Montagne **7**
Hôtel Le Germain **5**
Hôtel Omni Mont-Royal **4**

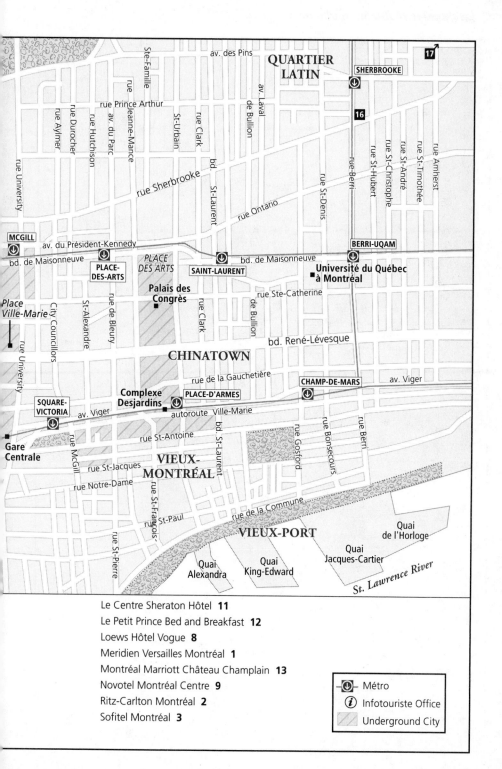

av. des Pins

QUARTIER LATIN

SHERBROOKE

MCGILL

av. du Président-Kennedy

bd. de Maisonneuve

PLACE-DES-ARTS

PLACE DES ARTS

SAINT-LAURENT

bd. de Maisonneuve

BERRI-UQAM

Université du Québec à Montréal

Place Ville-Marie

Palais des Congrès

rue Ste-Catherine

bd. René-Lévesque

CHINATOWN

rue de la Gauchetière

CHAMP-DE-MARS

av. Viger

Complexe Desjardins

PLACE-D'ARMES

SQUARE-VICTORIA

av. Viger

autoroute Ville-Marie

rue St-Antoine

Gare Centrale

rue St-Jacques

VIEUX-MONTRÉAL

rue Notre-Dame

rue St-Paul

rue de la Commune

VIEUX-PORT

Quai de l'Horloge

Quai Jacques-Cartier

Quai King-Edward

Quai Alexandra

St. Lawrence River

Le Centre Sheraton Hôtel **11**
Le Petit Prince Bed and Breakfast **12**
Loews Hôtel Vogue **8**
Meridien Versailles Montréal **1**
Montréal Marriott Château Champlain **13**
Novotel Montréal Centre **9**
Ritz-Carlton Montréal **2**
Sofitel Montréal **3**

- Métro
- *i* Infotouriste Office
- Underground City

Vieux-Montréal Accommodations

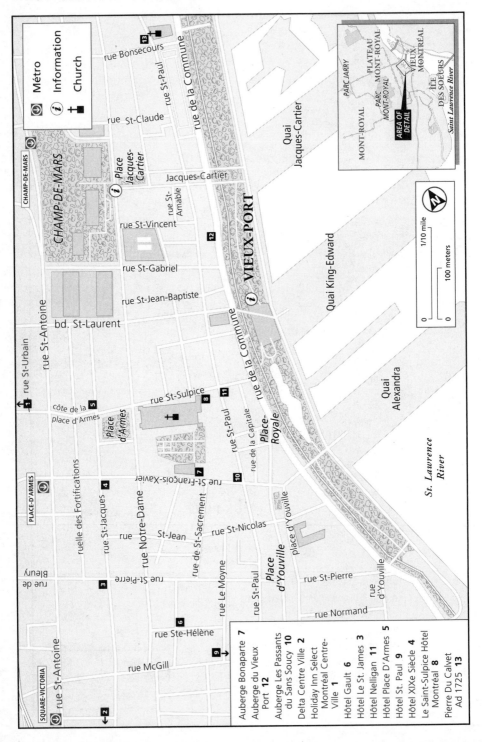

Métro
Information
Church

CHAMP-DE-MARS

rue Bonsecours

rue St-Claude

rue St-Paul

rue de la Commune

Place Jacques-Cartier

Jacques-Cartier

rue St-Amable

rue St-Vincent

rue St-Gabriel

rue St-Jean-Baptiste

bd. St-Laurent

rue St-Antoine

rue St-Urbain

rue St-Sulpice

côte de la place d'Armes

Place d'Armes

ruelle des Fortifications

rue St-Jacques

rue St-François-Xavier

rue Notre-Dame

rue St-Jean

rue de St-Sacrement

rue St-Nicolas

rue St-Pierre

rue de Bleury

rue Le Moyne

rue St-Paul

Place d'Youville

place d'Youville

rue St-Pierre

rue d'Youville

rue Normand

rue Ste-Hélène

rue McGill

rue St-Antoine

PLACE-D'ARMES

SQUARE-VICTORIA

CHAMP-DE-MARS

VIEUX-PORT

Place-Royale

rue St-Paul

rue de la Capitale

rue de la Commune

Quai Jacques-Cartier

Quai King-Edward

Quai Alexandra

St. Lawrence River

AREA OF DETAIL

PARC JARRY

PLATEAU MONT-ROYAL

PARC MONT-ROYAL

MONT-ROYAL

VIEUX MONTRÉAL

ÎLE DES SŒURS

Saint Lawrence River

1/10 mile

100 meters

Auberge Bonaparte **7**
Auberge du Vieux Port **12**
Auberge Les Passants du Sans Soucy **10**
Delta Centre Ville **2**
Holiday Inn Select Montréal Centre-Ville **1**
Hôtel Gault **6**
Hôtel Le St. James **3**
Hôtel Nelligan **11**
Hôtel Place D'Armes **5**
Hôtel St. Paul **9**
Hôtel XIXe Siècle **4**
Le Saint-Sulpice Hôtel Montréal **8**
Pierre Du Calvet Ad 1725 **13**

Hilton Montréal Bonaventure

$$–$$$ **Downtown**

A serene penthouse perched above Place Bonaventure — 17 floors up — this two-story Hilton comprises a perimeter of modular, concrete-walled rooms that surround an immense, landscaped park land inspired by the Canadian wilderness. The emphasis here is on quiet. All of the hotel's services are in a central hub, away from the rooms, which are spacious and come with bathrooms finished in marble. The hotel makes children feel at home by giving them a welcoming gift and stocking the concierge's desk with games to loan.

900 rue de la Gauchetiere Ouest. ☎ *800-267-2575 or 514-878-2332. Fax: 514-878-1442. Internet:* www.hilton.com. *Parking: C$15 (US$11) or valet C$22 (US$16). Rates: C$160–C$300 (US$120–US$225). AE, DC, DISC, MC, V. Métro: Bonaventure.*

Holiday Inn Select Montréal Centre-Ville

$$–$$$ **Downtown**

From the Chinese pagoda-like exterior to the central atrium lobby, feng shui principles influence the design of this 235-room hotel. For example, the hotel has no fourth floor because the Chinese consider the number bad luck. Conveniently located in Chinatown, the hotel's decor is Asian throughout, from the framed Chinese prints to the emerald bedspreads. On the whole, it's refreshing and unusual. The decor and the large rooms make this a select-level Holiday Inn, a notch above the brand's usual level of hospitality.

99 av. Viger. ☎ *888-878-9888 or 514-878-9888. Fax: 514-878-6341. Internet:* www.yul-downtown.hiselect.com. *Parking: C$14 (US$10). Rates: C$139–C$289 (US$104–US$216). AE, DC, DISC, MC, V. Métro: Place-d'Armes.*

Hotel de la Montagne

$$ **Downtown**

Elegance, location, and particularly large rooms are what recommend this hotel, a former 20-story apartment building. With 135 rooms in all, each floor offers a choice of nine different units, all of which have modern bathrooms with separate tub and shower. All rooms have balconies facing east or west and provide great views of Downtown. The back of the hotel fronts rue Crescent, a vibrant nightlife strip. If you're a particularly light sleeper, you may wish to request a room on the other side, away from the action.

1430 rue de la Montagne. ☎ *800-361-6262 or 514-288-5656. Fax: 514-288-9558. Internet:* www.hoteldelamontagne.com. *Parking: Valet C$12 (US$9). Rates: C$169–C$195 (US$126–US$146). Rates include breakfast on weekends. AE, DC, DISC, MC, V. Métro: Peel.*

Hotel Gault
$$$–$$$$ Vieux-Montréal

The immense rooms of this 30-room boutique hotel feel like loft apartments. The floors are of polished concrete, and the rooms are furnished with mobile, custom cabinetry made from white oak. Rooms include a wooden trellis at the door for increased privacy. Some rooms have secret terraces and ornate 19th-century wrought iron detailing in the windows. Most impressive are the bathrooms, with large tubs and heated floors. The furniture in the lobby, with a bar, seating area, and reading room, are all reproductions of design classics, like Harry Bertoia chairs and Artemide lamps.

449 rue Ste-Hélène. ☎ *866-904-1616 or 514-904-1616. Fax: 514-904-1717. Internet:* www.hotelgauld.com. *Parking: Valet C$18 (US$13). Rates: C$229–C$299 (US$172–US$224). Rates include breakfast. AE, DC, MC, V. Métro: Square-Victoria.*

Hotel Le Germain
$$$ Downtown

According to the concierge, "Art Deco minimalism with a touch of Zen" is what awaits you at this 99-room boutique hotel. Outside, the color scheme is dark and earthy, but inside it's clean and contemporary. The smaller scale of this hotel operation allows the staff to be meticulous in its service and upkeep. Fresh flowers, a sumptuous seating area, and a wood-burning fireplace greet guests in the subdued lobby. Perhaps the most intriguing detail is that each bathroom has a glass wall. The architects envisioned it as a way of allowing natural light into the bathroom.

2050 rue Mansfield. ☎ *877-333-2050 or 514-849-2050. Fax: 514-849-1437. Internet:* www.hotelboutique.com. *Parking: Valet C$18 (US$13). Rates: C$240–C$290 (US$180– US$217). Rates include breakfast. AE, DC, MC, V. Métro: McGill.*

Hôtel Le St-James
$$$$ Vieux-Montréal

The last time the Rolling Stones were on tour in Montréal, they booked this entire hotel. The 61 units, many of them suites, are among the most deluxe and expensive accommodations in Montréal, with huge marble bathrooms and working fireplaces. The lobby and guest rooms are ornate and decorated with art and antiques. At night, the building's Second Empire facade lights up and looks spectacular. Its Vieux-Montréal location is away from much of the tourist melee and slightly closer to Downtown than other hotels in this neighborhood.

355 rue St-James. ☎ *866-841-3111 or 514-841-3111. Fax: 514-841-1232. Internet:* www.hotellestjames.com. *Parking: Valet C$25 (US$18). Rates: C$400–C$475 (US$300–US$356). AE, DC, DISC, MC, V. Métro: Place-d'Armes.*

Hôtel Nelligan

$$$ **Vieux-Montréal**

This 63-room boutique hotel was named after Québec poet Emile Nelligan, whose verses are sprinkled on its interior walls. Located in two historic buildings on rue St-Paul, one of Vieux-Montréal's main strips, Hôtel Nelligan is filled with galleries, cafes, and boutiques. Originally built in 1850, the premises have exposed stone and brick walls that create a warm and welcoming aura. Guest rooms feature dark woods and leather furnishings along with high ceilings, fireplaces, and hot tubs. Nightly wine and cheese gatherings welcome hotel guests in the lobby's central atrium, which is also a popular restaurant and bar.

106 rue St-Paul Ouest. ☎ ***877-788-2040** or 514-788-2040. Fax: 514-788-2041. Internet:* www.hotelnelligan.com. *Parking: Valet C$17 (US$12). Rates: C$210–C$235 (US$158–US$176). Rates include breakfast and evening cocktail. AE, DC, DISC, MC, V. Métro: Place-d'Armes.*

Hotel Omni Mont-Royal

$$–$$$ **Downtown**

For a central downtown location, the Omni can't be beat. You can walk just about anywhere, and the Peel Métro station is close at hand. Be sure to ask for a room facing Mont-Royal for an excellent view. Plus, the rooftop pool is heated all year around. However, for the money, some guests feel that Montréal's Omni leaves something to be desired, with standard-size rooms that have a somewhat tired feeling, particularly in the '80s vintage bathrooms.

1050 rue Sherbrooke Ouest. ☎ ***800-843-6664** or 514-284-1110. Fax: 514-845-3025. Internet:* www.omnihotels.com. *Parking: C$14 (US$10) or valet C$26 (US$19). Rates: C$160–C$245 (US$120–US$184). AE, DC, DISC, MC, V. Métro: Peel.*

Hotel Place d'Armes

$$ **Vieux-Montréal**

This 44-room boutique hotel, located near the Basilique Notre-Dame and the Montréal Convention Center, has a rooftop terrace overlooking the many patinaed copper rooftops of Vieux-Montréal. The architects harnessed the beauty of the facade and carried it over into the design of the interior. The result is a welcoming environment that's cozy, contemporary, and comfortable. Brick walls and wood furnishings add to the warmth. Many of the black-and-white marble tiled bathrooms have a hot tub built for two.

701 côte de la Place d'Armes. ☎ ***888-450-1887** or 514-842-1887. Fax: 514-842-6469. Internet:* www.hotelplacedarmes.com. *Parking: Valet C$17 (US$12). Rates: C$185–C$190 (US$139–US$142). Rates include breakfast and an evening cocktail. AE, DC, DISC, MC, V. Métro: Place-d'Armes.*

Hotel St-Paul

$$$ **Vieux-Montréal**

Despite an imposing exterior, the inside of this 120-room boutique hotel is ephemeral and ultra-modern, making a good case for the less-is-more argument. The lighting is almost theatrical — definitely mood — from the mysterious hearth hovering in alabaster in the lobby to the knee-level, colored floodlights in the halls. The dark, 100-year-old wooden floors of the rooms are warm and welcoming. The rooms are sparsely furnished — intentionally, of course. Along with other custom pieces, a television screen in each room displays the room-service menu, which changes on a daily basis.

355 rue McGill. ☎ **514-380-2222** *or 866-380-2202. Fax: 514-380-2200. Internet:* www. hotelstpaul.com. *Parking: Valet C$17 (US$12). Rates: C$205–C$245 (US$154– US$184). Rates include breakfast. AE, DC, MC, V. Métro: Square-Victoria.*

Hotel XIXe Siècle

$$$–$$$$ **Vieux-Montréal**

A Victorian reading room — resembling a set on *Masterpiece Theatre* — with extremely high ceilings, sets a tone of intimate grandeur in this Vieux-Montréal boutique hotel in a renovated, 19th-century, neo-classical bank building. The 59 rooms are of the same scale and thoughtfully decorated in French Second Empire style. The large and luxurious bathrooms have black and white tiled floors, large marble countertops, and deep tubs. Rates include a lavish continental breakfast, featuring a selection of breads, jams, juices, yogurt, and so on, served in the main floor dining room.

262 rue St-Jacques Ouest. ☎ **877-553-0019** *or 514-985-0019. Fax: 514-985-0059. Internet:* www.hotelxixsiecle.com. *Parking: Valet C$18 (US$13). Rates: C$180– C$375 (US$135–US$281). AE, DC, MC, V. Métro: Place-d'Armes.*

Le Centre Sheraton Hotel

$$$–$$$$ **Downtown**

Montréal's Sheraton is in an excellent Downtown location: across the street from the Bell Centre, a block from rue Ste-Catherine, and a quick amble from the nightlife and restaurants on rue Crescent. All the rooms have all the latest amenities, including the Sheraton's own Sweet Sleeper bed (also for sale), minibars with infrared sensors, and automated billing systems. Built in 1982, the marble bathrooms lack nothing — except hot tubs.

1201 bd. René-Levesque Ouest. ☎ **888-627-7102** *or 514-878-2000. Fax: 514-878-3958. Internet:* www.sheraton.com/lecentre. *Parking: C$17 (US$12) or valet C$22 (US$16). Rates: C$209–C$309 (US$157– US$231). AE, DC, DISC, MC, V. Métro: Peel.*

Le Saint-Sulpice Hôtel Montréal
$$$–$$$$ **Vieux-Montréal**

Near Basilique Notre-Dame in the heart of Vieux-Montréal, this spacious and classy 108-suite hotel is splendid and lavish without being gaudy. Each condo-style suite, between 550 and 1,500 square feet, has a full kitchen, a living room with leather seating, and French doors that open to a courtyard or the streets of Vieux-Montréal. Many have their own fireplaces. The bathrooms are well lit, stocked with high-end toiletries, and have a large shower. The staff is helpful, energetic, and well trained in the art of pampering.

414 rue St-Sulpice. ☎ *877-785-7423 or 514-288-1000. Fax: 514-288-0077. Internet:* www.lesaintsulpice.com. *Parking: Valet C$25 (US$18). Rates: C$179–C$500 (US$134–US$375). Rates include American buffet breakfast. AE, DC, DISC, MC, V. Métro: Place-d'Armes.*

Loews Hotel Vogue
$$$–$$$$ **Downtown**

Loews, a luxury hotel brand, owns distinct properties in cities across North America. In Montréal, it's the 142-room Hotel Vogue, right downtown and a block away from rue Crescent. For some guests, the large marble bathrooms, featuring a two-person hot tub and a television, are absolutely to die for. However, you may be disappointed if you're expecting a room with a view. The black and white marble lobby is elegant, though.

1425 rue de la Montagne. ☎ *800-465-6654 or 514-285-5555. Fax: 514-849-8903. Internet:* www.loewshotels.com/vogue. *Parking: Valet C$25 (US$18). Rates: C$229–C$309 (US$172–US$232). AE, DC, DISC, MC, V. Métro: Peel.*

Meridien Versailles Montréal
$$–$$$ **Downtown**

A fancy name for a fancy hotel, the Versailles walks the walk with its understated elegance. Located in the western part of the downtown core, this 106-room hotel is at the end of a long stretch of antiques shops, art galleries, and designer boutiques on rue Sherbrooke. The lobby is small and cozy, just a front desk and a seating area. The rooms are large and tastefully finished in neutral tones and lush textures.

1808 rue Sherbrooke Ouest. ☎ *800-543-4300 or 514-933-8111. Fax: 514-933-7102. Internet:* www.versailleshotels.com. *Parking: Valet C$17 (US$12). Rates: C$195–C$235 (US$146–US$176). AE, DC, DISC, MC, V. Métro: Guy-Concordia.*

Montréal Marriott Château Champlain
$$–$$$ **Downtown**

This 36-floor high rise, halfway down the hill between Downtown and Vieux-Montréal, offers standard-size rooms, but with all the amenities and services of a first-class hotel. The north-facing view is the best, with a close-up of the other buildings in the downtown core. Inspired by glorious Windsor Station next door, the Moorish-style, semi-circular, floor-to-ceiling windows are particularly remarkable. Otherwise, the look and level of comfort are what you expect from a Marriott property.

1 Place du Canada. ☎ *800-200-5909 or 514-878-9000. Fax: 514-878-6761. Internet:* www.mariotthotels.com/yulcc. *Parking: C$16 (US$12). Rates: C$199–C$229 (US$149–US$171). Rates include breakfast on weekends. AE, DC, DISC, MC, V. Métro: Bonaventure.*

Novotel Montréal Centre
$–$$ Downtown

You detect subtle differences in this hotel's approach to hospitality from the minute you enter the lobby until you depart. For example, rather than a long front counter, guests check-in at individual islands. The service is considerate but expedient. The rooms have a modern feel with clean lines, warm tones, and accents of primary colors. It is just steps away from shopping on rue Ste-Catherine and restaurants and bars of rue Crescent.

1180 rue de la Montagne. ☎ *800-668-6835 or 514-861-6000. Fax: 514-861-2295. Internet:* www.novotel.com. *Parking: C$13 (US$9). Rates: C$119–C$220 (US$89–US$165). AE, DC, DISC, MC, V. Métro: Lucien-L'Allier or Peel.*

Ritz-Carlton Montréal
$$–$$$$ Downtown

Opened in 1912 and recently refurbished, Montréal's Ritz-Carlton, the only Ritz in Canada, remains a bastion of elegance — the crown jewel of Downtown's Golden Square Mile that's filled with art galleries, swank boutiques, and antiques shops. The quality of service is high; the staff seems to remember each guest's name. Surprisingly, it is not the most expensive hotel in town — although it is definitely the grandest. High tea is served daily and in the summer, you can sit in the garden. The rooms and suites are spacious with large closets, chandeliers, and marble bathrooms. Some have working fireplaces. Liz Taylor married Richard Burton here, many moons, and perhaps even more husbands, ago.

1228 rue Sherbrooke Ouest. ☎ *800-363-0366 or 514-842-4212. Fax: 514-842-3383. Internet:* www.ritzcarlton.com/hotels/montreal. *Parking: Valet C$25 (US$18). Rates: C$198–C$325 (US$150–US$243). AE, DC, DISC, MC, V. Métro: Peel.*

Sofitel Montréal
$$$–$$$$ Downtown

This 258-room hotel offers its guests modern European elegance and refinement on a grand scale in a part of downtown known as the

Golden Square Mile. Owned by a French hotel group, the Sofitel is a well-known brand throughout Europe. The hotel is allegedly designed on the principals of the *art de vivre* — something like a French version of feng shui. Despite its minimalist and understated decor, the luminous lobby's 18-foot ceilings make it an imposing space. The floor-to-ceiling windows in the rooms are only half as high and offer spectacular views of the downtown core. The rooms, with soft tones of taupe and rust, have original artwork on the walls and teak furniture. Large bathrooms of ochre marble and black granite countertops feature a glass-walled shower and a deep tub.

1155 rue Sherbrooke Ouest. ☎ **877-285-9001** *or 514-285-9000. Fax: 514-289-1155. Internet:* www.sofitel.com. *Parking: Valet, C$24 (US$17). Rates: C$159–C$319 (US$119–US$239). AE, DC, DISC, MC, V. Métro: Peel.*

Runner-up Hotels

Auberge Bonaparte

$$–$$$ Vieux-Montréal Located in Vieux-Montréal, this hotel has 30 rooms and delectable croissants for breakfast. With views of Basilique Notre-Dame, it offers Old World refinement on an intimate scale. *447 rue St-François-Xavier.* ☎ **514-844-1448**. *Fax: 514-844-0272. Internet:* www.bonaparte.ca.

Auberge du Vieux Port

$$–$$$ Vieux-Montréal This 27-room hotel in a late 19th-century building in Vieux-Montréal was once a warehouse and general store. The rooms have stone and brick walls, huge beams running across the ceilings, hardwood floors, and original artwork. *97 rue de la Commune Ouest.* ☎ **888-660-7678** *or 514-876-0081. Fax: 514-876-8923. Internet:* www.aubergedu vieuxport.com.

Auberge Les Passants du Sans Soucy

$$–$$$ Vieux-Montréal A small inn with nine spacious rooms and made-to-order breakfast. In Vieux-Montréal, the would-be lobby also serves as an art gallery. *171 rue St-Paul Ouest.* ☎ **514-842-2634**. *Fax: 514-842-2912. Internet:* www.lesanssoucy.com.

Le Petit Prince Bed and Breakfast

$$ Downtown This downtown B&B with four rooms is in the southwestern corner of the downtown's Golden Square Mile. The rooms feature fireplaces, hot tubs, wireless Internet, and large private balconies. *1384 av. Overdale.* ☎ **877-938-9750** *or 514-938-2277. Fax: 514-935-9750. Internet:* www.montrealbanb.com.

Pierre Du Calvet Ad 1725

$$$ Vieux-Montréal A romantic nine-room inn, this is in one of Vieux-Montréal's most historic residences; it features stone walls, original antiques, oriental rugs, and a fireplace. The rooms have canopy beds. *405 rue Bonsecours.* ☎ *866-544-1725 or 514-282-1725. Fax: 514-282-0456. Internet:* www.pierreducalvet.ca.

Index of Accommodations by Neighborhood

Chinatown
Holiday Inn Select Montréal
  Centre-Ville ($$–$$$)

Downtown
Best Western Hotel Europa ($–$$)
Château Royal Hotel & Suites ($$–$$$)
Delta Centre Ville ($$–$$$$)
Fairmont The Queen Elizabeth
  ($$–$$$)
Hilton Montréal Bonaventure ($$–$$$)
Hotel de la Montagne ($$)
Hotel Le Germain ($$$)
Hotel Omni Mont-Royal ($$–$$$)
Le Centre Sheraton Hotel ($$$–$$$$)
Le Petit Prince Bed and Breakfast ($$)
Loews Hotel Vogue ($$$–$$$$)
Meridien Versailles Montréal ($$–$$$)
Montréal Marriott Château Champlain
  ($$–$$$)
Novotel Montréal Centre ($–$$)

Ritz-Carlton Montréal ($$–$$$$)
Sofitel Montréal ($$–$$$$)

Vieux-Montréal
Auberge du Vieux Port ($$–$$$)
Auberge Les Passants du Sans Soucy
  ($$–$$$)
Auberge Bonaparte ($$–$$$)
Hotel Gault ($$$–$$$$)
Hôtel Le St-James ($$$$)
Hôtel Nelligan ($$$)
Hotel Place d'Armes ($$)
Hotel St-Paul ($$$)
Hotel XIXe Siècle ($$–$$$$)
Le Saint-Sulpice Hôtel Montréal
  ($$–$$$$)
Pierre Du Calvet Ad 1725 ($$$)

Plateau
Auberge de La Fontaine ($$–$$$)
Crowne Plaza ($$$–$$$$)

Index of Accommodations by Price

$–$$
Best Western Hotel Europa
  (Downtown)
Novotel Montréal Centre (Downtown)

$$
Hotel de la Montagne (Downtown)
Hotel Place d'Armes (Vieux-Montréal)
Le Petit Prince Bed and Breakfast
  (Downtown)

$$–$$$
Auberge Bonaparte (Vieux-Montréal)
Auberge de La Fontaine (Plateau)
Auberge du Vieux (Vieux-Montréal)
Auberge Les Passants du Sans Soucy
  (Vieux-Montréal)
Château Royal Hotel & Suites
  (Downtown)
Fairmont The Queen Elizabeth
  (Downtown)

Hilton Montréal Bonaventure
(Downtown)
Holiday Inn Select Montréal
Centre-Ville (Chinatown)
Hotel Omni Mont-Royal (Downtown)
Meridien Versailles Montréal
(Downtown)
Montréal Marriott Château Champlain
(Downtown)

$$–$$$$

Ritz-Carlton Montréal (Downtown)

$$$

Hotel Le Germain (Downtown)
Hôtel Nelligan (Vieux-Montréal)
Hotel St-Paul (Vieux-Montréal)
Pierre Du Calvet Ad 1725
(Vieux-Montréal)

$$$–$$$$

Crowne Plaza (Plateau)
Delta Centre Ville (Downtown)
Hotel Gault (Vieux-Montréal)
Hotel XIXe Siècle (Vieux-Montréal)
Le Centre Sheraton Hotel (Downtown)
Le Saint-Sulpice Hôtel Montréal
(Vieux-Montréal)
Loews Hotel Vogue (Downtown)
Sofitel Montréal (Downtown)

$$$$

Hôtel Le St-James (Vieux-Montréal)

Chapter 10

Dining and Snacking in Montréal

● ●

In This Chapter

▶ Understanding the ins and outs of dining in Montréal

▶ Finding Montréal's top dining spots

▶ Locating the best snacks and light meals

● ●

*Y*our options are staggering when dining in Montréal, one of the world's great restaurant cities and a food-lover's paradise. Montréalers eat out often, so the city is brimming with contenders hoping to be the next "it" restaurant with the in crowd.

But don't be intimidated. Eating in Montréal doesn't have to be an ordeal. Many restaurants offer tasty and diverse options at a good price, and the city has an endless variety of ethnic eats. In fact, Montréalers looking to score a quick bite are likely to choose a *shish-taouk* (Lebanese souvlaki), a *samosa* (meat or veggie Indian pastry), or sushi over a burger and fries. Don't fret: You can find burgers and fries, too.

In this chapter, we attempt to simplify your choices by offering a representative selection of Montréal's best places to eat, including fine dining, trendy spots, and some neighborhood gems. After that, we tell you where to find the best picnic food, coffee, BYOB restaurants, and more.

Recognizing Montréal's Hot Food Trends

Montréal's real specialty, of course, is French food. While the better French restaurants tend to be a little on the expensive side, we think they're worth every penny. If you leave Montréal without eating at least one great French meal, you miss out on one of the best things about the city.

Your terroir is my local ingredient

Many of Montréal's best restaurants offer some variation of French or contemporary continental cuisine. What's particularly new and exciting is the trend toward *terroir,* the French word describing high-quality, locally produced, seasonal ingredients. (Actually, the trend started in France about ten years ago.) Menus of finer restaurants are cluttered with names of specialty ingredients from Québec's bountiful rural regions. Thankfully, most of the best kitchens go beyond obvious Canadian staples like salmon and maple syrup and some offer items you've probably never heard of before.

The brunch bunch

Does anyone in Montréal have the makings of a sensible breakfast in their fridge anymore? Not if you judge by the action in the Plateau neighborhood. On weekends, Montréalers flock here looking for somewhere to land a late-morning or midday brunch. Lines are common at the better places, and new spots specializing in all-day breakfasts are popping up at an amazing rate. Brunch patrons are a mixed bag, a potentially volatile combination of chipper morning people and groups of extremely hungover friends. Everyone's happy, though, as waiters arrive with elaborate breakfasts on oversized plates accompanied by fresh juice and hot coffee. See "The big breakfast bonanza" section near the end of this chapter for locations.

Cutting Costs

Eating is not particularly expensive in Montréal, especially when you consider how good the food generally is. Still, you can find a few ways to cut corners on your food budget with sacrificing too much:

- ✔ **Pack a picnic.** This obviously isn't an option in mid-winter, but during the summer months, it makes sense. With plenty of parks across the city where you can find a shady corner to have a light meal, even if you splurge on some fancy cheese or pâté, you'll still save.

- ✔ **Enjoy a French breakfast.** An economical breakfast, which is typically French and easy enough to reconstruct in Montréal, is a croissant or two and bowl of *café au lait.* Dipping and jam are optional. See our picks for the best croissants in the "Coffee and pastries" section later in this chapter.

- ✔ **Eat your big meal at lunch.** Lunch menus are considerably cheaper than their equivalent at dinner. Check the lunch *table d'hôte,* a fixed menu including a starter and dessert, which is often a very good deal.

✔ **Check your memberships.** You may be eligible for discounts of 10% to 15% off your restaurant bill if you're a member of clubs like AAA. Always ask.

✔ **Eat in your own kitchen.** If your hotel room has a kitchenette, you can store some milk, bread, and a few staples. Eat in for breakfast, pack a picnic lunch, and save your dining dollars for the evening.

✔ **Bring your own wine.** Montréal has many BYOB restaurants. Taste-wise, you may have difficulty deciding on a wine when you have yet to look at the menu. But budget-wise, you'll come out ahead.

Honing in on Dining Etiquette

Here are a few do's and don'ts for dining out:

✔ **Dressing:** Montréal follows roughly the same confusing clothing rules as Paris. People look together when they go out to eat, but they don't really dress up. A clothing Catch-22? Our advice: Don't be a slob, but leave the glitz at home. For both men and women, a nice pair of pants or even jeans (*nice* jeans) and a decent top make you feel comfortable almost anywhere.

✔ **Smoking:** Until recently, the province of Québec was somewhat of a bastion for smokers, counter to the trend that's turning North American cities into paragons of smoke-free living. But change is in the air. Several higher-end restaurants are declaring themselves non-smoking environments. Other eateries may soon follow their lead. For the moment, though, expect most restaurants to have a smoking section.

✔ **Deciphering the menu:** Wouldn't France be wonderful without the French language? Wouldn't French food be great without French menus? Don't worry about language barriers between you and your plate. In most restaurants, the menu is available in English. When it's not, waiters are used to translating. Just take note of one common trap to spare yourself some confusion: an *entrée* in French actually means a starter. A main course, therefore, is not an entrée but a *plat principal*.

✔ **Dining hours:** Montréalers typically eat later than other North Americans. Many restaurants don't fill up until 10 p.m., especially on weekends. That's good news if you're an early eater and want a table at a popular restaurant: You can almost always find something available around 6:30 p.m. or so. The restaurant may be dead, but the food will be taste the same as it does at 10 p.m.

Montréal's Best Restaurants from A to Z

This section gives you our top choices for eating in Montréal, in alphabetical order. With so many great restaurants in Montréal, the decision wasn't easy! And remember, you can find tons more in addition to the ones we list here.

To simplify your choices, we give you two ways to evaluate how expensive each place is. The first is a dollar-sign rating. This represents the price of one complete meal (appetizer, main, and dessert) including tip; the dollars signs correspond with the following price ranges:

$	Less than C$10 (US$7.50)
$$	C$10–C$20 (US$7.50–US$15)
$$$	C$20–C$30 (US$15–US$22.50)
$$$$	More than C$30 (US$22.50)

The second way is that, in our reviews, we also include the price range of a main course, from lowest to highest, and that price does not include drinks, taxes, or tip. It just gives you an idea of what the prices on the menu will actually be.

These are great spots, so they're likely to fill up quickly. We tell you whether reservations are recommended, required, or not accepted. For places that accept reservations, calling early in the day is usually sufficient to snag a table.

Au Pied de Cochon
$$$–$$$$ **Plateau** **FRENCH CONTEMPORARY**

In 2002, *En Route,* Air Canada's in-flight magazine, named Au Pied de Cochon one of the ten best new restaurants in Canada. Chef-owner Martin Picard is the man behind the inspired and upscale French cooking. But a word to the wise: Delicate and decorative nouvelle cuisine this is not. Instead, the kitchen's forte is hearty, almost peasant-like comfort food, prepared with the finest ingredients and the greatest of care. Come hungry. As the name suggests, the restaurant specializes in pork and even serves pig's feet. You also find a choice of excellent venison, lamb, and duck plates. Foie gras (goose liver) is a bit of a fetish item on the menu, appearing in several new and unusual places, like in a foie gras burger and foie gras poutine. (See the "Eating like a local" section for more info about this local delicacy.) The restaurant is nonsmoking.

536 av. Duluth Est (near rue St-Hubert). ☎ *514-281-1114. Reservations recommended. Main courses: C$11.50–C$45 (US$8–US$36). AE, MC, V. Open: Dinner Tues–Sun. Wheelchair accessible. Métro: Sherbrooke.*

Beaver Club

$$$$ **Downtown   FRENCH**

Don't be put off by the dated, old-money feel of the Fairmont The Queen Elizabeth's restaurant, which actually was an exclusive men's club dating back to the 18th century. Beaver Club, a restaurant since 1959, ranks among the top 10 hotel restaurants in the world. Star chef Alain Pignard, hired to rework the menu in 1999, offers an absolutely delectable range of classic French dishes, many made with Canadian ingredients, including Québec veal, lobster, caviar, foie gras, and more. The French sommelier is a great fan of Canadian wines and will gladly find a way for you to taste as many as possible. Service is warm, congenial, and beyond reproach. Prices are surprisingly reasonable, considering the level of artistry you experience.

In Fairmont The Queen Elizabeth, 900 bd. René-Levesque Ouest. ☎ **514-861-3511.** *Reservations strongly recommended. Main courses: C$29–C$35 (US$22–US$26). AE, DC, MC, V. Open: Lunch Mon–Fri, dinner Tues–Sat. Wheelchair accessible. Métro: Bonaventure.*

Buona Notte

$$$–$$$$ **Plateau   CONTEMPORARY ITALIAN**

This snazzy, contemporary Italian restaurant is a fixture on boulevard St-Laurent and a popular destination for A-list celebrities like Bono, Jim Carrey, and Jacques Villeneuve. Check out the wall of signed plates at the back of the restaurant for proof of their passing through. Buona Notte has been one of the city's trendiest spots practically since it opened in 1992, thanks at least in part to the exceptionally statuesque and leggy waitresses that saunter about the quasi-industrial space. But the place doesn't get by on good looks alone: The kitchen is meticulous about it's cuisine, serving fresh takes on classic Italian ingredients. Along with delicate starters and fresh pasta dishes, the menu offers main courses of meats and fish. For three consecutive years, the restaurant's wine cellar, stocked exclusively with Italian wines, has won coveted awards from *Wine Spectator* magazine.

3518 bd. St-Laurent (north of rue Milton). ☎ **514-848-0644.** *Reservations recommended. Main courses: C$11–C$36 (US$8–US$27). AE, DC, MC, V. Open: Lunch Mon–Sat, dinner daily. Métro: Saint-Laurent or Sherbrooke.*

Chez L'Épicier

$$$$ **Vieux-Montréal   FRENCH CONTEMPORARY**

At first sight it's hard to figure out exactly what this establishment is. The first thing you see when you walk in are rows of jams and preserves on shelves. But if the name — which means grocery store — suggests the everyday and banal, wait until you taste. Plates are inventive and fun, like the oh-so-French foie gras glazed with tandoori sauce or the dessert club sandwiches. Whimsical as it sounds, the food is top notch.

Downtown and Vieux-Montréal Dining and Snacking

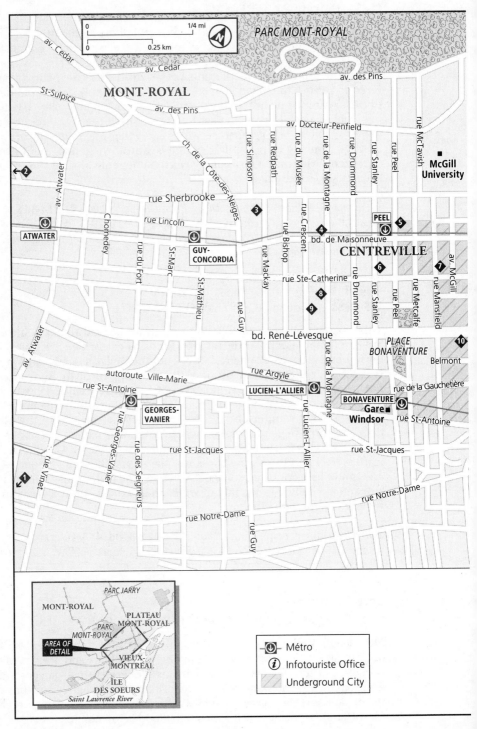

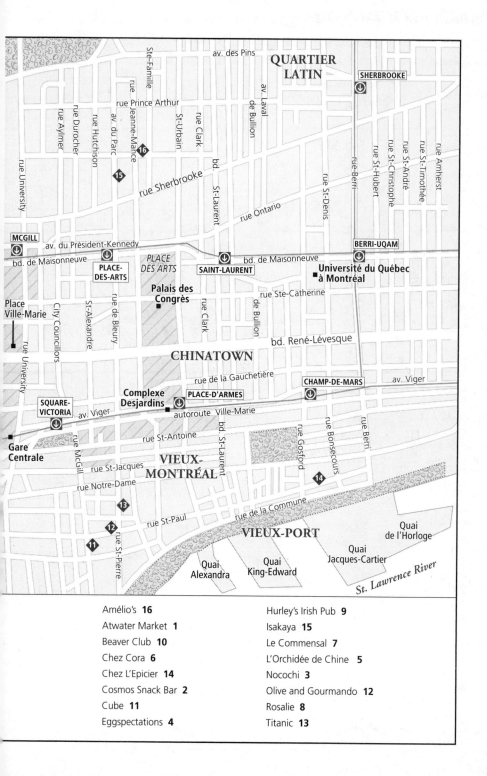

Amélio's **16**

Atwater Market **1**

Beaver Club **10**

Chez Cora **6**

Chez L'Epicier **14**

Cosmos Snack Bar **2**

Cube **11**

Eggspectations **4**

Hurley's Irish Pub **9**

Isakaya **15**

Le Commensal **7**

L'Orchidée de Chine **5**

Nocochi **3**

Olive and Gourmando **12**

Rosalie **8**

Titanic **13**

Plateau and Mile End Dining

Au Pied de Cochon **28**
Buona Notte **40**
Café Italia **6**
Café Olympico **5**
Cafe Santropol **30**
Chez Clo **43**
Eggspectations **13**
Epicerie Latina **3**
Euro Deli **37**
Fairmont Bagels **11**
Fondumentale **24**
Golden Curry House Restaurant **9**
Il Piatto Della Nonna **4**
Jean Talon Market **8**
L'Avenue **19**
L'Express **32**
La Binerie Mont-Royal **18**
La Cabane **33**
La Colombe **29**
La Croissanterie **10**
La Paryse **42**
La Veille Europe **35**
Le Commensal **45**
Le Continentale **26**
Le P'tit Plateau **23**
Le 2 **41**
Marché des Saveurs **8**
Moishe's Steak House **31**
Mount Royal Hot Dog **20**
Ouzeri **16**
PA Supermarché **14**
Patati Patata **25**
Philinos **15**
Piton de la Fournaise **27**
Pizzedélic **21, 46**
Pizzeria Napolitana **7**
Restaurant Lafleurs **38**
Rumi **12**
Schwartz's **34**
Shed Café **39**
Spirite Lounge **42**
St-Viateur Bagels **2**
Taquéria Mexicaine **22**
Toqué! **36**
Vaudeville **1**
Yoyo's **17**

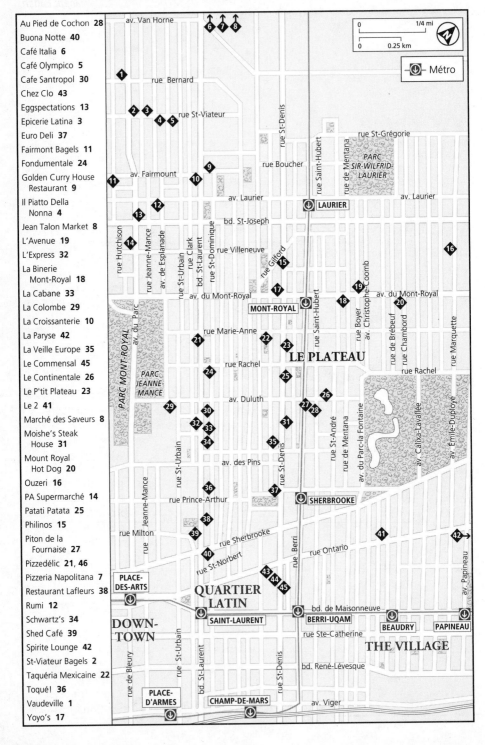

311 rue St-Paul Est (near rue St-Claude). ☎ **514-878-2232.** *Reservations recommended. Main courses: C$16–C$28 (US$12–US$21). AE, DC, MC, V. Open: Lunch, Mon–Fri, dinner daily. Métro: Champ-de-Mars.*

Cube

$$$$ Vieux-Montréal   FRENCH CONTEMPORARY

In the mood for a truly slick dining experience? The minimalist decor and rich-artist clients that linger about the tables at this hotel restaurant in Vieux-Montréal make you feel like you're eating among the gods of cool. Young as it feels, though, you have to be old enough to pay for it — this place is pricey. But like many fine eating destinations in Montréal, it's worth it. Cube offers a (need we say?) minimalist menu of modernized French classics, items such as oysters, foie gras, and warm goat salad for appetizers followed by fish, seafood, venison, and veal main dishes. Try some endives cooked in grapefruit juice, sample some fine Québec cheeses on raisin bread and hazelnut toasts, or nibble on scallops dressed in a mousse of Jerusalem artichoke. Everything is imaginatively conceived, exquisitely prepared, and immaculately presented.

355 rue McGill (in the Hotel St-Paul). ☎ **514-876-2823.** *Reservations recommended. Main courses: C$23–C$34 (US$17–US$26). AE, DC, MC V Open: Lunch Mon–Fri, dinner daily. Métro: Square-Victoria.*

Euro Deli

$ Plateau   ITALIAN AMERICAN

The campy approach of this cafeteria-style pizza and pasta spot attracts boulevard St-Laurent hipsters at all hours of the day. No one seems to mind the bright-red plastic trays, paper plates, and disposable cutlery, probably because the fresh pasta is so amazing. In terms of being seen on boulevard St-Laurent in the summer, there is nothing quite cooler than sipping an espresso on Euro Deli's marble stoop. Open late, there's often a mad rush of drunken revelers chowing down late-night eats after bars close at 2:00 a.m. During the day, it's perfect for a quick lunch. The pesto tortellini, the Caesar salad, and the plain cheese pizza are all good choices. Otherwise, you can select a type of pasta and sauce from a list or get a slice of pizza or *panzerotti* (pizza pockets) on display.

3619 bd. St-Laurent (north of rue Prince-Arthur). ☎ **514-843-7853.** *Reservations not accepted. Main courses: C$4–C$8 (US$3–US$6). Cash only. Open: Lunch and dinner daily until 4 a.m. Métro: Saint-Laurent or Sherbrooke.*

Fondumentale

$$–$$$$ Plateau   FONDUE

What better way to kick back with a friend than by dunking morsels of bread, meat, or veggies into a pot of fondue? If you crave fondue and a fun time, this is where it's at, right in the thick of the action on stylish rue St-Denis. Fondumentale's laid-back, slightly rumpled atmosphere makes it a perfect place to let your hair down. Fondue is not fine dining, but Fondumentale's cheese, broth, and oil fondues have kept locals coming back for years. Make an evening of it.

4325 rue St-Denis. ☎ 514-499-1446. Reservations essential. Main courses: C$14–C$25 (US$11–US$20). AE, DC, MC, V. Open: Dinner daily. Métro: Mont-Royal.

Golden Curry House Restaurant
$$–$$$ Plateau   INDIAN

Locals call this place the Golden Closet, but that's exaggerating a little. It's actually a narrow hallway packed with tables. In spite of the severe space restrictions — one table is even squished behind the front door, where you would normally expect to see a plant — this place is almost always packed. We can't say with absolute certainty that this is the best Indian food you'll find in Montréal, but popular opinion ranks it highly, the locale is great, and the prices are very reasonable, so it's hard to knock. The menu is classic Indian fare: nan bread; samosas; beef, lamb, and chicken curry; tandoori chicken; agaloo peas; and more. Wash it down with a pint of Guinness. Waiters are polite and do their job well with literally very little breathing room, so don't complain if service is on the perfunctory side.

5210 bd. St-Laurent. ☎ 514-270-2561. Reservations recommended on weekends. Main courses: C$8.25–C$9.25(US$6–US$7). AE, DC, MC, V. Open: Lunch Mon–Sat and dinner daily. Métro: Laurier.

Il Piatto Della Nonna
$$–$$$ Plateau-Mile End   ITALIAN

It sure is fun to find truly traditional Italian cooking in the Mile End, a neighborhood where most traditions are giving way to the yuppie tastes that are taking over the neighborhood. Il Piatto Della Nonna is a family-run establishment that offers fresh, homemade pasta and hearty dishes like grilled Italian sausage, chicken legs stuffed with cheese and breadcrumbs, and veal shank. This is a good place to fill up if you're on a budget. The menu, which changes regularly, is a *table d'hôte* (appetizer, main course, dessert, and coffee) posted on a chalkboard. Service is warm and informal (the owner's six-year-old daughter lends a hand to the wait staff every now and again). The coffee and biscotti are excellent.

176 rue St-Viateur Ouest. ☎ 514-278-6066. Nearby, there's a second location: 5171 bd. St-Laurent (☎ 514-843-6069). Reservations recommended on weekends. Table d'hôte: C$15–C$25 (US$11–US$19). AE, DC, MC, V. Open: Lunch Mon–Fri, dinner daily. Métro: Laurier.

Isakaya
$$$ Downtown   JAPANESE (SUSHI)

First things first: Isakaya has the best sushi in town. That said, *isakaya* is the generic word for Japan's informal eateries, so, true to form, this restaurant features a wide variety of what amounts to Japanese pub-fare favorites. Of course, these popular Japanese dishes are much more delicate than their western counterparts, and they're healthier, too. Start with an order of *edamame,* steamed and salted pods of baby soybeans, which go well with beer. *Gyoza* (browned dumplings of pork and cabbage) and *yakitori* (barbecued skewers of chicken) are also good starters. If you really want to wow your date with your sushi *savoir faire*, ask for a spot at the bar. Gently lean into the sushi chef and ask for, "a selection of what he thinks is best," some sashimi, some nigiri, and some maki rolls. A delightful parade of sushi will follow.

3469 av. du Parc (south of rue Milton). ☎ **514-845-8226.** *Reservations recommended. Main courses: C$17–C$23 (US$12–US$17). AE, MC, V. Open: Dinner daily. Wheelchair accessible. Métro: Place-des-Arts.*

La Croissanterie
$–$$$ Outremont   FRENCH

There's always a bit of action at La Croissanterie. People flow in and out as they please — for a late-morning coffee and croissant, a light midday meal, a late-night snack of French onion soup, or a glass of wine any time of the day. That's probably what makes it so charming — that, and the breezy, quiet, expansive outdoor terrace, which is a jewel in the hot summer months. If you're not feeling up to a full-force French feast, but you still have a hankering for something Gallic, not too pricey, and a place you can rest your hind quarters for a while without remorse, La Croissanterie is your destination. Soups and sandwiches are served all day long, and dishes like filet mignon, chicken breast, and fish are available in the evening.

5200 rue Hutchison. ☎ **514-278-6567.** *Reservations not accepted. Main courses: C$7–C$15 (US$5–US$11). AE, DC, MC, V. Open: Lunch and dinner daily. Métro: Laurier.*

Le 2
$–$$ Plateau   CONTEMPORARY CANADIAN

Perched atop the hill on boulevard St-Laurent at rue Sherbrooke, this former diner recently reinvented itself as a compact dining room with a bar. Its Asian-minimalist makeover won the much-coveted Commerce Design Montréal interior design award in 2003. In the meantime, the clientele traded in greasy spoons and crossword puzzles for chopsticks and cocktails. Actually, the restaurant sets the tables with cutlery, but like the new décor, the menu has a pronounced Asian accent. Their signature dish is a piece of tuna flash seared, rubbed with miso, sprinkled with hot pepper flakes, and served on a bed of jicama slaw. All the items are under C$10 (US$7.50). The portions are snack-sized but feature thoughtful combinations of ingredients. Order several; they're ideal for sharing. In fact, with a laid back, yet intimate, atmosphere, this hideaway of sorts is the perfect place to start the evening before heading into the madness of the nightlife to the north.

2 rue Sherbrooke Est (at the corner of boulevard St-Laurent). ☎ **514-843-8881.** *Reservations recommended. Main courses: C$3–C$10 (US$2–US$7.20). MC, V. Open: Dinner Sun–Wed 5–11 p.m., Thurs–Sat 5 p.m.–1 a.m. Wheelchair accessible. Métro: Saint-Laurent.*

Le Continentale

$$$–$$$$ **Plateau**   **FRENCH CONTEMPORARY**

This rue St-Denis restaurant is a long-time favorite among Montréalers in the know, because it's consistently good. The menu offers bistro classics, contemporary dishes with unique twists, and a good wine list. The kitchen excels at steak frites, duck confit, pasta carbonara, and seared tuna steak, served on a bed of exotic fruits. The chatty crowd creates a lively atmosphere, which becomes almost electric on a busy night, as everyone clamors over the colorful and attractively presented plates. The ever-changing nightly specials, such as salmon filet wrapped in nori and flash-fried in tempura batter, tend to get the most "oohs" and "aahs." The decor is based on early 20th-century air travel motifs, like black-and-white photos of propeller planes.

4169 rue St-Denis (at rue Rachel). ☎ **514-845-6842.** *Reservations recommended. Main courses: C$10–C$30 (US$7.50–US$23). AE, MC, V. Open: Dinner daily. Wheelchair accessible. Métro: Mont-Royal.*

Le Vaudeville

$$–$$$$ **Mile End**   **FRENCH BISTRO**

Looking for a good authentic French meal at a decent price? In Montréal, it takes a Greek to deliver this perfect formula: George Paradisis, a cook-entrepreneur who opened this place 15 years ago. Vaudeville is a super-quaint bistro on the northern tip of the Plateau neighborhood. A quasi-diner revamped with white cotton lampshades and walls speckled with the work of local artists (for sale), you feel like you're hiding out in some obscure town in France. On the small menu, hearty servings of variations on classics such as duck confit, warm goat cheese salad, and steak frites.

361 rue Bernard Ouest. ☎ **514-495-8258.** *Reservations recommended. Main courses: C$14–C$19 (US$11–US$14). AE, MC, V. Open: Dinner Tues–Sat, brunch Sat–Sun. Métro: Laurier.*

L'Express

$$–$$$$ Plateau FRENCH BISTRO

You may have heard the term *brasserie* floating around to describe a category of French cuisine and wondered whether it's a food or a place. The answer: It's both. L'Express, a Montréal landmark since 1979, is *brasserie* in the purest form — or at least in the purest North American form. A bustling restaurant-bar complete with black-and-white tiled floors and a zinc bar, L'Express serves steak and frites, duck confit, and other French comfort food with a jar of pickles and basket of baguette on the table. The white table clothes and bow-tied waiters may trick you into thinking that formality is de rigueur here, but don't be fooled. Brasseries are high-quality, but casual eating. Whether you want to linger over a leisurely meal or wolf down a swift lunch, the waiters will figure it out and cater to you accordingly. Just don't expect them to spend hours talking to you. They're busy!

3927 rue St-Denis. ☎ 514-845-5333. Reservations recommended. Main courses: C$11–C$20 (US$8–US$15). AE, DC, MC, V. Open: Lunch and dinner daily. Wheelchair accessible. Métro: Sherbrooke.

L'Orchidée de Chine

$$$–$$$$ Downtown CHINESE

Located in central Downtown, this four-floor restaurant with a pared-down decor may feel a bit cold at first, but the food will definitely warm you up. Don't come here looking for inexpensive, buffet-style Chinese food. L'Orchidée de Chine has been one of Montréal's most popular Chinese restaurants for years because of the sophistication and refinement of its fare. The uniform sea of soy sauce that plagues so much Chinese food is not to be seen here. Sauces are light and subtle. Don't miss the juicy five-flavored spare ribs and perfectly crispy fried spinach.

2017 rue Peel. ☎ 514-287-1878. Reservations essential. Main courses: C$13–C$19 (US$10–US$14). AE, DC, MC, V. Open: Lunch Mon–Fri, Dinner Mon–Sat. Métro: Peel.

Moishe's Steak House

$$$–$$$$ Plateau STEAK

A revered restaurant that has been in business for 65 years, Moishe's is Montréal's steak mecca, hands-down. A recent facelift has given the establishment a modern allure, but it is still very much a remnant of the days when The Main (boulevard St-Laurent) was the heart of Montréal's Jewish community. The Lighter brothers, who inherited this place from their father, consider the quest for quality meat a high art. Their steaks come exclusively from corn-fed beasts raised on a hand-picked ranch in Colorado, and the best cuts will melt in your mouth. Accompanying potatoes and vegetables are also top notch, and the walls are stocked with bottles of fine wine. Career waiters are knowledgeable and friendly, glad to entertain even the most obscure questions. Come with an appetite. English speakers feel very comfortable here.

3961 bd. St-Laurent. ☎ *514-845-3509. Reservations recommended. Main courses: C$24–C$45 (US$18–US$34). AE, DC, MC, V. Open: Lunch Mon–Fri, dinner daily. Métro: Sherbrooke.*

Ouzeri

$$ **Plateau** **CONTEMPORARY GREEK**

Exposed brick walls and storeroom shelves stocked with bottles of wine and vats of olive oil give Ouzeri a warm, yet stripped-down feel with a designer edge. A bit of a scene for Montréal's work-hard, play-hard crowd, this is where urbanites in their late 20s and 30s stop in for a late dinner. It's a great place for Greek tapas, the restaurant's specialty. Service is friendly and expedient as the waiters rush about the main dinning room. Two other spaces, one upstairs, the other down, are more intimate and less noisy.

4690 rue St-Denis (at the corner of rue Gilford). ☎ *514-845-1336. Reservations recommended. Main courses: C$7–C$18 (US$5–US$13). AE, DC, MC, V. Open: Lunch and dinner daily. Wheelchair accessible. Métro: Laurier.*

Patati Patata

$ **Plateau** **DINER**

Quirky is the word for this little fish-and-chips and burger joint on boulevard St-Laurent. The 20-something owners converted a minuscule old 12-chair diner into a miniscule new 12-chair diner. They whip up tasty, fresh fast food behind the counter while you watch — breading the fish, tossing the salad, and frying the burgers before your eyes. The entertainment value is great, but the food is even better. Don't scrimp on the skinny fries, even if you're on a diet. Homemade brownies also hit the spot.

4177 bd. St-Laurent (at corner of rue Rachel). ☎ *514-844-0216. Reservations not accepted. Main courses: C$1.50–C$6 (US$1–US$4.50) Cash only. Open: Breakfast, lunch, and dinner daily. Métro: Mont-Royal or Sherbrooke.*

Philinos

$$–$$$ **Plateau** **GREEK**

Avenue du Parc, just north of Parc Mont-Royal, is Montréal's traditional Greek neighborhood, and oodles of souvlaki joints and fish restaurants line this busy avenue and the smaller side streets nearby. Philinos stands out for its solid, satisfying food and inviting atmosphere. It's usually full of Greek customers, which is always a good sign. You can order from a selection of tapas-style appetizers, like szatiki, or go for generous plates of kebabs. Don't miss the divine dessert of thick yogurt drizzled with honey.

4806 av. du Parc. ☎ *514-271-9099. Reservations recommended. Main courses: C$11–C$30 (US$8–US$23). AE, DC, MC, V. Open: Lunch and dinner daily. Wheelchair accessible. Métro: Laurier.*

Rosalie

$$$$ **Downtown**   **CONTEMPORARY CONTINENTAL**

During the summer, the long narrow terrace with immense, black, canvas parasols in the front is a major draw for the suits from Downtown office buildings. They arrive for after-work drinks, and then linger for a big-ticket dinner. It's usually money well spent as Dave McMilllan, the restaurant's executive chef, devises contemporary yet refined dishes. Appetizers include a foie gras (goose liver) sundae and salmon tartare with mixed greens. The main courses feature a variety of meats, such as pork, fish, duck, sweetbreads, and rabbit, and come in robust and flavorful sauces. The restaurant's contemporary yet serene interior can be best summed up as retro-Scandinavian, with lots of wood, chrome, and black leather seats and banquettes. The pleasant sommelier can help you choose from the extensive wine list.

1232 rue de la Montagne (south of rue Ste-Catherine). ☎ *514-392-1970. Reservations recommended. Main courses: C$25–C$45 (US$20–US$33). MC, V. Open: Lunch Mon–Fri, dinner daily. Wheelchair accessible. Métro: Peel.*

Rumi

$$–$$$ **Outremont**   **MIDDLE EASTERN**

For atmosphere, this Middle Eastern cafe–style restaurant is hard to beat. The interior is warm, spacious, and comfortable, decorated with oriental trimmings. The sidewalk terrace, spanning half a block on the corner on two quiet streets, is one of the most relaxing in the city. A haven of peace, Rumi is a good place to put an end to a busy day. Tapas-style portions of Middle Eastern standards include hummus and marinated red peppers, as well as more substantial plates like veal kebabs and seasonal fish. In the summer, arrive before 7 p.m. if you want a spot on the terrace, or you can call to reserve a table.

5198 rue Hutchinson (at the corner of rue Fairmont). ☎ *514-490-1999. Reservations recommend. Main courses: C$11–C$22 (US$8–US$16). AE DC, MC, V. Open: Lunch and dinner Tues–Sun. Métro: Laurier.*

Schwartz's

$–$$ **Plateau**   **SMOKED MEAT**

This cramped deli, staffed mainly by surly seniors, is a fixture on boulevard St-Laurent and positively the best place to sample Montréal's famous smoked meat. While you'll find little else on the menu, order these juicy slices of beef brisket, cured, smoked, spiced, then heaped on rye bread and served with mustard. The sandwiches or plates come in lean, medium, or fatty varieties. The medium-fatty is our favorite. French fries, pickles, roasted red peppers, and coleslaw sides are available separately. Tradition dictates a black cherry soda to wash it all down. Most days bring a long line outside, but it's definitely worth the wait.

3895 bd. St-Laurent. ☎ 514-842-4813. Reservations not accepted. Main courses: C$8–C$18 (US$6–US$14). Cash only. Open: Lunch and dinner daily. Métro: Sherbrooke.

Taquéria Mexicaine
$ Plateau MEXICAN

Taquéria Mex offers the usual selection of tacos, burritos, quesadillas, and more — all in beef, chicken, and vegetarian versions, with a choice of salad, rice, or chips. The ingredients are fresh. The salad is never wilted and is always accompanied by perfectly ripe avocados. The fresh tomatoes even taste good all year round. We're not sure how they do it, actually, but we've never been disappointed. Kids will find familiar fare here, like tacos and tortilla chips. This place is hard to beat if you want a satisfying meal for under C$10 (US$7.20) a head.

4306 bd. St-Laurent. ☎ 514-982-9462. Reservations not accepted. Main courses: C$4–C$12 (US$3–US$9). V, MC. Open: Lunch and dinner daily. Métro: Mont-Royal or Sherbrooke.

Toqué!
$$$$ Downtown FRENCH CONTEMPORARY

If you're willing to lay down some big money for a serious gastronomic experience, don't miss this high-end French restaurant, considered one of the best in the province. Québec celebrity chef Normand Laprise uses as many fresh local ingredients as possible to make dishes like veal, scallops, red snapper, risotto, guinea hen, and delectable French desserts. The food is wildly imaginative, but it's dished out in small portions. The atmosphere is chic and intimate, and the same can be said about the crowd. Don't worry about dressing up, but most of all, don't be intimidated by the snobby-looking waiters. Many are chefs-in-training, along with decent types who know a lot about their vocation. They magically lose their attitude if you ask a straightforward question. Reserve a week ahead to get a table on the weekend and don't plan anything else for the evening. No smoking.

900 place Jean-Paul Riopelle. ☎ 514-499-2084. Reservations recommended. Main courses: C$26–C$38 (US$20–US$29). AE, DC, MC, V. Open: Lunch Tues–Fri, dinner Tues–Sat. Métro: Sherbrooke.

Index of restaurants by neighborhood

Downtown

Beaver Club ($$$–$$$$, French)
Isakaya ($$$, Japanese-Sushi)
L'Orchidée de Chine ($$$–$$$$, Chinese)
Rosalie ($$$$, Contemporary Continental)
Toqué! ($$$$ French Contemporary)

Mile End

Piatto Della Nonna ($$–$$$, Italian)
Le Vaudeville ($$–$$$$, French Bistro)

Vieux-Montréal

Chez L'Épicier ($$$$, French Contemporary)
Cube ($$$$, French Contemporary)

Outremont

La Croissanterie ($–$$$, French)
Rumi ($$–$$$, Middle Eastern)

Plateau

Au Pied de Cochon ($$$–$$$$, French Contemporary)
Buenna Notte ($$$–$$$$, Contemporary Italian)
Euro Deli ($, Italian American)
Fondumentale ($$–$$$$, Fondue)
Golden Curry House ($$–$$$, Indian)
Le Continentale ($$$–$$$$, French Contemporary)
Le 2 ($–$$, Contemporary Canadian)
L'Express ($$–$$$$, French Bistro)
Moishe's Steak House ($$$–$$$$, Steak)
Ouzeri ($$, Contemporary Greek)
Patati Patata ($, Diner)
Philinos ($$–$$$, Greek)
Schwarz's($–$$, Smoked Meat)
Taquéria Mexicaine ($, Mexican)

Index of restaurants by cuisine

Chinese

L'Orchidée de Chine (Downtown, $$$–$$$$)

Contemporary Canadian

Le 2 (Plateau, $–$$)

Continental

Rosalie (Downtown, $$$$)

Diner

Patati Patata (Plateau, $)

Fondue

Fondumentale (Plateau, $$–$$$$)

French

Beaver Club (Downtown, $$$–$$$$)
La Croissanterie (Outremont, $–$$$)

French Bistro

Le Vaudeville (Outremont, $$–$$$$)
L'Express (Plateau, $$–$$$$)

French Contemporary

Au Pied de Cochon (Plateau, $$$–$$$$)
Chez L'Épicier (Vieux-Montréal, $$$$)
Cube (Vieux-Montréal $$$$)
Le Continentale (Plateau, $$$–$$$$)
Toqué! (Downtown, $$$$)

Greek

Ouzeri (Plateau, $$)
Philinos (Plateau, $$–$$$)

Indian

Golden Curry House (Plateau, $$–$$$)

Italian
Buona Notte (Plateau, $$$–$$$$)
Euro Deli (Plateau, $)
Piatto della Nonna (Mile End, $$–$$$)

Japanese-Sushi
Isakaya (Downtown, $$$)

Mexican
Taquéria Mexicaine (Plateau, $–$$)

Middle Eastern
Rumi (Outremont, $$–$$$)

Smoked Meat
Schwarz's (Plateau, $–$$)

Steak
Moishe's (Plateau, $$$–$$$$)

Index of restaurants by price

$
Euro Deli (Plateau, Italian)
Patati Patata (Plateau, Diner)
Schwarz's (Plateau, Smoked Meat)
Taquéria Mexicaine (Plateau, Mexican)

$$
Golden Curry House (Plateau, Indian)
La Croissanterie (Outremont, French)
Ouzeri (Plateau, Greek)
Le 2 (Plateau, Contemporary Canadian)

$$$
Au Pied de Cochon (Plateau, French)
Fondumentale (Plateau, Fondue)
Isakaya (Downtown, Japanese–Sushi)
L'Express (Plateau, French Bistro
Le Vaudeville (Mile End, French)
L'Orchidée de Chine (Downtown, Chinese)

Philinos (Plateau, Greek)
Piatto Della Nonna (Mile End, Italian)
Rumi (Outremont, Middle Eastern)

$$$$
Beaver Club (Downtown, French)
Buenna Notte (Plateau, Contemporary Italian)
Chez l'Èpicier (Vieux-Montréal, Contemporary French)
Cube (Vieux-Montréal, Contemporary French)
Le Continentale (Plateau, Contemporary French)
Moishe's (Plateau, Steak)
Rosalie (Downtown, Contemporary French)
Toqué! (Downtown, Contemporary French)

Montréal's Best Snacks

In Montréal, fast food doesn't equal tasteless — not even close. If you don't want to go out for fine dining every night, don't despair. Montréal's food festival carries on in every corner of the city's dining experience, from pizza and picnicking to *poutine.*

Pizza and burgers

Almost everything you eat in Montréal has a distinct local twist, including these fast food staples. Like the French, many Montréalers prefer pizzas with very thin crusts. If you want to try one, hit a **Pizzadélic,** with various locations around town: at 1250 av. Mont-Royal Est (☎ 514-522-2286) and 1641 rue St-Denis (☎ 514-499-1444).

If you like the thicker crust variety of pizza, try **Pizzeria Napolitana,** 189 rue Dante (☎ 514-276-8226), in Little Italy or **Amélio's,** 201 rue Milton (☎ 845-8396), right Downtown. The tastiest delivery pizza in the city comes from **Tasty Food Pizza,** 6660 bd. Décarie (☎ 514-739-9333), as its name suggests.

Montréal isn't a big burger town, but if you get a craving, a few places seem to have perfected the genre. Downtown, try **La Paryse,** 302 rue Ontario Est (☎ 514-842-2040). On boulevard St-Laurent, there's **Shed Café,** 3515 bd. St-Laurent (☎ 514-842-0220), and **La Cabane,** 3872 bd. St-Laurent (☎ 514-843-7283). At 1225 rue Crescent, **Hurley's Irish Pub** (☎ 514-861-4111) has garnered quite a reputation for its fine burgers.

The best bagels

From time immemorial — okay, at least the last 20 years or so — Montréal has been battling it out with New York over who bakes the best bagels. Montréal bagels are denser and slightly crisp on the outside. We obviously don't have much to say about New York bagels. This is your chance to vote with your stomach, but beware. Even inside Montréal, there's a civil war of sorts between bagel lovers who love one of two major bagel bakeries in Montréal. Don't show your colors to locals until you know which side they're on.

St-Viateur Bagels, 102 rue St-Viateur Ouest (☎ 514-272-6548), is our favorite. Bagel come piping hot out of a wood-burning oven, drawing a faithful following from all corners of the city. From the fridges beside the counter, you can buy cream cheese, smoked salmon, and other toppings.

Fairmont Bagels, technically the Bagel Factory, 74 rue Fairmount Ouest (☎ 514-272-0667), offers several variations on its famous sesame-seed bagel. Here, you can try bagels with raisins and cinnamon or even olives and sun-dried tomatoes, plus a variety of toppings.

Sandwich, anyone?

Montréalers love good bread — in particular, long, thin, crusty baguettes, and that's good news for anyone looking for a sandwich. Whether you grab one on the run or settle into a cafe for a bite, this section gives you some options.

Olive and Gourmando, 351 rue St-Paul Ouest (☎ 514-285-1000), has some of the best sandwiches in town. Choose from the sausages and cheese or more exotic ingredients, like portobello mushrooms. The bread is always fresh.

Titanic, 445 rue St-Pierre (☎ 514-849-0894), in Vieux-Montréal, is also considered one of the city's best lunch spots. Sandwich-wise, it serves rather exotic combinations of ingredients on delicious crusty bread. Homemade soups, daily specials, and heaping antipasto plates are all delicious.

Au Pain Doré, one of Montréal's major bakery chains, has locations throughout the city. Each sells very respectable pre-wrapped sandwiches — classics like ham and cheese or smoked salmon. This is a good place to stop if you need to grab something on the run. Popular downtown locations include 556 rue Ste-Catherine Est (☎ 514-282-2220) and 1415 rue Peel (☎ 514-843-3151), and in the Plateau at 1145 av. Laurier Ouest (☎ 514-276-0947).

The big breakfast bonanza

Montréalers are extremely fond of working off their morning blues (or hangover) over a plate of eggs and bacon. Join a citywide ritual and load up on cholesterol at one of the following renowned breakfast joints. You can have it fancy, surrounding yourself with stylish locals, or go in for classic, greasy-spoon formula.

L'Avenue, 922 av. Mont-Royal Est (☎ 514-523-8780), located in the heart of the hip Plateau neighborhood, is the breakfast spot of the moment. Trendy denizens line up for the breakfasts; to beat them, aim to arrive before 11 a.m.

Mount Royal Hot Dog, 1001 av. Mont-Royal Est (☎ 514-523-3670), is one of the few remnants of this neighborhood's working class past. Breakfasts are generous and cheap, the gum-smacking waitresses give you exactly what you want, and you don't have to listen to any jazz while you're eating.

Eggspectations, 98 av. Laurier Ouest (☎ 514-278-6411) and 1313 bd. de Maisonneuve Ouest (☎ 514-842-3447), is a chain that serves eggs any which way, all day long. It's on the fancier side of the greasy-spoon scale, and so are the prices.

Chez Cora, another chain of breakfast cafes, has restaurants all over the city. For the basic variations on eggs, bacon, baked beans, and potatoes, you can't go wrong here. Downtown locations include 3465 Ave. du Parc (☎ 514-849-4932) and 1425 rue Stanley (☎ 514-286-6171).

Cosmos Snack Bar, 5843 rue Sherbrooke Ouest (☎ 514-486-3814), is a tiny, Greek family–owned restaurant that serves only breakfast. Sit at the counter and listen to the family at work. It's My Big Fat Greek Breakfast: a kind of comic-tragedy set in a greasy spoon. Breakfast here gets you through a lumberjack's day.

Chez Clo, 3199 rue Ontario Est (☎ **522-5348**), is a Montréal landmark. Authentic, Québec-style breakfast and lunch at absurdly low prices.

Picnicking and markets

The best place to picnic in Montréal, by far, is **Parc Mont-Royal.** See Chapter 11 for details. Prime spots are the slope in front of **Beaver Lake,** or the slope facing avenue du Parc. To pick up some bread, cheese, pâté, or cold cuts, visit nearby **PA Supermarché,** 5029 av. du Parc; **La Veille Europe,** 3855 bd. St-Laurent; or **Épicerie Latina,** 185 rue St-Viateur Ouest.

Montréal's two major outdoor markets are also great places to pick up some light fare and explore among the locals. Both are conveniently located next to Métro stops. To get to the **Atwater Market** in the west-end of downtown, get off either the orange or green line at Lionel-Groulx station. To get to the **Jean Talon Market** in Little Italy, go to Jean Talon station, at the intersection of the blue and orange lines.

These are great places to taste locally grown Québec *terroir* products. Both markets begin carrying local produce by mid-June and are usually going strong well into October. At the Jean Talon Market, don't miss the **Marché des Saveurs,** 280 Place du Marché-du-Nord, one of the best specialty food stores in the city, which carries Québec wines, cheese, maple syrup products and more.

As an added bonus, municipal authorities remain convinced that drinking wine in a park with a meal poses no greater danger to public morality than drinking wine at a sidewalk restaurant. As long as you're eating a meal, drinking wine and beer in parks is legal.

Eating like a local

Like the French, Québeckers love fine cuisine. But in the dietary staples here — notably *steamies* (steamed hot dogs), *bines* (baked beans), and *poutine* (fries served with gravy and cheese curds) — Québeckers distinguish themselves as a totally separate gastronomic race. These regional favorites are true fuel. Loaded with fat and dripping with grease, this is the kind of food that sticks to your stomach and keeps you warm on winter nights, although, come to think of it, people eat it all year round. Why Québeckers love it so much is anybody's guess, but local foods live on.

Give local delicacies a try, ideally on a very empty stomach. The legendary **La Binerie Mont-Royal,** 367 av. du Mont-Royal Est (☎ **514-285-9078**), is Québec's spiritual home of baked beans. **Restaurant Lafleurs,** 3620 rue St-Denis (☎ **514-848-1804**), is reputed to make the best *poutine* in Montréal, which makes it a *poutine* world leader. At **Chez Clo,**

3199 rue Ontario Est (☎ **522-5348**), you can move up the *habitant* (Québec native) food chain a little and eat Québec specialties like pea soup, meat ball *ragoût* (stew), or *toutière* (meat pie).

The vegetarian scene

Most Montréal restaurants are enlightened enough to offer at least one vegetarian option on their menus. But most of the time, the vegetarian choice seems like an afterthought.

Luckily, some restaurants around town cater exclusively to Montréal's vegetarians, who are no longer considered just patchouli-scented, placard-bearing, long-haired social-activists. No, Montréalers at large are eating healthier diets. And the city's vegetarian restaurants are gaining ground as legitimate dining destinations, rather than as once-in-a-blue-moon concessions to the pickier palates in a dinner party. Meat-and-potato lovers will not leave the table hungry or unsatisfied. Indeed, having come a long way from the stereotypes of serving tree bark, inventive combinations at the city's vegetarian restaurants can be as delightful as they are filling.

Right in the heart of the Quartier Latin, **Le Commensal,** 1720 rue St-Denis (☎ **514-845-2627**), was the first venue of what's now a vegetarian chain with several restaurants around the city. Its downtown location, 1204 av. McGill-College (☎ **514-871-1480**), is extremely popular at lunch with the business crowd. Food is sold by weight, and both spots offer three different buffets at three different rates: hot, cold, and dessert. An average meal costs about C$20 (US$15).

Cafe Santropol, 3990 rue St-Urbain (☎ **514-842-3110**), occupies the first floor of a house at the corner of avenue Duluth. The restaurant has a wonderful back garden with rocks, trees, and a babbling fountain, making it an urban oasis on a hot summer day. Inside, it's a cozy place to warm up over a bowl of vegetarian chili after walking up the mountain on a blustery fall day. Sandwiches of thick sliced bread, stuffed with fresh and original flavor combinations (cream cheese is a staple) are the main attraction. A couple of sandwiches include meat, so you can bring your carnivore friends, but the rest of the menu is all vegetarian.

Spirite Lounge, 1205 rue Ontario Est (☎ **514-522-5353**), is an outlandish dining experience by any standard. Located in a sort of no-man's-land between the Quartier Latin and the Gay Village, its walls are covered with crumpled aluminum foil. This is deep-vegetarianism with a fascist bent. At the beginning, a waiter brandishing a riding crop lays down the exact rules. There is no menu, but a meal is three courses, each consisting of a dizzying list of ingredients, organic whenever possible. Choose your portion-size wisely, because if you don't finish your main course or starter, you don't get dessert . . . plus you have to pay a fine of C$2

(US$1.50). The restaurant matches the two dollars and gives it to charity. If you don't finish your dessert, you're banned from the restaurant for life. If you use your cellphone, you're thrown out on your other ear.

BYOB

One thing that makes Montréal's dining landscape unique in Canada is the availability — abundance, even — of restaurants that don't serve alcohol but allow you to Bring Your Own Bottle (BYOB) of wine to accompany your meals.

This arrangement is ideal. It allows you to save substantially on alcohol or afford a better bottle of wine than you would normally order. We recommend striving to do both.

Unfortunately, in an attempt to compensate for its nonexistent liquor sales, the majority of Montréal's BYOB restaurants, particularly those concentrated along the pedestrian part of rue Prince-Arthur, try to compensate by turning tables quickly. Quality and care can suffer, and the wham-bam approach to service can ruin your appetite as you begin to feel you are part of a giant, feeding herd. L'Academie, spanning three floors on the corner of rue St-Denis and avenue Duluth, packed most nights, is the worst offender in this regard.

However, a select few BYOBs are owned by artful restaurateurs, rather than proprietors blinded by their bottom lines. These are the hidden gems of Montréal's restaurant scene. Because they are usually small and extremely popular, you may need to reserve a couple of days in advance in order to get a table. Walking in on a weekend night is a gamble, but you may get lucky if you're looking only for a table for two. At these places, you can expect to pay between C$20 and C$30 (US$15–US$22) per person, before tip and taxes, for a three-course meal.

Somewhat far-flung, **Yoyo's,** 4720 rue Marquette (☎ **514-524-4187**), is located in the northeastern reaches of the Plateau, on an otherwise mainly residential street. It is considered one of the best BYOBs in town. The warmly lit rooms with dark wood trim are sedate and intimate, and the service is conscientious. The most serious gastronomes among the clientele bring magnums of cherished vintages from their own cellars for decanting, because they are confident that the kitchen will come through with food to match.

Named after an active volcano, **Piton de la Fournaise,** 835 av. Duluth Est (☎ **514-526-3936**), is the only restaurant in town that serves Creole cuisine from Reunion Island, a former French colony in the Indian Ocean. The flavorful dishes are combination of French, African, and Indian influences. They are heavily seasoned, but not necessarily spicy. Bring a light red, slightly chilled wine.

La Colombe, 554 av. Duluth Est (☎ **514-849-8844**), is a French BYOB that incorporates North African influences. Fish first, then meat are the specialties here. Of the four main courses, two are usually fish, although the menu items change daily, based on what the chef finds on his morning shop at the market.

Reserve a table for the second of the two seatings (at 7 p.m.) at **Le P'tit Plateau,** 330 rue Marie-Anne Est (☎ **514-282-6342**). The first seating at 5:30 p.m. can feel a tad rushed. But no matter when you dine here, the classic French is first rate. The chalkboard menu changes regularly but usually features beef, pork, fish, and game.

Coffee and pastries

Montréalers who are serious about their coffee regularly trek to the northeastern reaches of the city to get their fix. In Mile End, **Café Olympico,** at the corner of rue Waverly and rue St-Viateur, is a neighborhood hangout for young couples, artsy types, grad students, and a supporting cast of colorful characters. A fair number of regulars hang out here, and everyone acts as though they're nonchalantly in the know. In terms of coffee, they are. Grab a *café au lait,* served in tall glass, sit back, and watch the action.

Further up boulevard St-Laurent, in Little Italy, **Café Italia,** 6840 bd. St-Laurent (☎ **514-495-0059**), is also reputed for its coffee. Here, too, the *café au lait* comes in a glass. You can also order a cappuccino or an espresso. The remnant 1950s decor and the elderly Italian men give the place an Old World feel. Like the great bagel debate among Montréalers (see "The best bagels" section, earlier in this chapter), which of the two cafes is best remains a divisive topic among coffee aficionados.

Downtown, near rue Crescent, the Montréal Museum of Fine Art, and Concordia University's downtown campus, **Nocochi,** 2156 rue Mackay (☎ **514-989-7514**), makes a curious selection of delicate Middle Eastern pastries, cookies, and treats.

If you're trippin' out about how French everything is, you may have a hankering for a croissant to top it off. The best in the city are baked at the **Duc de Lorraine Patisserie Francaise,** 5002 Cote-des-Neiges (☎ **514-731-4128**). They're good enough to give a Frenchman pause.

Au Pain Doré and **Première Moisson** operate several outlets for their baked goods around the city. Their croissants, baguettes, and pastries are all good. These are excellent places to start your day with something fresh-baked or, later on, to launch an impromptu picnic in a nearby park.

Chapter 11

Exploring Montréal

. . . .

In This Chapter

▶ Checking out Montréal's best sights and activities

▶ Choosing a guided tour

▶ Following three great itineraries

. . . .

*I*n this chapter, we give you Montréal's top sights and activities and tell you how to see them yourself or with the help of a guided tour. We also suggest three themed itineraries you can follow to soak up the different flavors of the city.

Discovering Montréal's Top Sights from A to Z

Wondering what to do while in Montréal? Read through our suggestions in this section and choose the attractions that interest you most. You probably won't have enough time to see them all, so don't run yourself ragged trying.

Basilique Notre-Dame
Vieux-Montréal

Basilique Notre-Dame is a New World version of Paris's Notre Dame Cathedral, a grandiose church overlooking a broad *place,* or square, in the heart of the historical city. Okay, so the style is Gothic Revival, not Gothic, and it was built in the 19th century, not the 12th. But still, this Catholic church is feast for the eyes, from the intricately carved altar to the gilded ornamentation throughout. The effect is so moving that the basilica's Protestant architect, James O'Donnell, actually converted to Catholicism when it was completed. You can explore on your own or take a guided tour (available in English) at various times, starting at 9 a.m. Sound and light shows were recently introduced, with two performances nightly Tuesday through Saturday.

Downtown Montréal Attractions

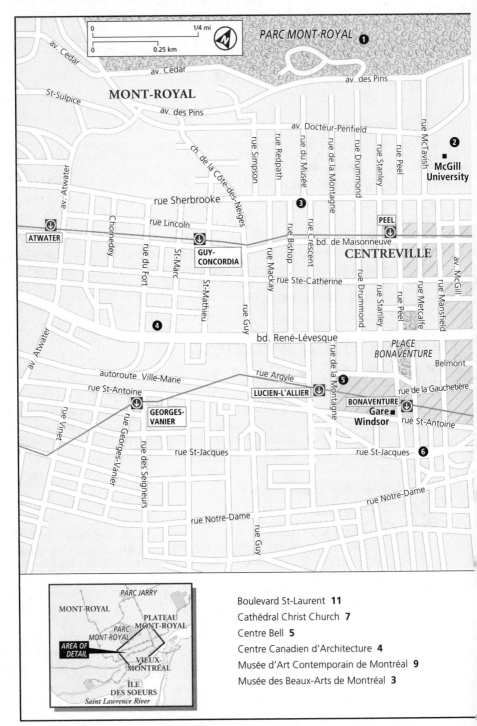

Boulevard St-Laurent 11

Cathédral Christ Church 7

Centre Bell 5

Centre Canadien d'Architecture 4

Musée d'Art Contemporain de Montréal 9

Musée des Beaux-Arts de Montréal 3

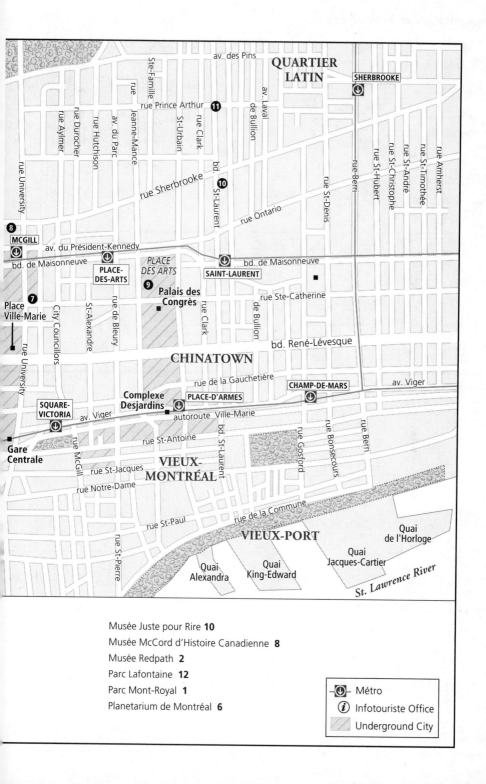

av. des Pins

QUARTIER
LATIN

SHERBROOKE

rue Prince Arthur **11**

10

rue Sherbrooke

rue Ontario

8
MCGILL

av. du Président-Kennedy

bd. de Maisonneuve

PLACE
DES ARTS

bd. de Maisonneuve

PLACE-
DES-ARTS

SAINT-LAURENT

9 Palais des
Congrès

rue Ste-Catherine

7
Place
Ville-Marie

bd. René-Lévesque

CHINATOWN

rue de la Gauchetière

av. Viger

CHAMP-DE-MARS

SQUARE-
VICTORIA

Complexe
Desjardins

PLACE-D'ARMES

av. Viger

autoroute Ville-Marie

Gare
Centrale

rue St-Antoine

VIEUX-
MONTRÉAL

rue St-Jacques

rue Notre-Dame

rue St-Paul

rue de la Commune

VIEUX-PORT

Quai
de l'Horloge

Quai
Jacques-Cartier

Quai
Alexandra

Quai
King-Edward

St. Lawrence River

Musée Juste pour Rire **10**

Musée McCord d'Histoire Canadienne **8**

Musée Redpath **2**

Parc Lafontaine **12**

Parc Mont-Royal **1**

Planetarium de Montréal **6**

⊙ Métro

ⓘ Infotouriste Office

Underground City

Vieux-Montréal Attractions

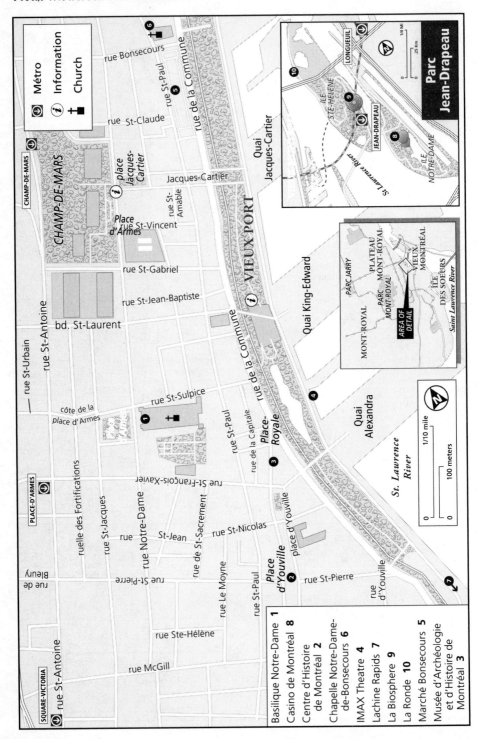

Métro 🚇
Information ⓘ
Church ✝▪

CHAMP-DE-MARS

rue Bonsecours

rue St-Paul

rue St-Claude

rue de la Commune

CHAMP-DE-MARS

place Jacques-Cartier

Jacques-Cartier

rue St-Amable

Place d'Armes

rue St-Vincent

rue St-Gabriel

rue St-Jean-Baptiste

bd. St-Laurent

rue St-Antoine

rue St-Urbain

côte de la place d'Armes

rue St-Sulpice

rue St-Paul

rue de la capitale

Place-Royale

Quai Jacques-Cartier

VIEUX-PORT

Quai King-Edward

rue de la Commune

Quai Alexandra

St. Laurence River

rue St-François-Xavier

PLACE-D'ARMES

ruelle des Fortifications

rue St-Jacques

rue Notre-Dame

rue St-Jean

St-Jean

rue de St-Sacrement

rue St-Nicolas

Place d'Youville

place d'Youville

rue St-Pierre

rue d'Youville

rue St-Pierre

rue Le Moyne

rue St-Paul

rue de Bleury

SQUARE-VICTORIA

rue St-Antoine

rue Ste-Hélène

rue McGill

Parc Jean-Drapeau

LONGUEUIL

ÎLE STE-HÉLÈNE

JEAN-DRAPEAU

ÎLE NOTRE-DAME

St. Laurence River

¼ Mi
.25 Km

PARC JARRY

PLATEAU

PARC MONT-ROYAL

MONT-ROYAL

MONT-ROYAL

VIEUX-MONTRÉAL

ÎLE DES SŒURS

Saint Laurence River

AREA OF DETAIL

1/10 mile

100 meters

Basilique Notre-Dame **1**
Casino de Montréal **8**
Centre d'Histoire de Montréal **2**
Chapelle Notre-Dame-de-Bonsecours **6**
IMAX Theatre **4**
Lachine Rapids **7**
La Biosphère **9**
La Ronde **10**
Marché Bonsecours **5**
Musée d'Archéologie et d'Histoire de Montréal **3**

East Montréal Attractions

110 rue Notre-Dame Ouest (on Place d'Armes). ☎ **514-849-1070**. Admission: Free for praying; otherwise: Adults C$2 (US$1.50), students C$1 (US75¢); Light show: Adults C$10 (US$7.50), senior C$9 (US$7), children 7–17 C$5 (US$4), children under 6 free. Light show open Tues–Fri 6:30 p.m. and 8:30 p.m., Sat 7 p.m. and 8:30 pm. Métro: Place-d'Armes or Square-Victoria.

Biodôme de Montréal
East Montréal

Built to fill the velodrome from the 1976 Olympics, Montréal's Biodôme is like a zoo and an indoor nature walk combined. You start at the penguin pool, a universal favorite among kids and grownups. Then you follow the trail through four different ecosystems: a Laurentian forest, the

St. Lawrence marine system, a tropical rain forest, and a polar environment, each complete with its own plants and animals. Guests spend their
visit largely in temperate surroundings, but you may want to bring a
pullover for the Polar World segment. Our 10-year-old source proclaims
the Biodôme "excellent," and adds, "the animals seem very happy." Kids
go nuts here. Allow 1 hour.

4777 av. Pierre-de-Coubertin (next to Stade Olympique). ☎ 514-868-3000. Internet:
www.biodome.qc.ca. *Admission: Adults C$10.50 (US$8), seniors $7.50 (US$5.50),*
students under 17 C$8 (US$5.60), children 5–17 C$5.25 (US$4), children under 5, free.
Open: Daily 9 a.m.–4 p.m. (until 6 p.m. in summer). Métro: Viau.

Boulevard St-Laurent
Plateau

The Main, as it is known to English Montréalers, is the city's oldest north-
south artery. It extends up from Vieux-Montréal through Chinatown and
beyond Little Italy and the Jean Talon Market to the furthest reaches of the
island. It also divides the city's street addresses between Est and Ouest.
There are many interesting parts to boulevard St-Laurent. The most colorful and liveliest stretch runs between rue Sherbrooke and avenue Mont-
Royal, where the foot traffic is heavy all day and well into the night; a
multitude of cafes, boutiques, delis, restaurants, and shops are frequented
by a cosmopolitan clientele. By night, boulevard St-Laurent is one of the
city's booming nightlife strips. It's a major destination and quite a scene
for debonair dons and flesh-bearing divas who cram behind velvet ropes
and crowd burly bouncers looking to get into *the* spot. And where the
eternal big question is, "Are you on the list?" Just say that you are.

☎ *514-286-0334. Internet:* www.boulevardsaintlaurent.com.

Casino de Montréal
Vieux-Montréal

The Casino de Montréal opened in 1993, occupying the French and
Québec pavilions built for Expo '67 on the banks of Île Notre-Dame. Lit
up at night, it looks like a remnant building from Superman's home planet
of Krypton. Minutes from downtown, past Habitat '67, another architectural gem from the World Fair, and over *Pont de la Concorde,* the casino's
chiming machines and velvety gaming tables span five floors. Every year,
six million guests pass through its doors to gamble, to catch a show at
the cabaret theater, or to dine at one of the four restaurants. One of them,
Nuances, nestled away on the fifth floor and offering spectacular views
of the St. Lawrence and the downtown skyline, is one of two five-star
restaurants in Montréal. You can also join the all-night cronies and early-
morning gamblers — who must be quite a sight to behold — for brunch
on Saturdays and Sundays starting at 9:30 a.m.

1 av. du Casino. ☎ 800-665-2274 or 514-392-2746. Internet: www.casino-de-
montreal.com. *Admission: Free; tickets to matinee and evening shows at*

Le Cabaret are C$15 (US$11.50). Open: 24-hours, 365 days per year. Métro: Jean-Drapeau; take the shuttle from there.

Centre Canadien d'Architecture
East Montréal

Tucked away on the southwestern edge of the downtown neighborhood, the impressive grounds of the CCA occupy a whole city block. The two buildings, — one austere and contemporary, the other a grandiose late-19th-century home — combine to make up the 130,000 square feet of exhibition galleries, a library and study center, a theater, and a bookstore, all devoted to the understanding, appreciation, and betterment of architecture. As museum-going goes, the photography, blueprints, and three-dimensional models can be a refreshing change from the paintings and sculptures of most art museums. The CCA's exhibits focus on architecture, urban planning, and landscape design. While CCA attracts architecture enthusiasts from around the globe, it is usually interesting and accessible enough for regular folk, too. Across boulevard René-Levesque, to the south, the CCA Garden is a unique sculpture garden — ideal at sunset.

1920 rue Baile (between rue du Fort and rue St-Marc). ☎ **514-939-7026** *Internet:* www.cca.qc.ca. *Admission: Adults C$6 (US$3.75), seniors C$4 (US$3), students C$3 (US$1.95). Open: June–Sept: Tues–Sun 11 a.m.–6 p.m. (until 9 p.m. on Thurs); rest of year Wed–Fri 11 a.m.–6 p.m. (until 8 p.m. on Thurs), Sat–Sun 11 a.m.–5p.m. Métro: Atwater, Georges-Vanier, or Guy-Concordia.*

Jardins Botanique
East Montréal

Montréal's Jardins Botanique offer a respite from the concrete jungle within the city's limits. By combining a visit here with the nearby Biodôme and Insectarium (see the "Finding More Cool Things to See and Do" section), you can make nature the theme of this daylong urban excursion. Spread over 72 hectares (178 acres) just north of the Stade Olympique, the gardens contain more than 22,000 plant species and offers a different treat for every season. In May, expect acres of fragrant lilac trees. Roses bloom from mid-June until fall. In winter, ten greenhouses shelter bonsai and tropical plants. In the fall, don't miss the Magic of Lanterns, a cooperative effort between Montréal and Shanghai, and the biggest of its type outside China. During this lantern exhibit, the gardens are particularly pretty at sunset. Picnics permitted.

4101 rue Sherbrooke Est (opposite Stade Olympique). ☎ **514-872-1400.** *Internet:* www.ville.montreal.qc.ca/jardin. *Admission: May–Oct: Adults C$10.50 (US$8), seniors and students C$8 (US$6), children 5–17 C$5.25 (US$4). Nov–April: Adults C$8 (US$6), seniors and students C$6 US$4.50), children 4–17 C$4 (US$3). Open: from 9 a.m. year-round. Closing hours vary. Métro: Pie-IX.*

Lachine Rapids
Vieux-Montréal

La chine is French for China, which is where early French explorers thought they were when first thwarted in navigating this impressive stretch of rapids in the St. Lawrence River south of Montréal. Montréal has done a lot of work on its waterfront areas in recent years, and more improvements are planned. It's still hard to believe Montréal is surrounded by so much moving water, but you'll see for yourself strolling, cycling, or in-line skating down the riverside path along the rapids. The rapids look tame from a distance, but watch for the odd, brave kayaker bobbing at breakneck speed and you'll get the gist. Several companies offer rafting trips through the rapids. **Lachine Rapids Tours** (☎ 514-284-9607) has 90-minute jet boat trips leaving from Vieux-Montréal. **Rafting Hydrojet** (☎ 514-842-3871) offers shorter, rubber rafting trips. Call for prices, schedules, and ocations.

Métro: De l'Église station and walk south several blocks south to boulevard LaSalle.

La Ronde
Vieux-Montréal

Located on the former grounds of Expo '67, this amusement park is the pinnacle of a Montréal kid's summer fun. Six Flags recently bought La Ronde, and then renovated the grounds to the tune of C$90 (US$64.8) million — and it shows. It's clean, slick, and packed with 35 rides. If you have a sturdy stomach, give Le Monstre, a classic wooden roller coaster, a try. Or venture onto Le Cobra, a stand-up roller coaster that reaches speeds of 60mph and will definitely bring your last meal to mind. There's only one catch: La Ronde is packed in the summer, especially on weekends. According to our 10-year-old source, who waited an hour to get onto Le Monstre, the lines can almost take the fun out of the whole experience. Luckily, though, waits are short for kiddy rides like the Tchou Tchou Train. If you need to take a break between rides, try the rock-climbing wall or carnival booths galore.

22 MacDonald Way (on Île Ste-Hélène). ☎ *800-797-4537. Internet:* www.laronde. com. *Admission: Grounds: C$20 (US$14); Rides: Age 12 and over C$28 (US$20), ages 3–11 C$17 (US$13); Parking: C$8.70 (US$6.50). Open: Last week in May, Sat–Sun only; June–Aug and Labour Day weekend from 10 a.m.–9 p.m. Métro: Papineau, then bus No. 169.*

Marché Bonsecours
Vieux-Montréal

You'll be sorely disappointed if you come expecting the vibrant market that closed in 1963. Today, the inside of the market building is a slick mall selling up-market tourist trinkets, mainly Québec jewelry, native crafts, and contemporary shelf furnishings. Yet, the Marché Bonsecours is an impressive neo-classical building in its own right, with many columns and a silver dome. It remains an important Vieux-Montréal landmark and one of the top ten heritage buildings in Canada. Since its completion in 1847, it also served (alternately) as a meeting place of Montréal's hob-nobbing men-only Beaver Club, as a theater where a young Charles Dickens performed as part of a touring troupe, as City Hall and, briefly, as the Parliament of United Canada.

350 rue St-Paul Est (at the bottom of rue Gosford). ☎ **514-872-7730.** *Internet:* www. marchebonsecours.qc.ca. *Open: Daily from 10 a.m.–6 p.m., and until 9 p.m. on some nights. Métro: Champs-de-Mars.*

Musée d'Archéologie et d'Histoire de Montréal
Vieux-Montréal

If you visit just one museum while in Montréal, this is our choice. And because it's a great introduction to Montréal's history, for the benefit of the rest of your stay, visit this superb and unusual museum first. Officially opened on the city's 350th anniversary in 1992, this museum is located in the **Point à Callière building,** an uber-modern construction by Montréal architect Dan Hanganu. It was built on the site of the original French set-tlement of 1642 — what would become today's Montréal. After a brief multimedia presentation, a self-guided tour takes visitors underground to discover, literally, layers of artifacts from the centuries of civilization and the partially excavated ruins of the city's first buildings, canal system, and cemetery. Along the way, five historical figures engage the willing in a virtual conversation. A cafe on the third floor is popular for lunch among the office workers in Vieux-Montréal.

350 Place Royale (at rue de la Commune). ☎ **514-872-9150.** *Internet* www. pacmusee.qc.ca. *Admission: Adults C$10 (US$7.50) families C$20 (US$14), chil-dren aged 6–12 C$3.50 (US$2.75), students C$6 (US$4.30), seniors C$7.50 (US$5.40). Open: Sept–June: Tues–Fri 10 a.m.–5 p.m., Sat–Sun 11 a.m.–5 p.m.; July–Aug: Mon–Fri 10 a.m.–6 p.m. Sat–Sun 11 a.m. –6 p.m. Métro: Square-Victoria or Place-d'Armes.*

Musée d'Art Contemporain de Montréal
Downtown

Everything about this new museum is light and airy, as if it were custom-designed for daydreamers and escapists. Situated just off the sprawling plaza of **Place des Arts,** it's a great place to take a breather from the bustle of downtown. About 60 percent of the museum's permanent col-lection comprises works by contemporary Québec painters. There are also works from international painters such as Jean Dubuffet, Max Ernst, Jean Arp, Larry Poons, and Antoni Tàpies, as well as photographers Robert Mapplethorpe and Ansel Adams. The museum is a little light on explanations, but it does offer a few of the guiding principles of the major schools of modern art.

185 rue Ste-Catherine Ouest. ☎ **514-847-6226.** *Internet:* www.macm.org. *Admission: Adults, C$6 (US$4.50), seniors C$4 (US$3), students C$3 (US$2), children under 12 free, families C$12 (US$9). Free on Wed 6–9 p.m. Open: Tues–Sun 11 a.m.–6 p.m. (until 9 p.m. Wed). Métro: Place-des-Arts.*

Musée des Beaux-Arts de Montréal
Downtown

Since Toronto took over as Canada's business center 20 years ago, Montréal has been repositioning itself as the nation's cultural and artistic capital. Hence, the role and profile of the MMFA (Montréal Museum of Fine Arts) continues to grow. The permanent exhibit features an excellent survey of modern and contemporary Canadian art, including works by the Group of Seven and Emily Carr. It also displays paintings and sculptures by a number of the art world's international heavy weights, like El Greco, Renoir, Monet, Picasso, and Cézanne. In 1991, the completion of a modern-looking wing, directly across the street from the original neo-classical building, tripled the exhibition floor space. Throughout the year, the MMFA hosts temporary exhibits of an international caliber.

1380 rue Sherbrooke Ouest (at rue Crescent). ☎ **800-899-6873** *or 514-285-2000. Internet:* www.mmfa.qc.ca. *Admission: Entrance to the permanent collection is by donation; tickets for temporary exhibits vary but are half price Wed, from 5:30–9 p.m. Métro: Guy-Concordia.*

Musée McCord d'Histoire Canadienne
Downtown

In the mood for some local history? This is the place to discover the past of Canada, Québec, and Montréal. The displays of clothing and artifacts may feel a little hokey by today's slick museum standards, but the collections are intelligently planned and well presented. Moderate history buffs will leave the museum with a concrete idea of how Québec's native population lived and how early settlers survived in hostile conditions with few comforts. Actually, you may leave wondering what kind of crazed, ice- and snow-loving souls decided to come here in the first place. Texts are in English and French. There's a cafe by the entrance and a great gift shop with books and work from local artisans, including jewelry, scarves, and other souvenir-friendly items.

690 Sherbrooke Ouest (at rue Victoria). ☎ **514-398-7100.** *Internet:* www.mccordmuseum.qc.ca. *Admission: Adults, C$7 (US$5), seniors C$5 (US$3), students C$4 (US$3), kids 7–11 C$1.50 (US$1), kids under 7 free, families C$14 (US$10). Open: Tues–Fri 10 a.m.–6 p.m. Sat–Sun 10 a.m–5 p.m. During the summer, open daily as of 9 a.m. Métro: McGill.*

Parc Jean-Drapeau
Vieux-Montréal

Let the expansive green spaces and varied leisure activities offered by these two islands in the St. Lawrence River take you away from the stop and go of the downtown. Directly south of Vieux-Montréal and minutes away by ferry, Métro, or bridge, **Île Notre-Dame** and **Île Ste-Hélène** make up the park, recently renamed after the mayor who built them. Mayor Drapeau's city workers constructed Île Notre-Dame entirely, out of the landfill excavated from the tunnels for Métro. They also enlarged Île Ste-Hélène. The two islands were the site for the '67 Expo, widely considered the best World Fair of the last century. Now, the parklands of the islands have some of city's main attractions, like Casino de Montréal, the Biosphère, and La Ronde, but they are also a haven for swimming, canoeing, sailing, cycling, in-line skating, picnicking, and strolling through the landscaped gardens. In the winter, for three successive weekends in February, Île Ste-Hélène is the site for Montréal's winter carnival, the *Fête des Neiges.*

Île Ste-Hélène and Île Notre-Dame. ☎ *514-872-6120. Internet:* www.parc jeandrapeau.com. *Métro: Jean-Drapeau.*

Parc Mont-Royal
Plateau

Montréalers from all walks of life agree that Parc Mont-Royal is a gem. Built 125 years ago, the park is the brainchild of Frederick Olmstead, who also designed New York's Central Park. If you follow the wide trail that starts at the monument, you circle around the mountain all the way to the top. It's an easy walk and you won't feel like you're climbing, although there's not much to see except trees and other walkers until you get to the top. From there, the lookout onto the city and the river is spectacular. There's a chalet where you can rest and buy refreshments. Keep following the trail until you reach Montréal's famous cross, a huge, lit cross on the top of the mountain that's visible from the east side of the city. The whole walk takes about two hours. While not particularly dangerous, the park is not lit, so plan to be out before sunset. Watch out for the odd mountain biker who springs out of the woods onto the trail.

Access from avenue du Parc. ☎ *514-843-8240. Internet:* www.lemontroyal.qc. ca. *Métro: Place-des-Arts, then take bus No. 80 and get off at the Monument Sir George-Étienne Cartier.*

Stade Olympique
East Montréal

Known locally as the Big O, the facilities of the 1976 Olympics are considered either a feat of architectural prowess, an enormous concrete debt, or perhaps both, depending on which local you ask. Built by French architect Roger Taillibert, the gigantic, 60,000 to 80,000 capacity, white dome-shaped stadium topped by a sloping Eiffel-like tower is an impressive structure. And no matter what your tastes, it's worth seeing up close. Okay, so the retracting roof has never worked and parts of the sloping tower ceded to the combined forces of time and gravity. The grounds of the complex still give you a distinct back-to-the-future experience, and the view of the city from the tower is incredible. The tour gives some highlights of the '76 Games and explains the municipal drama of preparing for the Montréal Olympics.

4141 rue Pierre-de-Coubertin. ☎ *514-252-8687. Admission: To the tower: Adults, C$10 (US$7.50), students and seniors C$7.50 (US$5.50), children C$5 (US$4); stadium tours: Adults C$5.50 (US$4), seniors C$5 (US$4), children and students C$4.25 (US$3). Open: Daily, English tours depart at 12:40 and 3:40 p.m.; the hours of the observation deck vary throughout the year. Métro: Pie-IX or Viau.*

The Underground City
Downtown

Eighteen miles of underground corridors, passageways, galleries, and atriums full of shops, boutiques, food courts, an indoor ice rink, Métro stations, and movie theaters comprise Montréal's *ville souterraine,* the largest network of its kind in the world. It all began innocently enough in 1962, with the completion of the Ville-Marie skyscraper, which boasted as much retail space underground as the total square footage of its 47 stories of office space above. Other downtown buildings soon followed suit, converting their lower levels into retail malls. Over time, they began to connect haphazardly. **The Infotouriste Centre** has a good map of what's not much more than a maze of stores. It's handy as a scenic alternate route or as a hideout from any harsh weather, because it's always warm in the winter and cool in the summer. Ideal conditions — a shopper's paradise.

Vieux-Montréal

Settled in the 17th century, much of Vieux-Montréal's magic is due to its European flair, unique in North America. You feel eons away from the rest of the city's 21st-century hubbub. Today, Vieux-Montréal is at once a port, a waterfront park, and a financial district, chock full of cafes, boutiques, art galleries, and hotels. After you've explored **rue St-Paul, Place Jacques-Cartier,** and **rue des Artistes,** head down to the waterfront. This narrow parkland stretches down several peers, along the St. Lawrence River, and eventually gives way to a network of bike paths. One leads to the Formula One track on nearby **Île Ste-Hélène.** In-line skates and bikes are available for rent from several shops along rue de la Commune and the boardwalk.

Internet: www.tourism-montreal.org, www.oldportofmontreal.com, www.old.montreal.qc.ca. *Métro: Champs-de-Mars, Place-d'Armes, or Square-Victoria.*

Index of top sights by neighborhood

East Montréal
Biodôme de Montréal
Jardins Botanique
Stade Olympique

Downtown
Centre Canadien de'Architecture
Musée des Beaux-Arts
Musée McCord d'Histoire Canadienne
The Underground City

Quartier Latin
Musée d'Art Contemporain de
    Montréal

Vieux-Montréal
Basilique Notre-Dame
Casino de Montréal
La Ronde
Lachine Rapids
Marché Bonsecours
Musée d'Archéologie et d'Histoire de
    Montréal
Parc Jean-Drapeau
Vieux-Montréal

Plateau
Boulevard St-Laurent
Parc Mont-Royal

Index of top sights by type

Gardens, Parks, and Natural Settings
Biodôme de Montréal
Jardin BotaniqueLachine Rapids
Parc Jean-Drapeau
Parc Mont-Royal

Galleries, Museums, and Historic Buildings
Basilique Notre-Dame
Centre Canadien de'Architecture
    Marché Bonsecours
Musée d'Archéologie et d'Histoire de
    Montréal

Musée d'Art Contemporain de
    Montréal
Musée des Beaux-Arts
Musée McCord d'Histoire Canadienne
Stade Olympique

Neighborhoods or Streets
Boulevard St-Laurent
Vieux-Montréal

Entertainment
Casino de Montréal
La Ronde
Underground City

Finding More Cool Things to See and Do

If the preceding section of top sights isn't enough to keep you busy, don't fret. There's plenty more to see and do in Montréal. The following sections give you some ideas for how to entertain kids and ways to get outside, plus museums, churches, and sports teams.

Kid-pleasers

In this section, you find some all-time favorite Montréal kids' attractions guaranteed to amuse.

Insectarium de Montréal
East Montréal

If you go to the Jardins Botanique, the Insectarium is included in the admission. See over 3,000 varieties of bugs, from butterflies to beetles and maggots. In November and December — delight of delights — you can even indulge in an Insect Tasting.

4581 rue Sherbrooke Est (at Jardins Botanique). ☎ *514-872-1400. Admission: May–Oct: Adults C$10.50 (US$8), seniors and students C$8 (US$6), children 5–17 C$5.25 (US$4); Nov–April: Adults C$8 (US$6), seniors and students C$6 (US$4.50), children 4–17 C$4 (US$3). Open: Daily in summer daily 9 a.m.–7 p.m.; daily rest of year 9 a.m.–5 p.m. Métro: Pie-IX or Viau.*

La Biosphère
Parc Jean-Drapeau

Located in the former American pavilion of Expo '67, this interactive nature museum is much more focused on ecology than the Biodôme. With exhibits on the Great Lakes and St. Lawrence River ecosystem, this museum explains the effects of pollution and other environmental issues.

160 Tour-de-l'Île Rd. (on Île Ste-Hélène). ☎ *514-283-5000. Admission: Adults C$8.50 (US$ 6.25), students and seniors C$6.50 (US$5), children 5–17 C$5 (US$4), families C$19 (US$14.25). Open: Late June–Labour Day, daily 10 a.m.–6 p.m.; Labour Day– Late June, Tues–Sat, 10 a.m.–4 p.m. Métro: Jean-Drapeau.*

Planetarium de Montréal
Downtown

For junior astronomers or any stargazers, this domed center explains it at all: how the stars change with the seasons, space travel, the collisions of stars, and more. Every other show is in English.

1000 rue St-Jacques (corner of rue Peel). ☎ *514-972-4530. Internet: . Admission: Adults C$6.50 (US$5), students and seniors C$5 (US$4), children under 18 C$3.25 (US$2.50). Open: Summer, Mon 12:30–5:00 p.m., Tues–Thurs 10 a.m.–5 p.m., Fri 10 a.m.–5 p.m., 6:45–8:30 p.m., Sat–Sun 12:30–5 p.m., 6:45–8:30 p.m. Off season, Mon– Thurs, 9:30 a.m.–5 p.m., Fri 9:30 a.m.–5 p.m. and 6:45–8:30 p.m., Sat–Sun 9:45 a.m.–5 p.m., 6:45–8:30 p.m. Métro: Bonaventure.*

1MAX Theatre
Vieux-Montréal

Kids get giddy watching hikers scale Mount Everest, divers explore coral reefs in Mexico, or cameras swoop through the Grand Canyon on a seven-story screen.

King Edward Pier (in the Old Port, at the end of boulevard. St-Laurent). ☎ *514-496-4724. Admission: Adults, C$9.95 (US$7.50), seniors and students C$8.95 (US$6.75), kids C$7.95 (US$6). Call for current schedule of shows in English. Métro: Place-d'Armes.*

Best city parks

If people-watching or just plain hanging out is on your agenda, don't miss these green spaces.

Parc Lafontaine
Plateau

Lovers loll about the shaded, grassy slopes of this park, while ducks and paddle boaters swirl about its large kidney-shaped pond. Parc Lafontaine is a very European-style park and as idyllic as it sounds. A great spot for a picnic or even a nap. Throughout the summer, the open-air theater, **Théâtre de Verdure,** presents many free music concerts and modern dance performances in the evenings from the end of June through August.

Between rue Sherbrooke and rue Rachel, on avenue Parc-Lafontaine. ☎ *872-2644. Métro: Sherbrooke.*

Parc Maisonneuve
East Montréal

Near the Stade Olympique, this former golf course is now one of the most popular and vibrant parks in Montréal, so score a point for the good guys. It's always buzzing with action, from in-line skating, cycling, and Ultimate Frisbee to cultural festivals and the annual celebrations of Québec's national holiday, June 24 — St-Jean-Baptiste Day. The remains of the golf course's 19th hole now serve as the park's restaurant and facilities.

4601 rue Sherbrooke Est. ☎ *514-872-6211. Métro: Pie-XI or Viau.*

Museums

Museum-wise, Montréal has much more than just art. Get your fill of natural history, local history, or even some humorous history while you're at it.

Centre d'Histoire de Montréal
Vieux-Montréal

Learn about Montréal's First Nations residents and the early European settlers, who started arriving in the 17th century. The museum tells about famous historical figures and gives you a pretty good idea of what everyday life was like over the past four centuries.

335 place d'Youville (at rue St-Pierre). ☎ 514-872-3207. Admission: Adults C$4.50 (US$3.50); seniors, students, children 7–17 C$3 (US$2.25), children under 6 free. Open: Summer daily 10 a.m.–5 p.m. Off season, Tues–Sun 10 a.m.–5 p.m. Métro: Square-Victoria.

Musée Just pour Rire
Downtown

An offshoot of Montréal's acclaimed **Just pour Rire/Just for Laughs Comedy Festival,** this museum explores laughter from all its angles in the International Comedy Hall of Fame. Real magicians teach magic tricks in the Abracadabra workshops. Phone ahead to check the programming schedule.

2111 bd. St-Laurent. ☎ 514-845-4000. Internet: www.hahaha.com. Admission: Comedy Hall of Fame, Adults and children C$5 (US$4). Abracadabra: Adults C$9 (US$6.75) children C$5 (US$4). Group rates are available. Open: Hall of Fame, Tues–Sat, 10 a.m.–5 p.m.; Abracadabra, Tues–Fri 9 a.m.–5 p.m. and Sat–Sun 10 a.m.–5 p.m. Métro: Saint-Laurent.

Musée Redpath
Downtown

This small natural science museum may seem quirky by today's slick standards, with it's old-school museology style, but it happens to have Canada's second largest collection of artifacts from ancient Egypt, for one. If fossils and geological fragments are your cup of tea, check it out.

859 rue Sherbrooke Ouest (on the campus of McGill University). ☎ 514-398-4086. Internet: www.mcgill.ca/redpath. Admission: free. Open: July–Aug, Mon–Thurs 9 a.m.–5 p.m. and Sun 1–5 p.m. Sept–June, Mon–Fri 9 a.m.–5 p.m. and Sun 1–5 p.m. Métro: McGill.

Churches

Montréal's religious hey-day is long gone but, luckily, many of the city's glorious church buildings remain. Here are two of the best.

Chapelle Notre-Dame-de-Bonsecours
Vieux-Montréal

Originally built in the 17th century, this church is known as the Sailor's Church, thanks to its proximity to Montréal's port. Enjoy excellent views of the harbor and the Old City from the church's tower.

400 rue St-Paul Est (near the Bonsecours Market). ☎ *514-282-8670. Internet:* www. marguerite-bourgeoys.com/index_new_en.html. *Admission: Free for praying and attending mass; otherwise: adults C$6 (US$4.50), senior C$4 (US$3), student C$4 (US$3), children 6–12 C$3 (US$2.25), children under 6 free. Open: Tues–Sun May–Oct 10 a.m.–5:30 p.m., Nov–mid-Jan and Mar–Apr 11 a.m.–3:30 p.m., mid-Jan–Feb closed. Sunday mass in English from Mar–mid-Jan 10:30 a.m. Métro: Champ-de-Mars.*

Christ Church Cathedral
Downtown

Located on one of the busiest, most commercial streets in the city, this graceful, 19th century, Gothic-style cathedral has an elegant interior that's worth exploring. Local musicians give concerts here year round.

635 rue Ste-Catherine Est. ☎ *514-843-6577. Internet:* www.montreal.anglican. org/cathedral. *Open: Daily 8 a.m.–6 p.m. Sunday services. Métro: McGill.*

Spectator sports

Hey sports fans! Montréal is a great sports town and currently home to professional hockey, football, baseball, and soccer teams. Montréal is, first and foremost, a hockey town, and the Montréal Canadiens are the most storied team in the history of the game. Since 1929, the Canadiens have won a record 24 Stanley Cup Championships while playing in the National Hockey League.

Canadiens (hockey)

The relationship between the team and its city runs deep and is infinitely complex. The red, white, and blue jerseys are part of Montréal's cultural fiber. After all, this is one of the disputed birthplaces of Canada's national game: Not coincidentally, the distance between rue Stanley and rue Drummond is the exact official length of a modern-day hockey rink. Unlike any other city in Canada, Montréalers feel so passionately about their Canadiens, or *Les Glorieux,* that riots mark the major moments in the team's history. The last one was in 1993, when the Canadiens won their last Stanley Cup.

There's been less civil unrest as of late, thanks to the Canadiens struggle to merely make the playoffs in recent years. Every season, from mid-September to the beginning of April, they play about half of their

82-game schedule downtown at the **Bell Centre,** also called the New Forum or the Phone Booth. The original Montréal Forum, at the corner of rue Atwater and rue Ste-Catherine, is now a movie megaplex.

If you're in town for a Canadiens' home game, definitely check it out. Buying a ticket on game day isn't easy, though; try buying them in person at the **Bell Centre Ticket Office,** located at 1260 rue de la Gauchetière Ouest, or phone the **Admission Ticket Line** at ☎ **800-361-4595** or 514-790-1245. You can get also your seats on the Web at either www.admission.com or www.canadiens.com. If the game is sold out, on most nights you'll find people outside the Bell Centre with extra tickets, and some may be willing to negotiate a price.

Alouettes (football)

The Canadian Football League's Montréal Alouettes — yes, the bird from that famous French song (*"Alouette, gentille alouette . . ."*) — returned in 1996 to roost in Montréal. The previous flock folded because of financial troubles about a decade earlier.

Canadian football is like the football played in the United States, but the field is longer and wider. Also, on offense, teams only have three tries to advance ten yards for a first down. The season, including exhibition games and playoffs, runs from early-June to mid-November.

The Alouettes weren't much of a draw for some time. When they made the playoffs in their second season back, there was a scheduling conflict with a U2 concert at the Stade Olympique (the Big O); the Irish rockers won out, and the Alouettes had to make alternate arrangements. Their recent move to McGill University's Percival Molson Stadium downtown revitalized the franchise, and they now sell out games on a regular basis, tripling the paltry attendance of their games at the cavernous Big O.

In 2002, the Montréal Alouettes won the Grey Cup Championship, so they're enjoying an all-time high in popularity and their tickets are hot. The Alouette's home field is at the top of avenue University, halfway up Mont-Royal.

Watching the Als and their *gentille* cheerleaders can be a pleasant outing on a Saturday afternoon in the late summer or fall. The **Alouettes' Ticket Office** (☎ **514-871-2255**) is downtown at 646 rue Ste-Catherine Ouest. You can also purchase tickets by phone (**Admission Ticket** hotline: ☎ **800-361-4595** or 514-790-1245) or on the Web at www.admission.com.

Expos (baseball)

The troubled Montréal Expos seem to be on their way out of town — possibly to San Juan — faster than you can say, "piña colada." This gutsy small-market team played some formidable seasons in recent years, but, even so, attendance at the Stade Olympique is poor.

If our boys of summer are still around when you get to Montréal, catching a game at the Big O is everything an outing to the ballpark ought to be — but in French. It shouldn't be too difficult to figure-out what the aisle vendors are selling — it's all the usual ballpark fare: beer, peanuts, hot dogs, and so on.

You can buy tickets for an Expos' game at the **Stade Olympique** (4549 av. Pierre-de-Coubertin; Métro: Pie-IX), open Monday to Friday from 9:00 a.m. to 6:00 p.m. and Saturday from 10:00 a.m. to 4:00 p.m. or call **Admission Tickets** at ☎ 800-361-4595 or 514-790-1245. On the Web, visit www.admission.com and montreal.expos.mlb.com.

Impact (soccer)

The new kids on the sports block, the Montréal Impact (☎ **514-328-3668;** www.montrealimpact.com), started in 1992 by a local cheese company, are already perennial contenders in the American Professional Soccer League (APSL). Soccer, not hockey, is currently Canada's fastest-growing sport in the amateur ranks, which translates into capacity crowds packed into the 7,500-seat Claude Robillard Stadium (1000 av. Émile-Journault; Métro: Crémazie) for the Impact season, from late-April to early-September.

Buy ticket by phone from **Admission Network** (☎ **800-361-4595** or 514-790-1245) or on the Web at www.admission.com.

Seeing Montréal by Guided Tour

Want to explore with an expert? In the mood to let someone else lead for a while? The following sections give you some options for guided tours to Montréal — by foot, by boat, or by bus. Call a day ahead to reserve a spot.

What's in a tour for me?

Will a guided tour give you a better excursion than going it alone? It depends on what you want. If you want specialized explanations of neighborhoods or themes, or you want to see sights that are difficult to access on your own, a guided tour is hard to beat. Someone else takes care of the planning and answers your questions, to boot. If meeting and talking to locals is your thing, you can take a pass on the guided tours.

One bit of advice for lone travelers: Guided tours are an excellent way to break the solitude when you're traveling on your own. They are the best of both worlds, really. You can share your impressions and experience with some other travelers, but you won't be stuck in group-mode with the same people for your whole trip.

No matter how good it sounds on paper, call ahead to find out if the tour is right for you. Ask how long the tour lasts, what you'll see, how much it costs, what's included (and not), how many people will be on it, whether the tour is in English, and whether there is anything you should bring along.

Walking it

Montréal is a great city for walking because it's full of interesting neighborhoods with their own architecture, history, and flavor. Most of the walking tours available in Montréal focus on particular neighborhoods. These are the most popular ones.

Guidatour (☎ 514-844-4012; www.guidatour.qc.ca) offers daily tours of Vieux-Montréal in the summer. Tours depart from Basilique Notre-Dame at 11 a.m. and 3 p.m. Tickets are C$14 (US$10.50) for adults, C$12 (US$9) for students and seniors, and C$6 (US$3.50) for children 6–12. Tickets are available 15 min. before departure, but try to buy them earlier. The two-and-a-half-hour tour is available in English.

Visites de Montréal (☎ 514-933-6674; www.visitesdemontreal.com) offers walking tours of Vieux-Montréal, including the Basilique Notre-Dame, for groups of up to 20 people. Reserve one week ahead of time. Prices vary for the two-hour tour, but are about C$34 (US$25).

Heritage Montréal (☎ 514-286-2662; www.heritagemontreal.qc.ca) offers architectural tours of various Montréal neighborhoods on foot or bicycle from June to September. Popular tours include the Plateau neighborhood, downtown churches, the Mile End neighborhood, and a tour of Montréal's Métro system. Tickets are C$10 (US$7.50) for adults, C$8 (US$6) for seniors and students.

Riding It

Feel like a break from the walking? Want to sit back and let someone else run the show for a while? Because Montréal is such a great walking city, we don't recommend bus tours. However, bus tours do have their merits, especially if you have trouble walking long distances. Here are your options:

✔ **Gray Line** (☎ 514-934-1222; www.grayline.com) operates 11 different sightseeing tours, departing from the tourism office on Square Dorchester. The basic city tour lasts about an hour and a half and costs C$20 (US$15) for adults and children; children under 5 are free. Call for information on more specialized trips.

✔ **Impérial Autocar** (☎ 514-871-4733; www.autocarimperial.com) offers narrated trips on open-top double-decker buses. Tours lasts 6 hours. Tickets are C$15 (US $11.25) for adults, C$12 (US$8.65) for students and C$8 (US$5.75) for children 5–12. Buses depart from Square Dorchester. On some tours, you can get on and off the buses as you please.

✔ **Amphi-Bus** (☎ 514-849-5181) offers tours of Vieux-Montréal with a twist. At the end of the tour, the bus waddles into the harbor. Reservations required. The basic one-hour tour costs C$16 (US$12) for adults, C$15 (US$11.25) for seniors and children under 12.

Boating it

Nothing beats the view of the city from the waters of the St. Lawrence. These companies offer short tours and longer dinner cruises:

✔ *Le Bateau-Mouche* (☎ 800-361-9952; www.bateau-mouche.com) offers 90-minute excursions in air-conditioned, glass-enclosed barges (like the ones on the Seine in Paris) leaving the Jacques Cartier Pier at 10 a.m., noon, 2 p.m., and 4 p.m. daily mid-May–mid-Oct. Tours cost C$20 (US$15) for adults, C$17 (US$12) for students and seniors, C$9 (US$6.75) for children 6–17, children under 5 free. Call for information on dinner cruises.

✔ **Croisières du Port de Montréal/AML Cruises** (☎ 800-667-3131; www.croisieresaml.com) offers Montréal harbor cruises daily, from May to October, departing from the Clock Tower Pier (at the foot of rue Berri). This company also cruises from Montréal to Québec City. Call for departures times and rates. Fares are C$15 to C$35 (US$9.70–US$26) adults, C$13 to C$33 (US$8.40–US$21) students and seniors, C$7 to C$25 (US$4.50–US$16) children 12 and under, C$35 to C$65 (US$23–US$42) families of 2 adults and 2 children. The higher prices are for dinner cruises.

✔ The *Nouvelle Orleans,* a Mississippi-style paddle-wheeler, leaves King Edward Quay for 90-minute narrated cruises at noon, 2 p.m., and 4 p.m. daily. Closed in winter. The tour costs C$20 (US$15) for adults, C$18 (US$13) for seniors and students and C$10 (US$7.50) for kids.

Hoofing it

You can also tour around Vieux-Montréal or Parc Mont-Royal in a horse-drawn carriage, known as a *calèche*. No need to reserve. You see them along **rue de la Commune** in the Old Port, and they line up at **Place d'Armes** (corner rue Notre-Dame and rue St-Sulpice). Count on spending C$35 (US$25) per half hour or $60 (US$43) per hour. Carriages take four or five people, and drivers usually explain historical and architectural sights along the way. In winter, there are also horse-drawn sled-carriages.

Taking Three Great Montréal Itineraries

The Montréal experience is greater than the sum of its architecture, shopping, entertainment, dining, and attractions. There is something quintessentially Montréal happening in the city's streets all the time, whether you're on commercial strips, landscaped parks, outdoor terraces, or among the festival crowds. You feel the city's attitude and spend your whole holiday trying to put in words just what it is — and that's *je ne sais quoi*.

Residents and visitors alike spend many an hour contemplating the question. (Answer: It's many things.) If you're in a car, though, chances are, Montréal's ephemeral nature will pass you by. If you're on foot and still don't know what we mean, go for a drink on the back patio of **Bar St-Sulpice** on rue St-Denis on a busy summer night. Experience, wonder, discuss.

What follows are three suggested itineraries that will let you experience the city like a Montréaler. They are less about getting around between various attractions, and more about exploring neighborhoods and indulging in experiences and rituals that are favorites here.

Itinerary #1: Connecting with your French roots

The term "two solitudes" describes coexisting universes of English and French in the province of Québec — and the abyss between them. Despite anyone's best efforts toward bilingualism in Montréal, two separate camps remain. They are not exclusive clubs, but they remain distinct for their differing senses of humor and ways of living the city life.

Assuming you're more comfortable in English than in French, you are going to experience the city as an *Anglophone* (English speaker). But keep in mind, there's a whole *Francophone* (French-speaking) world out there, with its own politicians, city officials, celebrities, rock stars, hockey players, biker gangs, talk radio, newspaper tabloids, sit-coms, music videos, and workplace humor.

You can visit Montréal and remain blissfully unaware of the French around you, partly because everyone in the service and tourism industries speaks very passable, if not impeccable, English. There's also plenty of English spoken around town, and most menus are bilingual. But, at any one time, the majority of the Montréalers surrounding you (over 60%) are French speaking and lead somewhat different lives than the English minority.

Itinerary #1: Connecting with Your French Roots

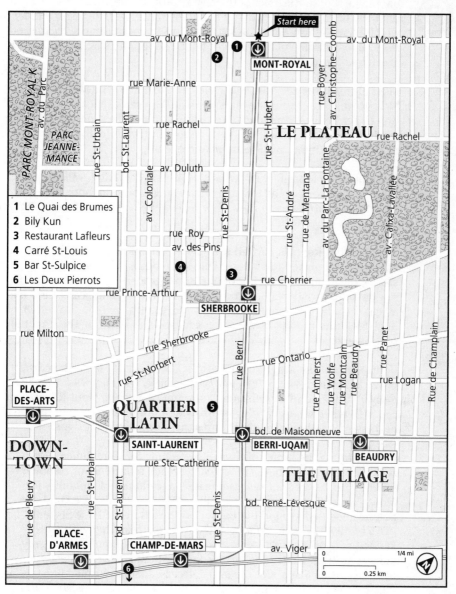

Start here

av. du Mont-Royal

av. du Mont-Royal

1
2
MONT-ROYAL

rue Marie-Anne

rue Rachel

LE PLATEAU

rue Rachel

PARC MONT-ROYAL K

av. du Parc

PARC JEANNE-MANCE

rue St-Urbain

bd. St-Laurent

av. Duluth

rue St-Hubert

rue Boyer

av. Christophe-Coomb

1 Le Quai des Brumes
2 Bily Kun
3 Restaurant Lafleurs
4 Carré St-Louis
5 Bar St-Sulpice
6 Les Deux Pierrots

av. Coloniale

rue St-Denis

rue St-André

rue de Mentana

av. du Parc-La Fontaine

av. Calixa-Lavallée

rue Roy
av. des Pins

4

3

rue Cherrier

rue Prince-Arthur

SHERBROOKE

rue Milton

rue Sherbrooke

rue St-Norbert

rue Berri

rue Ontario

rue Amherst

rue Wolfe

rue Montcalm

rue Beaudry

rue Panet

rue Logan

Rue de Champlain

PLACE-DES-ARTS

QUARTIER LATIN

5

bd. de Maisonneuve

DOWN-TOWN

rue St-Urbain

SAINT-LAURENT

BERRI-UQAM

BEAUDRY

rue Bleury

bd. St-Laurent

rue Ste-Catherine

rue St-Denis

THE VILLAGE

bd. René-Lévesque

PLACE-D'ARMES

CHAMP-DE-MARS

av. Viger

0   1/4 mi
0   0.25 km

6

After Paris, Montréal is the second largest French-speaking city in the world, so it stands to reason that there would be plenty to do in French, as well. This itinerary is a gentle introduction to Montréal's French side, guiding you on a stroll among the many shoppers and denizens on the Plateau's main commercial streets. There are no real destinations along the way, just suggested landmarks to guide your journey.

If you are a true *Francophile* (lover of all things French) and want to dabble further in this part of the city's cultural calendar, try to decipher the listings in either of the two free French weeklies, *Voir* and *Ici*, which come out on Thursdays. Their English counterparts, *Mirror* and *Hour*, also list some of the Francophone community's events, but they are not as thorough.

Most of this itinerary runs along the Orange Line of the Métro, between Mont-Royal and Champs-de-Mars stations. You can use it at your discretion to get between the most interesting parts of the different segments we describe. You can walk this whole route quickly, in about two hours, or stretch it out into an afternoon and evening.

Starting at the Mont-Royal Métro station, turn right and walk along the central artery of the trendy Plateau neighborhood, once a hotbed for bohemian artists and now a hot real-estate market and shopping district.

Avenue Mont-Royal is packed with every kind of merchant imaginable. Small, locally owned businesses rule the blocks. Used book and CD stores, designer clothing boutiques, small grocers, health-food shops, salons, outdoor sports outfitters, bakeries, restaurants, cafes, and bars all cater to the locals, who justifiably feel that they are in the center of it all. Meander until you've had your fill and the return in the direction of the Métro.

Continue past the Mont-Royal Métro station and pause on the corner of rue St-Denis. If you're into vintage clothing, you may want to make a detour at this point by continuing straight on avenue Mont-Royal, past rue St-Denis. For several blocks up a slight grade, shops on both sides of the street sell retro clothing and some of their own designs.

Depending on the hour, this may also be time for refreshment. Both bars we recommend here are typically French Montréal but completely different. The first spot represents a somewhat dated mentality in Montréal, while the second is all about Montréal today. **Le Quai des Brumes,** located around the corner on the left at 4481 rue St-Denis (☎ **514-499-0467**), is a smoky and dark place festering with anti-Federalist sentiment and known as a hang out for staunch, but graying, separatists. Do try to start a conversation, but we suggest not opening with a line about the late, former Canadian Prime Minister, Pierre Trudeau. **Bily Kun,** 354 av. Mont-Royal Est (☎ **514-845-5392**), is a block to the west. It's populated with good-looking but casual 20- and 30-somethings, engaged in animated chatter over microbrewery beer and light snacks. Ostrich-head trophies high on the walls overlook the scene.

Back on rue St-Denis, you're faced with a similar scene to where this walk started on Mont-Royal, but the storefronts are glitzier, the foot traffic heavier, and the pace faster. It goes on at this rate for four long city blocks.

At the bottom of this strip, there's a break in the action, but soon, on your right, you see the illuminated yellow sign of **Restaurant Lafleurs,** 3620 rue St-Denis (☎ **514-848-1804**) — *the* place to sample *poutine,* a local delicacy of French fries, cheese curds, and gravy. Lafleurs is the benchmark for all *poutines.*

Poutine, while delicious, is best consumed in small quantities. Finishing a small at Lafleurs is a feat in itself. Sharing is probably a good idea. Do not order the *familiale* size — ever — under any circumstances.

If the weather is pleasant, you may as well ask for your *poutine* to go and enjoy it in nearby **Carré St-Louis,** where nineteenth-century townhouses surround and enhance an already beautiful square with a multi-layered, birdbath fountain as its core. Benign loafers of all kinds hang out on the benches and on the ledge of the fountain.

Continue south on rue St-Denis. After crossing rue Sherbrooke, you descend into the Quartier Latin. We suggest you plan your arrival for the early evening, after the shops close on upper St-Denis. That's when the night start to get going in the streets below, surrounding the Université de Québec à Montréal (UQAM). The neighborhood's central location makes it a favorite destination for locals heading out for libations. It is jammed with choices, but the **Bar St-Sulpice,** 1680 rue St-Denis (☎ **514-844-9458**) is the most popular place to meet up for pitchers of beer or sangria, particularly in the summer, when the bar opens its immense back patio.

At this point, you may wish to take the Métro at the Berri-UQAM station. The entrance is just a bit farther down rue St-Denis on the same side, just across boulevard Maisonneuve. You take it for only one stop, to Champs-de-Mars, but the walk isn't scenic — actually, it's a bit of a hike, and it goes through something of a no-man's land. Plus, you may be feeling a tad sluggish after all that *poutine.* If you still want to walk, keep going straight down St-Denis for several blocks until you come to rue Notre-Dame. Turn left.

Out of the Champs-de-Mars Métro station, follow the arrows to Vieux-Montréal, walk up the hill to rue Notre-Dame, and turn left.

On the right, you pass City Hall, and on the left is Place Jacques-Cartier, which bustles in the summer with street performers and bands of tourists. Cross the square diagonally and aim for two blocks down, at rue St-Paul. A couple of doors farther west, you hit our final destination. By now it should be late at night, and **Les Deux Pierrots,** 104 rue St-Paul Est (☎ **514-861-1270**), is in full swing. This is a traditional *boîte à chansons,* where legions of French Montréalers gather to sing and clap along to Québec folk favorites. The songs won't be familiar, but they're catchy nonetheless. You'll be tapping your feet in no time, but it may take you considerably longer to learn the lyrics.

Itinerary #2: The English establishment

The historic conflict between the French and English in Québec was not only about two separate languages, religions, and identities, but also about two social classes. After 1759, when the English took over Montréal and the city began to industrialize, an increasing divide grew between the blue-collar French and the white-collar English. By the 1800s and early into the next century, much of Canada's wealth was concentrated in the **Golden Square Mile,** what's now the western part of Montréal's downtown.

Canada's post-industrial economy has gone a long way toward leveling the playing field, but the stately, nineteenth-century, grey stone town-houses of the Golden Square Mile have thankfully stood the test of time and can be seen in and among the city's modern office buildings.

Begin at the **corner of avenue McGill-College and rue Ste-Catherine** (Métro: McGill), one of the downtown's major intersections. McGill College is usually the recipient of the city's best landscaping efforts, including outdoor photo exhibits in the summer and millions of white Christmas lights during the winter.

Walk north up the slight grade on avenue McGill-College; at the top you see huge wrought iron gates. Along the way, on the right-hand side of the street, you pass a sculpture that looks like it's made out of butter. The numerous near life-size figures stand together making up *The Illuminated Crowd,* a 1979 sculpture by Raymond Mason.

At the top of the street, you are at the main entrance to **McGill University,** a gated campus and a serene and scenic retreat, right in the downtown core. You are welcome to go in and walk around. Go up the central drive, which comes to a fork after the playing field. Hang a left. The building on your right is the **Musée Redpath.** Admission is free.

From the museum, continue traveling in the same direction (west) through a smaller set of gates. Turn left, down rue McTavish, and walk past the university's student union and bookstore.

At rue Sherbrooke, turn right. Then take a left at the first light, onto rue Peel. The red-brick building that dominates the right hand side of the block is the **Montréal Amateur Athletic Association.** Now a posh sport's club, it's a holdover of the era of English-speaking private men's clubs.

Almost at the end of the next block is the **Seagram House,** a 1929 castle-like structure and former headquarters of the Bronfman family, who built a liquor empire during the prohibition.

Itinerary #2: The English Establishment

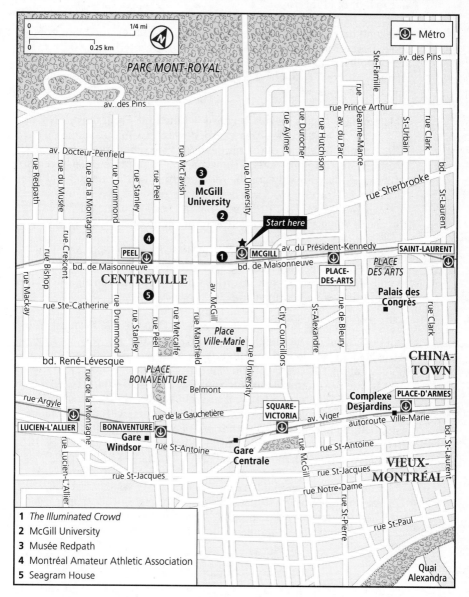

1 *The Illuminated Crowd*
2 McGill University
3 Musée Redpath
4 Montréal Amateur Athletic Association
5 Seagram House

Itinerary #3: Brunch, tam-tams, and beyond

Summer Sundays are still sacred in Montréal but are no longer a strictly Catholic affair. The day's main events are **brunch** (whenever) and **Tam-tams**, an all-afternoon drum-circle with dancers and a hippie crafts market at the Monument Sir George-Étienne Cartier at the foot of Mont-Royal.

Weekend brunch spots do brisk business on Saturday and Sunday. Most places serve breakfast specials until late in the afternoon, so there's absolutely no rush to get out of bed. And no one does. You see plenty of mussy-haired, rosy-cheeked couples grinning sleepily at each other and their menus.

This itinerary begins on **rue Bernard** in **Mile End.** From downtown, hop on bus no. 80 at Place-des-Arts Métro, heading north up avenue du Parc. After brunching at one of the hidden spots we recommend, you criss-cross avenue du Parc several times as you explore its cross streets, while working your way south. You end up amid the masses in Parc Mont-Royal. The city blocks in between are particularly long in this part of town, but the route is really not that far. At any point, you can catch the no. 80 going south to get between the different stops we suggest.

Ideally, attempt this itinerary on a sunny Sunday, beginning by late morning or in the early afternoon, before scoring breakfast. You can even follow this route on a Saturday or on weekends during the winter, but no one will be beating drums at the last stop.

Start by taking the no. 80 bus up avenue du Parc to rue Bernard. You will be in front of the **Théâtre Rialto,** 5723 av. du Parc, with its striking Art Nouveau facade and marquee. Take your pick of excellent brunch choices along rue Bernard: You can turn right and go a block to the east to the Brazilian **Restaurant Senzala,** 177 rue Bernard Ouest (☎ **514-274-1464),** for a tropical brunch. We like the Tropicana: poached eggs in avocado- or mango-halves topped with tomato sauce and melted cheese, served with fried plantains and grilled fruit. Or, from the starting point in front of the Rialto, turn left and go west to **Café Souvenir,** 1261 rue Bernard Ouest (☎ **514-948-5259),** which is several blocks down. Its menu is clever: Within each item are more choices allowing you to customize, to a certain extent, what will appear on your breakfast plate. It's a small, neighborhood spot that also harks of faraway destinations, because dioramas of European capitals adorn the walls. During the summer, the seating spills out onto a sidewalk terrace.

After your nth refill of coffee, make your way back to the intersection of rue Bernard and avenue du Parc. Turn south on avenue du Parc and walk toward downtown.

At the next intersection, avenue St-Viateur, you find **Le Petit Milos,** 5551 av. du Parc (☎ **514-274-9991),** a gourmet shop selling Greek specialty items, like fine olive oils. Around the corner, to the left, is **St-Viateur Bagels,** 263 av. St-Viateur Ouest (☎ **514-276-8044).** Although food may be the furthest thing from your imagination after a big brunch, tasting one of this bakery's famous bagels,

Itinerary #3: Brunch, Tam-Tams, and Beyond

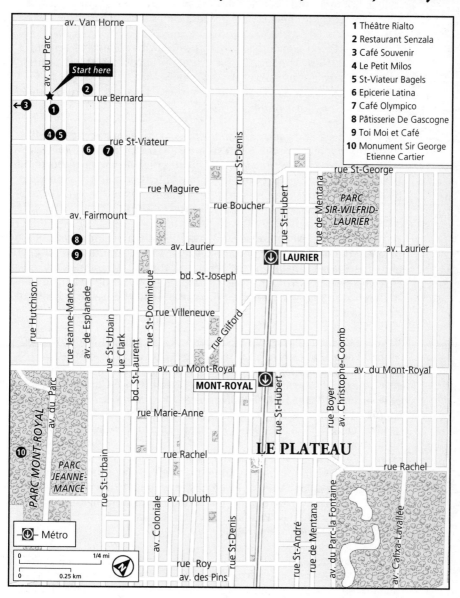

1	Théâtre Rialto
2	Restaurant Senzala
3	Café Souvenir
4	Le Petit Milos
5	St-Viateur Bagels
6	Epicerie Latina
7	Café Olympico
8	Pâtisserie De Gascogne
9	Toi Moi et Café
10	Monument Sir George Etienne Cartier

fresh out of the oven, is a must — at least, we strongly suggest it. If you can't do another bite, pick some up for a light picnic that you will unveil at Tam-tams, the last stop along your route.

You can also find lots of small shops farther along avenue St-Viateur, on both sides of the street. At the next corner, **Epicerie Latina**, 185 av. St-Viateur Ouest (☎ **514-273-6561**), is a gourmet grocery store, specializing in Italian ingredients. The market has produce as well as butcher- and cheese-counters. If you're even slightly curious about any of their cheeses, the grocers slices you off a sample taste.

At this point, you may already be saturated with coffee and seeking a bathroom, rather than looking for more. But if you can stand another cup, the coffee at **Café Olympico,** 185 av. St-Viateur Ouest (☎ 514-273-6561), is as good as it gets in Montréal. The scene there is worth taking in, if only for a moment.

Now, turn back and walk a block towards avenue du Parc. Turn left, going south along **avenue de l'Esplanade.** The townhouses on this street are some of the prettiest and most typical in the neighborhood. When you reach the next street, **avenue Fairmount,** jog to your right, by turning first to the right, and then immediately to the left, continuing down rue Jeanne-Mance, until **avenue Laurier.**

This street, to the east and west of avenue du Parc is an upscale shopping district, with clothing boutiques, cafes, restaurants, and magazine and video stores, mainly at the service of the sedate and upscale clientele who putter in from the uber-affluent neighborhood of Outremont. It's where they go when they don't want to fight the traffic and riffraff downtown.

If you're coming all the way from rue Bernard, you can window shop along avenue Laurier to your heart's content. You can also locate several brunch options around here, offering an abridged version of this itinerary. You will be right beside **Pâtisserie De Gascogne,** 237 av. Laurier Ouest (☎ 514-490-0235), a French bakery with bread, pastries, a coffee bar, and seating. Across the street, **Toi Moi et Café,** 244 av. Laurier Ouest (☎ 514-369-1150), roasts its own coffees and serves a brunch menu that's consistently good.

When you're ready to leave avenue Laurier, head south along avenue du Parc, once again. After three blocks, you come to avenue Mont-Royal (the Mountain) on your right. A bit farther, beyond the lights, you come to the Sunday ritual of **Tam-tam's,** which has grown to such an extent that tour buses now stop to gawk.

Beginning at 2:00 p.m., drummers and percussionists from all over Montréal converge on the **Monument Sir George-Étienne Cartier,** on avenue du Parc at the foot of the Mountain — you're in Parc Mont-Royal. After they begin, their beats roll up its slopes and drone on for the rest of the afternoon. A crowd of dancers forms in front of them, and the whole thing gathers momentum. People keep coming from every direction armed with blankets, Frisbees, dogs — the works — and they set up camp on the grassy hills surrounding the monument, which are all within earshot of the incessant drums. It is a veritable circus, and everyone gets in on the act, including children. Out on the fringes, there's even a group of Dungeons and Dragons kids whacking each other with foam and duct-tape swords.

Chapter 12

A Shopper's Guide to Montréal

. . . .

In This Chapter

▶ Getting to know Montréal's shopping scene

▶ Checking out the best neighborhoods

▶ Locating the big names and big centers

. . . .

Call it the French connection. If you're looking to adorn yourself, unearth unique treasures, or bring home something special for friends and family, Montréal is something of a shopper's horn of plenty. From the thriving fashion industry, vibrant gallery scene, and numerous shopping malls to the underground city, Montréal has your shopping needs covered.

Figuring Out the Scene

This section gives you the lowdown on shopping hours, shopping districts, taxes, and the amount of stuff you can take home with you.

Shopping hours in Montréal are similar to those in the rest of Canada. Stores generally open at 9:30 or 10 a.m. and close at 5 or 6 p.m., Monday through Wednesday. On Thursdays and Fridays, most stores stay open until 9 p.m. On Saturdays, the hours swing back to 9 or 10 a.m. to 5 or 6 p.m. Most stores are also open on Sundays: Hours vary, but you can usually count on finding stores open from noon to 5 p.m.

These are the standard hours for stores in commercial areas. In neighborhoods like avenue Laurier or rue St-Denis, which have many small boutiques, the hours can vary from one store to another, and owners of small shops sometimes close without warning to take a coffee break.

In Montréal, you can find pretty much any major brand-name item available anywhere else in North America. But you can also find a lot of items you probably can't find elsewhere. If you're looking for something unique, the following are Montréal's areas of strength:

✔ **Clothes:** The city's fashion industry gets better practically every season, and you can often buy clothing directly from the designers themselves. **Rue St-Denis** (between rue Sherbrooke and avenue Mont-Royal) are full of boutiques of local designers, with unique, quality fashion at reasonable prices. **Boulevard St-Laurent** specializes in extremely cool clothes for a youthful clientele, while **downtown** has a great mix of homegrown clothing chains for both men and women, plus big name shops of major designers. More and more new designers are also setting up shop in Vieux-Montréal.

✔ **Antiques:** French-speaking Québeckers don't actually care much for the old, rustic look, which means that tons of antiques and vintage pieces are available to you at good prices. (Antiques dealers from New York flock to the city to skim off the best of them.) **Rue Notre-Dame,** way west, is Montréal's Antiques Alley, with dozens of shops to pick through, whether you're looking for furniture, home accessories, or memorabilia.

✔ **Art:** Several high-quality fine arts schools supply Montréal with what seems like a never-ending source of new talent. In addition, established painters sell their work in the city's traditional gallery strip on **rue Sherbrooke** around **rue Crescent.** The **Plateau** neighborhood has many smaller galleries featuring younger, more affordable artists. **Vieux-Montréal** has serious galleries, as well as an artists' cooperative featuring drawing, lithographs, etchings, and more.

✔ **Home decor:** If you like knick-knacks and cool home accessories, you'll be in heaven. Boutiques specializing in household decorations can be found all over the city, including downtown, but especially on **rue St-Denis** and **avenue Laurier.**

✔ **Specialty foods and liquor:** The last decade in Québec has seen a surge of interest in local culinary specialties — from maple syrup and blueberry liqueurs to fine chocolates and Québec cheeses. The **Jean-Talon** and **Atwater markets** are good places to pick up local delicacies, as is **avenue Laurier.**

✔ **Books:** Not one other place in North America comes close to offering the quantity and variety of books in French that Montréal does. And the selection in English is good, too. Montréal has even managed to hold on to several independent English-language booksellers. Most of the English scene is **downtown,** while French bookstores are practically everywhere.

✔ **Music:** What we say about books is also true of music in Montréal. Compared to New York or even Toronto, Montréal can hardly be called CD city, but after Paris, this is probably one of the best places in the world to sample French-language music. Several large chains, mostly **downtown,** pretty much dominate the market.

Sounds great, but how much stuff can you bring home? If you spend more than two days in Canada, you're entitled to bring back US$400 worth of goods duty-free. Included in that price, you're allowed to take home 45 ounces (a little more than 1 liter) of alcohol.

Hold onto your receipts in case you have to prove your case at the border. Actually, hold onto your receipts so you can keep track of your spending and count up the cost of your loot _before_ you get to the border. Customs agents aren't known to provide calculators to frenzied travelers.

If you bring more than US$400 in goods back to the U.S. with you, don't worry, no one is going to throw you in jail. You just have to pay a small tax on your purchases. And if you stay less than 48 hours in Canada, your duty-free limit drops to US$200 per person.

Taxes, taxes. They're rather steep in the Great White North. Don't forget that almost 15% will be tacked onto your purchases. For more information on taxes and how to get a refund, see Chapter 3.

Casing the Top Shopping Neighborhoods

Montréal is a great shopping city, but like all cities of plenty, you need to know where to go to get the goods. The following sections show you the prime stomping grounds of the city's consumer culture.

Downtown

You can always go — downtown. The noise and the hurry can help your worries. And so can a little retail therapy at the shops, boutiques, and department stores along Montréal's main shopping drags. You'll feel better and look great in no time at all.

Rue Ste-Catherine

Montréal's downtown area is definitely not the most charming or quaint part of the city; parts of rue Ste-Catherine are actually pretty crass. Still, while it's not really a neighborhood for strolling among unique boutiques, it's _the_ place to find the city's big department stores (see the "Finding Big-Name Stores" section later in this chapter). It's where you find most of the shopping centers, movie theaters, and large bookstores. You also get a great concentration of chain stores of all sorts, although most are Canadian.

The downtown is also home to Montréal's famous **underground city**, with over 1,500 boutiques. The 18-mile underground complex links up many of the major hotels, major shopping complexes, and most of the downtown Métro stations. You are likely to happen upon underground city shops as you pop in and out of it via a shopping center, Métro station, or hotel. The underground city is full of chain stores and cheap outlets for everything from shoes to electronics. Very few Montréalers actually shop in the underground city, because better stores exist above ground.

Unless the weather is particularly vicious (making the underground city particularly attractive), your best bet for downtown is shopping on rue **Ste-Catherine,** between rue Guy on the west and avenue du Parc on the east. Here are the shopping complexes you'll find there:

- ✔ **Centre Eaton,** 705 rue Ste-Catherine Ouest (☎ **514-288-3708**). Eaton's used to be Canada's main mid- to high-end department store. It went out of business several years ago, but this five-floor shopping complex with 175 shops, cinemas, and eateries has retained the name. Métro: McGill.

- ✔ **Cours Mont-Royal,** 1455 rue Peel (☎ **514-842-7777**). The shops in this center are a little more chic, and the whole effect is slightly more elegant than at the Centre Eaton. Métro: Peel.

- ✔ **Les Ailes de la Mode,** 677 rue Ste-Catherine Ouest (☎ **514-282-4537**). Montréal's newest shopping complex is also the sleekest and the priciest. When it opened in 2002, it was hyped as a "new concept in shopping." Unfortunately, most shoppers report that they just can't find their way around the place. Métro: McGill.

- ✔ **Les Promenades de la Cathédrale,** at the corner of avenue University and rue Ste-Catherine (☎ **514-849-9925**). Located right next to the Centre Eaton, this shopping center is virtually indistinguishable from it. Métro: McGill.

Also of note are some Montréal shops worth mentioning on their own. For contemporary Canadiana — leather, shoes, bags, clothes and accessories — check out the sporty classic **Roots,** 1035 rue Ste-Catherine Ouest (☎ **514-845-7995**). For home decor and stylish modern kitchenware, try the new lifestyle store, **Caban,** 777 rue Ste-Catherine Ouest (☎ **514-844-9300**), a spinoff of the clothing chain Club Monaco.

Chapters Bookstore, 1171 rue Ste-Catherine Ouest (☎ **514-849-8825**), is Canada's largest chain bookstore. The Montréal store is four floors high and includes an Internet cafe. A few blocks west at 1500 av. McGill-College, **Indigo** (☎ **514-281-5549**) is part of the same chain and has a huge selection of books and a comfortable cafe. If you prefer a more intimate environment, check out the independent bookseller **Paragraphe Bookstore** at 2220 av. McGill-College (☎ **514-845-5811**). For the best selection of French books, check out one of the **Renault Bray** stores, either at 4380 rue St-Denis (☎ **514-844-1781**) or at 5117 av. du Parc (☎ **514-276-7651**).

Underground City

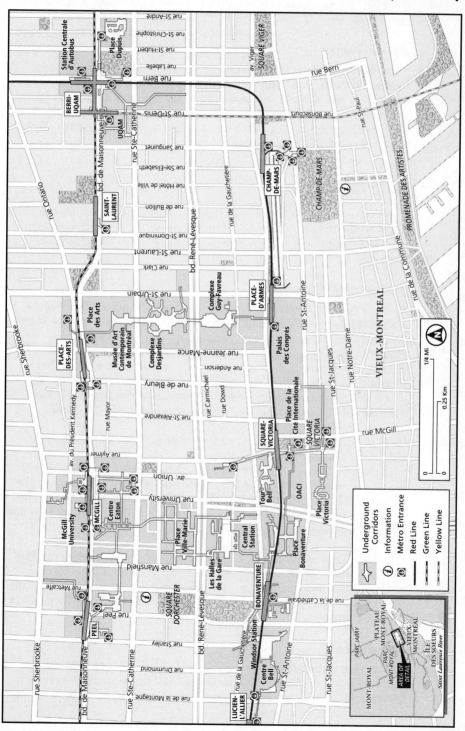

For CDs, visit **HMV,** 1020 rue Ste-Catherine Ouest (☎ 514-875-0765). For a better selection of French CDs, try the big **Archambault** store near Place des Arts at 500 rue Ste-Catherine Est (☎ 514-849-6201).

Rue Crescent

If you head west along rue Ste-Catherine, away from the department stores and malls, you soon hit **rue Crescent,** which has a handful of chic shops and upscale stores, including art galleries, antiques stores, and clothes stores. This is a nice neighborhood in which to stroll about after visiting the Montréal Museum of Fine Art, and you can also find plenty of cafes and bars to choose from.

The Plateau

If you've noticed that Montréalers are a particularly fashionable bunch, this is where they come to perfect their look. While you find more famil-iar offerings at the big stores downtown, the Plateau is the best place to go native.

Boulevard St-Laurent

South of rue Sherbrooke, boulevard St-Laurent is home to Montréal's small, slightly rundown China Town. Walk north on boulevard St-Laurent and cross rue Sherbrooke, and St-Laurent turns into one of the hippest streets in the city — chock full of trendy hair studios; even trendier clothes stores; and fashionable lounges, bars, and restaurants that recruit their wait staffs from local modeling agencies. For cosmetics, check out the St-Laurent store of the Canadian blockbuster makeup company **MAC Cosmetics,** 3487 bd. St-Laurent (☎ 514-287-9297).

Head north on St-Laurent, and your shopping opportunities diversify and food options abound until just before avenue Mont-Royal. There, you find yourself smack in the middle of Montréal's up-and-coming fur-niture and interior design neighborhood, including popular stores like **Montok,** 4404 bd. St-Laurent (☎ 514-845-8285), and **Biltmore** 5685 bd. St-Laurent (☎ 514-844-3000). Farther north, you find antiques, framing stores, clothing stores, galleries, and more.

For used CDs, vintage clothes, and more small clothes designers, head east on **avenue Mont-Royal** from boulevard St-Laurent. This former working-class neighborhood is reaching the peak of a decade-long colo-nization process led by students and young professionals. The result is tons of interesting little boutiques and shops.

Rue St-Denis

The stretch between rue Sherbrooke and avenue Mont-Royal is the spiritual home of Montréal's bourgeoisie and the location of several higher-end, more established Montréal fashion designers. Rue St-Denis is a great shopping street featuring elegant clothing and unique home accessories. Alas, the last few years have been a little hard on the area, with stores coming and going a little faster than normal. It remains a lovely street to stroll, with many inviting cafes.

Check out the big **Mexx** store at the corner of rue Rachel, 4190 rue St-Denis (☎ **514-843-6399**). Farther north, don't miss the increasingly popular **Boutique Do** (4439 rue St-Denis; ☎ **514-844-0041**) with reasonably priced, local designs for women. **Révenge,** 3852 rue St-Denis (☎ **514-843-4379**), is another great store with local designs. **Artéfact,** 4117 rue St-Denis (☎ **514-842-2780**) has lovely and unusual suits and dresses by Québec designers.

For home decor and gourmet kitchenware, check out **Arthur Quentin,** 3960 rue St-Denis (☎ **514-843-7513**).

Mile End/Outremont (avenue Laurier)

This upscale shopping street, the playground of Montréal's well-heeled Outremont residents, was hit hard by the recession that gripped the city in the early 1990s, but it's making a remarkable comeback at the moment. West of avenue Parc, you find great gourmet food stores like **Gourmet Laurier,** 1042 av. Laurier Ouest (☎ **514-274-5601**) and **Anjou Québec,** 1025 av. Laurier Ouest (☎ **514-272-4065**). The boutiques between avenue du Parc and boulevard St-Laurent sell upscale goods ranging from clothing for an older, more conservative shopper to kitchenware and home furnishings.

For a wide choice of travel supplies, like bags, suitcases, sun hats, money pouches, electricity converters, and more, visit **Jet-Setter,** 66 av. Laurier Ouest (☎ **514-271-5058**).

St-Henri (rue Notre-Dame)

While it looks a little downtrodden at first sight, the western strip of **rue Notre-Dame,** between rue Guy and avenue Atwater, is Montréal's Antiques Alley, with dozens of shops selling collectible furniture and memorabilia.

Check out **Lucie Favreau Antiques** (1904 rue Notre-Dame Ouest; ☎ **514-989-5117**) for crazy collectibles, **Les Antiquités Grand Central** (2448 rue Notre-Dame Ouest; ☎ **514-935-1467**) for more elegant pieces, and **Lussier Antiques** (3645 rue Notre-Dame Ouest; ☎ **514-938-2224**) for bargains on lamps, chests, and fixtures.

At avenue Atwater, just to the south, is the **Atwater Market,** with farmers, butchers, fishmongers, and gourmet shops.

Vieux-Montréal (rue St-Paul)

Until several years ago, Vieux-Montréal was not considered much of a shopping area, unless you were in the market for cheesy tourist souvenirs. Large cash injections over the last decade changed all that, and **rue St-Paul** in particular has profited from the renaissance. This is *the* street to scout for arts and crafts. Check out **La Guilde Graphique** (9 rue St-Paul Ouest; ☎ 514-844-3438), where more than 200 artists display their work, or visit a craftspeople's collective **L'Empreinte** at 272 rue St-Paul Ouest (☎ 514-861-4427).

For modern art galleries, try **Gallery 2000** (45 rue St-Paul Ouest; ☎ 844-1812), **Galerie Parchemine** across the street at 40 rue St-Paul Ouest; (☎ 514-845-3368), or **Galerie St-Dizier** (20 rue St-Paul Ouest; ☎ 514-845-8411).

Westmount (rue Sherbrooke Ouest)

Rue Sherbrooke Ouest around avenue Greene is very much the traditional English area of the city. You can find the usual selection of upscale clothing, shoes, and home furnishings. Over the last few years, perhaps because more and more French-speakers are moving into the neighborhood, stores in this district have taken on a more European flavor. In particular, don't miss **L'Occitane,** a popular French cosmetics chain, full of luxurious soaps, moisturizers, and perfumes from Provence at 4972 rue Sherbrooke Ouest (☎ 514-482-8188).

Finding Big-Name Stores

Department stores have taken a beating over the last decade, but downtown Montréal still has several venerable old stores that sell goods the old-fashioned way:

- ✔ **Holt Renfrew,** 1300 rue Sherbrooke Ouest (☎ 514-842-5111), is a luxury clothing store for the well-heeled and label-conscious.

- ✔ **La Baie,** 585 rue Ste-Catherine Ouest (☎ 514-281-4422), also known as the Hudson's Bay Company, is a three-century-old Canadian institution. The Montréal store sells everything from cosmetics to clothing to kitchen appliances, and it's a great place to pick up crystal, China, and bedding.

- ✔ **La Maison Simons,** 977 rue Ste-Catherine Ouest (☎ 514-282-1840), originally a Québec City chain, is the new kid in town. Great for clothes, coats, and accessories.

- ✔ **Ogilvy,** 1307 rue Ste-Catherine Ouest (☎ 514-842-7711), is an upscale department store that feels like a collection of rather fancy boutiques.

Index of Stores by Merchandise

Antiques

Antiques Grande Centrale (rue Notre-Dame)
Antiques Lussier (rue Notre-Dame)
Lucie Favreau Antiques (rue Notre-Dame)

Art

Galerie St-Dizier (Vieux-Montréal)
Galerie Parchemine (Vieux-Montréal)
Gallery 2000 (Vieux-Montréal)
La Guilde Graphique (Vieux-Montréal)
L'empreinte (Vieux-Montréal)

Books

Chapters (Downtown)
Indigo (Downtown)
Paragraphe Bookstore (Downtown)
Renaud Bray (Plateau)

Clothing

Artéfact (rue St-Denis)
Boutique Do (rue St-Denis)
Holt Renfrew (Downtown)
La Baie (Downtown
Mexx (rue St-Denis)
Ogilvy (Downtown)
Révenge (rue St-Denis)
Roots (Downtown)
Simon's (Downtown)

Cosmetics

L'Occitane (rue Sherbrooke Ouest)
MAC (boulevard St-Laurent)

Department Stores

La Baie (Downtown)
Ogilvy (Downtown)
Simon's (Downtown)

Furniture and Home Accessories

Caban (Downtown)
Biltmore (boulevard St-Laurent)
Montauk (boulevard St-Laurent)

Gourmet Foods

Anjou Québec (avenue Laurier)
Gourmet Laurier (avenue Laurier)

Kitchenware

Arthur Quentin (rue St-Denis)
Caban (Downtown)

Music

HMV (Downtown)
Archambault (Downtown)

Chapter 13

Living It Up After the Sun Goes Down: Montréal Nightlife

● ●

In This Chapter

▶ Figuring out where the beautiful people go at night

▶ Dancing the night away

▶ Hitting the right bars and clubs in the right order

▶ Watching performing arts for a dose of culture

● ●

*W*hether you prefer a quiet cocktail at a jazz club or a night on the town flitting from one hot spot to the next, Montréal delivers an awesome nightlife — you can paint the town whatever color you choose. Activities peak between Thursday and Sunday, but something's always going down.

It all begins at quitting time on Thursday with the *cinq à sept* (the hours from 5:00 to 7:00), the unofficial opening ceremonies of the weekend, when Montréal's office workers flock to their favorite watering holes to drink and snack, commiserate and socialize, and, of course, see and be seen. The party then carries on in the bars, cafes, pubs, restaurants, live music venues, and dance clubs well into the night. Saturday is definitely the pinnacle of Montréal's frenzied nightlife activities. If it's a long weekend (a Monday holiday), concerts and all-night dance parties continue on Sunday, too.

In this chapter, we organize the nightlife scene by category, giving you our top choices for each type of nightlife pursuit, regardless of where they're located. We also open the curtains on Montréal's vibrant performing arts scene. Much of it takes place in French, but you can find a good number of shows in English and plenty of other performances where spoken language doesn't matter. Montréal's performing arts scene tends to be on the edgy and daring side.

True to its Latin spirit, Montréal's nocturnal activities start later and end later than other cities in North America. Last call is at 3 a.m., so don't be surprised if the pace doesn't really pick up until after 11 p.m. — a lot of people are just finishing dinner at that hour — and peak around 1 a.m. Québec's legal drinking age is 18.

So where are the city's hot spots? Great spots are everywhere, but many can be found on rue Crescent and boulevard St-Laurent, the city's two main nightlife strips. You don't need to be excessively concerned about safety in these neighborhoods. Montréal's streets are relatively safe at night, partly because so many people are out. Everyone's very friendly, as people tend to be after a drink or two.

The cost of a night out can vary greatly. Many bars and clubs charge a cover, which ranges from C$5 to C$25 dollars (US$3.75–US$18). Drinks can cost anywhere from C$5 to C$8 (US$3.75–US$6), depending on how snazzy the bar deems itself to be.

Getting the Lowdown

The *Montréal Gazette,* the city's only English daily newspaper, as well as *Hour* and *Mirror,* two free English weeklies, cover the city's cultural calendar. These publications list films, art venues, events, music shows, and more. The weekly publications come out on Thursday mornings and preview the coming week. You can find them in the entranceways of many boutiques, cafes, restaurants, and bars and in Montréal's neighborhoods.

NightLife, a free glossy magazine with articles in both English and French, is also a good source. Each issue includes an exhaustive nightlife directory for the whole city, with a series of icons describing each establishment.

Also keep your eyes open for the events and acts advertised via guerilla marketing techniques: flyers and posters littering the downtown core, left on windshields, taped to poles, or pasted to the plywood barriers surrounding a construction site. For environmental reasons, we don't sanction them. But when you're looking for the latest nightlife happenings, they are hard to beat.

Checking Out the Scene

With four university campuses scattered around the downtown core, students rule the night and set the tone. Everywhere you go, all night, you're bound to see packs of students staggering about. Don't worry, though. Few bars in Montréal cater exclusively to students, so you don't risk stumbling into a scene from *Animal House.*

In fact, stepping out in Montréal requires a touch of class. No one in Montréal really dresses up at night, but people are still pretty chic on the whole. You won't see any baseball caps, fraternity sweatshirts, or running shoes. Some places even enforce a dress code. If you are unsure of what to wear, just don black.

In terms of music, rock is almost dead and DJs rule the city. But you can find great live music if you like funk, jazz, world beat, Latin, bluegrass, blues, or punk. A number of venues host big-name acts passing through on the northeastern legs of their North American Tours. The free weeklies are the best place to find out about whose playing where and when. Heck, you can spend the night as a groupie.

Hitting the Dance Floor

The following sections list venues where the dance floor is the main attraction.

The hottest clubs

DJs rule the night at these clubs, where the bold and beautiful clientele dance the night away. So go ahead: Strut your stuff and make the scene.

- ✔ **Blizzart,** 3956-A bd. St-Laurent, Plateau (☎ **514-843-4860**), is a long, narrow spot that feels like a cafe and oozes with street-cred. Each night of the week local DJs play a different sound: dancehall, reggae, drum 'n' bass, and so on. Cover: C$3—C$5 (US$2—US$3.75) Wed, Fri, Sat. Métro: Sherbrooke.

- ✔ At **Funkytown,** 1454 rue Peel, Downtown (☎ **514-282-8387**), an older clientele gathers to reminisce to a medley of re-mixed disco classics. When a '70s anthem plays, everyone rushes to the dance floor, where they sing along at the top of their lungs. Doors open at 10 p.m., Fri–Sat. Cover: C$6 (US$4.50). Métro: Peel.

- ✔ **Mile End Bar,** 5322 bd. St-Laurent, Mile End (☎ **514-279-0200**), north of the main St-Laurent strip, has become a fixture of Thursday's *cinq à sept* landscape. Droves of flirting office workers, fresh from a hard day on the job, jam the bar downstairs. The action later moves to the nightclub upstairs, where's there a lofted seating area and a suspended catwalk. Open Tues–Sat. Cover: usually C$5 (US$3.75) Fri–Sat. Métro: Laurier.

- ✔ **Society of Art and Technology** (SAT), 1195 bd. St-Laurent, Quartier Latin (☎ **514-844-2033**), is the leader of the underground music scene. Its main room features video projections that play along with the music. The SAT often hosts parties in association with new-media, and also hosts music, festivals and events, which

Downtown Montréal Nightlife

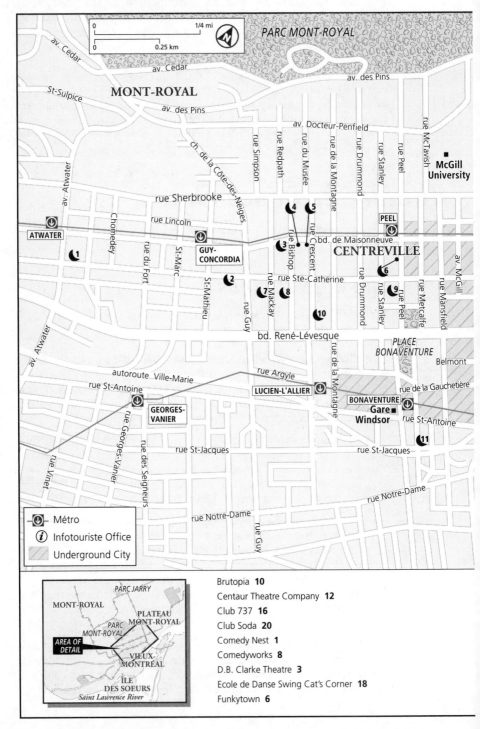

Brutopia **10**
Centaur Theatre Company **12**
Club 737 **16**
Club Soda **20**
Comedy Nest **1**
Comedyworks **8**
D.B. Clarke Theatre **3**
Ecole de Danse Swing Cat's Corner **18**
Funkytown **6**

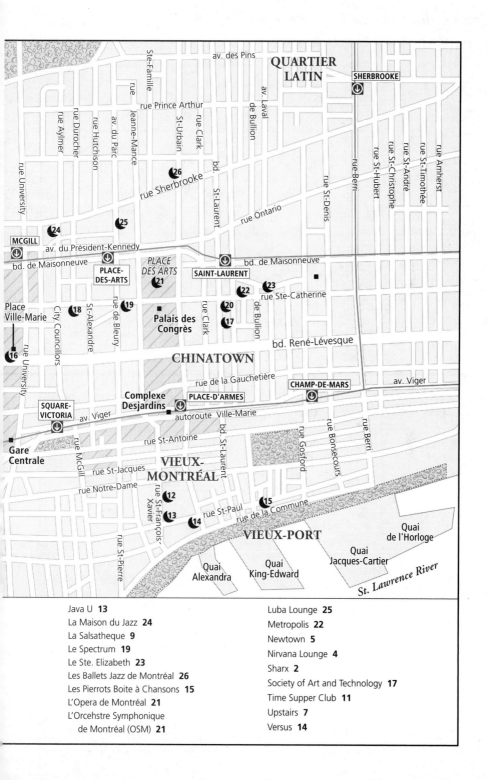

Plateau, Mile End, and Gay Village Nightlife

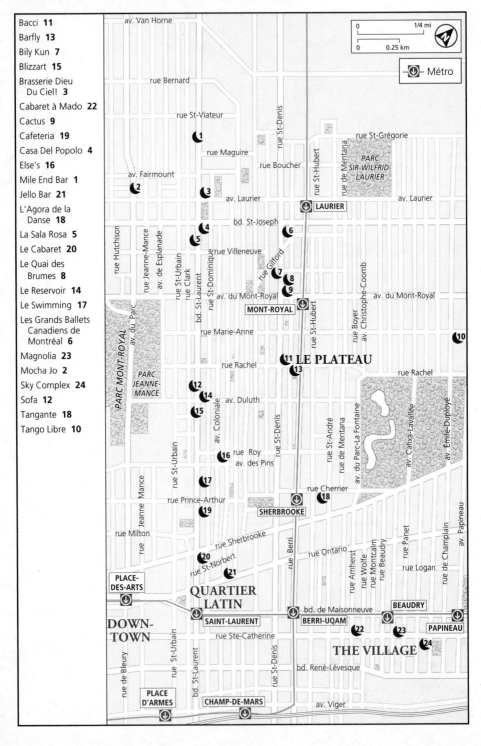

makes nights here varied and eclectic, as is the clientele. The schedule is erratic, but there is usually something going on. Call or check its Web site (www.sat.qc.ca). Métro: Saint-Laurent.

✔ **Time Supper Club,** 997 rue St-Jacques, Downtown (☎ **514-392-9292**), is wildly popular after dinner, when the chairs are cleared from the main floor and everybody gets up to dance. The party carries on at a feverish pace, as people crowd the bar, mingle in the walkways, and take turns dancing on the island in the middle of the dining room. Open Thurs–Sat. Cover: C$15 (US$11). Métro: Bonaventure.

Salsa, swing, and tango

Ever since disco bottomed out in the '80s, there's been a growing nostalgia for couples dancing, in Montréal as everywhere else. These days, swing is not the only dance in town. Salsa and tango are also extremely popular. Whichever style you opt for, couples dancing makes for a great night out. You can dance, watch, or learn — we hope a bit of each.

Most of the following places give free lessons or crash courses earlier in the evening, before the real party starts. So you can walk in a complete beginner and tango home like a pro. Well, sort of. Call to find out when the sessions are on.

✔ **Cactus,** 4461 rue St-Denis, Plateau (☎ **514-849-0349**), Montréal's other salsa hot spot, is on two floors of a townhouse just around the corner from the Mont-Royal Métro station. It's a little less intimidating than La Salsatheque, perhaps because the setting is more intimate. Beginners try out their moves on the upstairs dance floor, while the regulars tear it up front and center. Thurs–Sun. Cover: C$4 (US$3). Métro: Mont-Royal.

✔ **Ecole de Danse Swing Cat's Corner,** 486 rue Ste-Catherine Ouest, Suite 303, Downtown (☎ **514-874-9846**), this place hosts the biggest swing night in Montréal on Saturday's, with a crash course from 9 to 10 p.m., and then dancing until whatever hour. Cover: C$7 (US$5.25). Métro: Place-des-Arts.

✔ **La Salsatheque,** 1220 rue Peel, Downtown (☎ **514-875-0016**), is Montréal's oldest Latin club. The decor is somewhat dated, but no one seems to mind. The action's on the steel dance floor as couples shimmy and spin to a variety of Latin rhythms, predominantly salsa, meringue, and bachata. Open Wed–Sun. Cover: C$5 (US$3.75) Fri–Sat. Métro: Peel.

✔ **Mocha Jo,** 5175A av. du Parc, Mile End (☎ **514-277-5575**), is a dance studio with a bar and cafe, serving drinks and a light menu. Throughout the week, the space hosts evenings of tango (Tues, Sat), swing (Fri), and salsa (Wed, Thurs). Sunday's Tango Brunch is from 1:30 to 7:30 p.m. Even if you have no intention of dancing, it's a romantic spot to spend a lazy Sunday afternoon. Cover: C$5–C$8 (US$3.75–US$6). Métro: Laurier.

✔ **Tango Libre,** 1650 rue Marie-Anne Est, Plateau (☎ **514-527-5197**), an intimate dance floor tucked away on a mainly residential street, has tango evenings beginning at 9:30 p.m. Friday and Saturday (Cover: C$7/US$5.25). Supervised practice sessions are Thursday and Sunday (Cover: C$6/US$4.50). In summertime, this tango studio organizes Sunday evening dances at parks around the city. Métro: Mont-Royal.

Grooving to Live Music

DJs may rule the city, but you can still find plenty of live, local music in the bars and clubs around town. And the summer festivals supercharge Montréal's concert schedule, drawing top talent and delighted crowds to city venues.

Intimate settings . . .

Do you feel like live music for a change? This doesn't necessarily mean rocking out at a concert in a stadium. Instead, here are several spots around town where live music is the main draw — where you can hear up-and-coming talent or an offbeat sound.

✔ **Barfly,** 4062A bd. St-Laurent (☎ **514-993-5154**), is a tiny spot on one of the city's main nightlife strips with a pool table and a stage. An eclectic mix of local talent plays lively and boisterous sets of folk music. Some nights are more brooding, when speakers and poets take the stage. Cover: C$3–C$5 (US$2–US$3.75) Fri–Sat. Métro: Sherbrooke.

✔ **Casa Del Popolo,** 4873 bd. St-Laurent, Plateau (☎ **514-284 3804**), bills itself as a vegetarian hotspot. During the day it's a cafe; by night, it's an intimate bar and live music venue. Along with the musical acts, the owners book a variety of performances, which can be broadly categorized as urban folk and include DJ nights, traveling video road shows, and spoken word. Casa also runs La Sala Rosa, a space across the street at 4848 bd. St-Laurent, which is for larger happenings. A sometimes cover charge costs C$5–C$8 (US$3.75–US$6). Métro: Laurier.

✔ **La Maison du Jazz,** 2060 rue Aylmer, Downtown (☎ **514-842-8656**), formerly called Biddle's, was the haunt of late Montréal jazzman Charlie Biddle. Live jazz is played nightly on a small stage, with several tiers of seating in an Art Nouveau setting. Dinner is available and includes La Maison's famous ribs. The lounge and bar are just far enough removed to allow for quiet conversation. Cover: C$3 (US$2) added to your bill. Métro: McGill.

- ✔ **Le Quai des Brumes,** 4481 rue St-Denis, Plateau (☎ **514-499-0467**), is a dark and smoky bar frequented by an older, mainly French-speaking clientele. The brick walls and wood paneling give it a warm ambience. Jazz, blues, or rock bands play on small stage in the back every Wed and Sat. Cover: Depending on the talent, cover can vary from C$3–C$8 (US$2–US$6). Métro: Mont-Royal.

- ✔ **Les Pierrots Boite à Chansons,** 104 rue St-Paul Est, Vieux-Montréal (☎ **514-861-1270**), is the premier spot to hear traditional Québec folk music, from Thursday through Saturday, when the place is usually rockin'. If you don't speak French, you won't be able to sing along, but you can still clap. For most of the crowd, the night is highly sentimental and emotionally charged as they sing along to the ballads they learned growing up. It's a memorable night out. Cover: C$5–C$6 (US$3.75–US$4.50). Métro: Champ-de-Mars.

- ✔ **Le Swimming,** 3643 bd. St-Laurent (☎ **514-282-7665**), part show bar, part pool hall, is where rock and funk bands jam late into the night for a college-aged crowd, Thursday through Saturday. There's ample seating around the stage and a small space for dancing in between. Street level, the door to this upstairs bar is hard to miss. It's under a pixel-board marquee, topped by a fifteen-foot-high statue of a '50s-era guitarist. Cover: C$5–C$10 (US$3.75–US$7.50) Wed–Sun. Métro: Sherbrooke or Saint-Laurent.

- ✔ **Sofa,** 451 rue Rachel Est, Plateau (☎ **514-285-1011**), a lounge with a cigar humidor and many bottles of port, has live acts, usually of the funk, soul, or R&B varieties, Thursday through Sunday. The bar is an island in the middle of the establishment. In front of it, a narrow space creates a sort of gauntlet for mingling 25- to 35-year-olds. Behind, groups of friends chill in the large alcoves with booths. Cover: C$4–C$9 (US$3–US$6.75). Métro: Mont-Royal.

- ✔ **Upstairs,** 1254 rue Mackay, Downtown (☎ **514-931-6808**), also offers jazz nightly, but in a more intimate setting. The stage seems no more than a windowsill, as ensembles of up to six musicians jam together in close quarters. Mondays and Tuesdays are "Fresh Jazz" nights, featuring the latest talent of McGill University's music students. Shows start at 9:00 p.m. Dining available. Cover: C$15–C$20 (US$11–US$15) Fri–Sat; C$10 (US$7.50) Sun. Métro: Guy-Concordia.

. . . and concert venues

The clubs, or show bars, discussed in this section net a surprising amount of top talent on tour. They open only when there's a show, but that seems to be most nights. So, who's playing while you're in town? Find out by browsing Montréal's free weeklies, calling the box offices, or visiting the clubs' Web sites. You can also book your tickets in person, by phone, or on the Web. Be sure to check out the following:

- **Club Soda,** 1225 bd. St-Laurent, Quartier Latin (☎ 514-286-1010; www.clubsoda.ca). Métro: Saint-Laurent.

- **Le Cabaret,** 111 bd. St-Laurent, Quartier Latin (☎ 514-845-2014). Métro: Saint-Laurent.

- **Le Spectrum,** 318 rue Ste-Catherine Ouest, Downtown (☎ 514-861-5851; www.spectrumdemontreal.ca). Métro: Place-des-Arts.

- **Metropolis,** 59 rue Ste-Catherine Est, Quartier Latin (☎ 514-844-3500; www.metropolismontreal.ca). Métro: Saint-Laurent.

Hopping Between Hot Spots: Montréal's Cafes and Bars

Montréal's nightlife begins early, carries on at a torrid pace, and ends late. Seasoned denizens look to hit at least two or three spots over the course of an evening. Choreographing the perfect night out is all about timing, variety, and keeping your options open.

Montréalers like to mix-and-match. The city's cafes and bars are perfect for this: meeting friends before a night of dancing or sharing impressions after a live show. Rather than clubs and concerts, where music is the main draw — and usually too loud for sustained conversation — the city's cafes and bars are definitely more social. This is also the best place to meet and mingle with the locals.

The expression in French is "*M'as tu vu?*" (pronounced mah-tu-vu, and literally meaning "Have you seen me?"). The following places are very that:

- **Cafeteria,** 3581 bd. St-Laurent, Plateau (☎ 514-849-3855), is really a restaurant. However, it is increasingly becoming a destination for drinks among the young and fashionable set. True to it's name, the tables of the dining room are packed together, allowing for plenty of social mingling. Others mill around the bar. It's quite a scene that goes late into the night. Métro: Sherbrooke or Saint-Laurent.

- **Club 737,** 1 place Ville-Marie, Downtown (☎ 514-397-0737), atop Montréal's tallest skyscraper, is easy to locate: Just find the source of the spotlights that stretch across the night's sky. On the ground floor, patrons line up for an elevator to shuttle them to the club on the 42nd and 43rd floors. Undeniably, the vistas of Montréal by night are spectacular! The experience is even better during the summer months, when the club allows patrons out onto one of the observation decks. We think the view is the main attraction here; otherwise, the two floors are dark, hot, and sweaty. Open Fri–Sat only. Cover: C$10–C$12 (US$7.50–$9). Métro: Bonaventure.

✔ **Newtown,** 1476 rue Crescent, Downtown (☎ **514-284-6555**), bears the nickname of its owner, former Formula One (F1) driver Jacques Villeneuve. It is a literal translation of his last name and what his pals called him on the F1 circuit. The three floors of his establishment include a restaurant and terrace upstairs and a club in the basement. The main-floor bar draws an older clientele than most other places on rue Crescent. The decor is sleek and sophisticated. Cover: C$10 (US$7.50) Fri–Sat. Métro: Guy-Concordia.

✔ **Versus,** 106 rue St-Paul Ouest, Vieux-Montréal (☎ **514-788-2040**), is the bar of the Hotel Nelligan. It is particularly popular for after-work drinks among slick professionals working in the area. It seems to be the boutique hotel of choice among visiting A-list celebrities, which adds further mystique to the contemporary, yet warm, decor. Métro: Place-d'Armes.

Lounging like lizards

Sipping cosmopolitan martinis and other candy-colored concoctions — this has been "in" for a terribly long time. In the mid-1990s, even before the lounge scene became a widespread trend in North American urban centers, Montréal had already started opening places with comfy seating, retro decor, and long drink lists of elaborate cocktails with fancy names, all served in martini glasses.

Following are the lounges we recommend:

✔ **Java U,** 191 rue St-Paul Ouest, Vieux-Montréal (☎ **514-849-8881**), serves cafe snacks during the day and a dinner menu in the evening, but by 11 p.m. (Tues–Sat), it's just drinks and DJs. Yes, here you can get martinis — both the classic and newfangled versions. It's probably the most legit spot in Vieux-Montréal — sleek, but not necessarily packaged for tourists, unlike most of the other places in the city's historic district. Métro: Place-d'Armes.

✔ **Jello Bar,** 151 rue Ontario Est, Quartier Latin (☎ **514-285-2621**), was one of the forerunners of the Montréal's martini movement. Its success in recreating a '70s lounge environment coincided with the public's sudden and insatiable appetite for all things retro and a newfound and considerable thirst for sophisticated-looking drinks. DJs and live bands enhance the ambience in the form of jazz, Latin, funk, soul, R&B and other lounge-friendly musical tangents. Open Mon–Sat. Cover: C$5–C$8 (US$3.75–US$6). Métro: Saint-Laurent.

✔ **Luba Lounge,** 2109 rue Bleury, Downtown (☎ **514-288-5822**), is intimate, informal, and relaxed. The deep comfort level has much to do with the decor: Red votives flicker and cast a warm glow over the various mid-20th-century living-room sets, coffee tables, and lamps. It could be your grandmother's parlor in a surreal dream. Open nightly, DJs mix records, with an emphasis on hip-hop, trip-hop, and other urban grooves, but, in keeping with the setting, nothing with too much oomph. Métro: Place-des-Arts.

✔ **Nirvana Lounge,** 2nd floor, 1445 rue Bishop, Downtown (☎ 514-842-3301), is a swank piano bar done up in Middle Eastern style. Sometimes, a jazz singer provides the accompaniment. It's ideal for after-dinner drinks before you head off into the night. Métro: Guy-Concordia.

Dropping into neighborhood bars

At the establishments in this section, you'll find plenty of locals and not many tourists. But don't be shy: Belly up to the bar, order a drink, and strike up a conversation with a regular.

✔ **Bily Kun,** 354 av. Mont-Royal Est, Plateau (☎ 514-845-5392), is a dimly lit and somewhat cavernous room, finished with bold lines, a beautiful tile-floor, and ostrich-head trophies on the walls. It is a modern-day pub that attracts a hip but unpretentious clientele in their mid-twenties and up. Order your drinks from the waiter; ask the busboy about the menu of light snacks. Métro: Mont-Royal.

✔ **Else's,** 156 rue Roy Est, Plateau (☎ 514-286-6689), is a comfortable, intimate spot that seems like a well-kept secret, with its inconspicuous location, soft lighting, and the constant murmur of conversation. Actually, it is quite popular. The bar's liquor license is such that you have to buy a token snack with your alcohol. On tap is an interesting selection of beer from Québec's microbreweries, as well as cider. Métro: Sherbrooke.

✔ **Le Ste-Elizabeth,** 1412 rue Ste-Elizabeth, Quartier Latin (☎ 514-286-4302), is hidden away, just off a seedy stretch of rue Ste-Catherine. But put any apprehension aside and persevere, and you will be rewarded. It's a real gem on a summer night: an intimate outdoor terrace with tables and chairs on two levels, surrounded by ivy-covered walls, several stories high. And it is right between the downtown's two festival sites, Place des Arts and rue St-Denis. Monday, all year around, the bar has a special: C$3 (US$2.25) for pints of Boreal beer. Métro: Berri-UQAM.

What's brewing in Montréal?

If you take your obligations as a tourist seriously, you should try as many of the locally brewed beers as possible. Not only are there a wide variety of suds brewed by the provinces' microbreweries, but several brewpubs also craft their own beer, which is not available anywhere else. Here are our recommendations:

✔ **Brasserie Dieu Du Ciel!,** 9 av. Laurier Ouest, Mile End (☎ 514-490-9555), features over 30 house recipes brewed on-premise. The bar is dark and cozy, ideal for a quiet time on a cold night. A window allows patrons to peer down into the basement to see where the beer's made. Métro: Laurier.

✔ **Brutopia,** 1219 rue Crescent, Downtown (☎ 514-868-9916), consists of two bars and several rooms spread over two floors. By the main bar, there's a small stage for the nightly, live music. Sundays are a popular open mic. During the warmer months, the brewery offers seating outside, both in back and out front. Brutopia brews its house beers in large brass barrels in the room behind the bar; try Indian Pale Ale, Raspberry Blonde, or Apricot Wheat. Métro: Guy-Concordia.

✔ **Le Reservoir,** 9 av. Duluth Est, Plateau (☎ 514-849-7779), has a window on its brewing operation to the right of the bar. Groups of friends and couples chat, seated at tables with votive candles. During the summer, the main floor windows open onto the street, and the second-floor terrace is in full swing. Métro: Sherbrooke.

Racking up in a pool hall

You don't have to be a shark or a rounder to frequent a pool hall these days. In Montréal, they're practically chic. You can play for rounds of drinks, but be sure to size up your competition before making such a suggestion — lest you get fleeced. Here are two of the more popular places to play pool, where you can rent tables by the hour:

✔ **Bacci,** 4175 rue St-Denis, Plateau (☎ 514-884-3929). Métro: Mont-Royal.

✔ **Sharx,** 1606 rue Ste-Catherine Ouest, Downtown (☎ 514-934-3105). Métro: Guy-Concordia.

Yucking it up at comedy clubs

As the annual **Just For Laughs Festival** continues to grow, Montréal is increasingly a mecca for stand-up and improv comedians. They say it's the hardest profession in the world. Here are two places to try:

✔ **Comedy Nest,** 2313 rue Ste-Catherine Ouest, Downtown (☎ 514-932-6378). Métro: Guy-Concordia.

✔ **Comedyworks,** 1238 rue Bishop, Downtown (☎ 514-398-9661). Métro: Atwater.

Being out and proud in Gay Village

Montréal is quickly becoming the hottest gay destination in North America, and the city's gay community has a thriving nightlife scene. Gay Pride and the Black and Blue weekends are annual highlights on the city's nightlife calendar. Rue Ste-Catherine, east of rue St-Hubert, is packed with innumerable restaurants, cafes, bars, and clubs that are always hopping throughout the year. Following are some of the hottest spots.

- **Cabaret à Mado,** 1115 rue Ste-Catherine Est, Gay Village (☎ 514-525-7566), has drag queens strutting in cabaret shows on some nights. The rest of the time they emcee for karaoke, stand-up comedy, and theme parties. Cover: C$3–C$6 (US$2–US$4.50). Métro: Beaudry.

- **Magnolia,** 1329 rue Ste-Catherine Est, Gay Village (☎ 514-526-6011), is Montréal's only lesbian bar — frequented by a good-looking, friendly crowd — but on Sundays everyone's welcome. DJs play what the bar calls *lesbian house.* Open Thurs–Sun, with two-for-one specials every day from 4 to 8 p.m. Cover: C$3–C$5 (US$2–US$3.75). Métro: Beaudry.

- **Sky Complex,** 1474 rue Ste-Catherine Est, Gay Village (☎ 514-529-6969), is a pub, restaurant, cabaret, male strip club, mega-dance club, and rooftop terrace in one. For gay men, it's a sort of one-stop shop. Cover: C$3 (US$2) Fri–Sat. Métro: Papineau.

Doing the Arts Scene

Although much of Montréal's cultural scene is conducted in French, you can find plenty in English; besides, music and dance need little translation. Check the free weekly newspapers for listings.

Attending the performing arts these days is a surprisingly casual affair. People seem to go in all sorts of dress — whatever makes them most comfortable. You should, too, although you won't be out of place if you dress up for the occasion.

Deserving special mention, partly because it defies quick and easy categorization, is Québec's own **Cirque du Soleil** (www.cirquedusoleil.com), a performance spectacle under a big top, but eons and galaxies beyond the corny entertainment that people sometimes associate with a circus.

Founded in Québec, now an international entertainment empire, a Cirque du Soleil performance is a human zoo of acrobats, contortionists, singers, dancers, and musicians all taking part in an elaborate fantasy. Although the shows tours the world, a troupe usually returns home to Montréal every year in the spring.

Theater

Most of Canada's English-language television and film productions, as well as the Broadway musical performances, happen in Toronto. This leaves Montréal's *Anglophone* (English-speaking) actors to fill the roles of the city's small-scale, short-run stage productions. But this situation can be a recipe for excellent theater. Before *Mambo Italiano* was a moderately successful movie, it was a hit play in Montréal, written by a local playwright. Here are some of the best venues for Montréal theater today:

- ✔ **Centaur Theatre Company,** 453 rue St-François-Xavier, Vieux-Montréal (☎ 514-288-3161), occupies a 1903 building, once the city's first stock exchange. Over the course of a season (end of Sept–end of May), Montréal's premier English-language theater company presents several plays on its two stages, including productions of modern classics, works of contemporary Canadian playwrights, and foreign adaptations. Métro: Place-d'Armes.

- ✔ **Geordie Theatre Productions** (☎ 514-845-9810), a professional children's theater company, stages a season's worth of kids classics. Intended for grade- and high-school audiences, the company's main stage is the **D.B. Clarke Theatre**, 1455 bd. de Maisonneuve Ouest (☎ 514-848-4742), on Concordia University's downtown campus. Métro: Guy-Concordia.

- ✔ **Saidye Bronfman Centre for the Arts,** 5170 côte Ste-Catherine, West Montréal (☎ 514-739-2301), has a full season of plays that runs from late fall to early summer. This multidisciplinary arts center, which includes a gallery and fine art school, presents dramatic works from around the world, both contemporary and modern. Métro: Côte-Sainte-Catherine.

Dance

Following is a selection of Montréal's best dance offerings:

- ✔ **L'Agora de la Danse,** 840 rue Cherrier, Plateau (☎ 514- 525-1500), is a part of the Université de Québec à Montréal's (University of Québec at Montréal) department of dance. **Le Studio,** its 256-seat venue, is the center of Canada's modern dance community. Métro: Sherbrooke.

- ✔ **Les Ballets Jazz de Montréal,** 3450 rue St-Urbain, 4th floor, Plateau (☎ 514-982-6771), is a contemporary dance troupe that tours internationally. Its reputation is solidly established for translating the latest artistic trends into dance. Métro: Place-des-Arts.

- ✔ **Les Grands Ballets Canadiens de Montréal,** 4816 rue Rivard (☎ 514-849-8681), produces four shows throughout its season and welcomes several visiting companies. The company adds fresh choreography to this classic ballet. Métro: Laurier.

✔ **Tangante,** 840 rue Cherrier (☎ 514-525-5584), bills itself as intimate laboratory theater. Dedicated to contemporary dance and experimental performance art, Tangante attempts upward of 90 performance projects during its September-to-June season. Métro: Sherbrooke.

Classical music and opera

Classical music and opera are the pinnacle of high-brow cultural consumption. For some, the challenge is to stay awake; for the true connoisseurs, it's a waking dream. Consider the following options:

✔ **L'Opera de Montréal,** 260 bd. de Maisonneuve Ouest, Downtown (☎ 514-985-2258), marries music, singing, plot, costumes, and set design in six elaborate productions per season. Métro: Place-des-Arts.

✔ **L'Orchestre Symphonique de Montréal** (OSM), 260 bd. de Maisonneuve Ouest, Downtown (☎ 514-842-9951), one of Canada's major orchestras, performs in the Salle Wilfrid-Pelletier of the Place-des-Arts. The OSM performs regularly at New York's Carnegie Hall. Métro: Place-des-Arts.

Chapter 14

Exploring Beyond Montréal: Three Great Day Trips

. . . .

In This Chapter

▶ Stretching your legs beyond the city limits

▶ Visiting Ottawa, the nation's capital

▶ Day tripping into rural Québec

. . . .

"**P**aris is Paris, but it's not France," goes the French expression. The same holds true for Montréal, which is not quite representative of the rest of the province of Québec. Montréal is Babylon by comparison. Beyond the bright lights of the big city, the province of Québec is a vast landscape, at times rural, at times rugged, dotted with many charming small towns, whose inhabitants are by and large French speaking, and where hockey and Catholicism are still the predominant religions.

Depending on how much time you have, you may want to escape Montréal and explore its surrounding regions. A jaunt into the hills of the countryside can be especially magical from late September to mid-October, when the leaves change colors. Ditto for anytime it snows, although the driving can be treacherous in heavy snowfall.

Of course, the first place you want to check out after Montréal is Québec City (see Part IV of this book). And it's doable in a day. You may want to stay longer, though; Québec City is perfect for an overnight visit — very romantic. We strongly recommend fitting this historic capital into your travel itinerary, if at all possible. It's very different from Montréal.

In this chapter, we present three other trips you can do in a day. For each, we also provide lodging information, should you decide to stay overnight. All three trips are between an hour and two hours by highway from Montréal.

For the first day trip to Ottawa, you can get there by bus, train, or airplane, but renting a car is probably the most practical route. You don't need a car, however, because taxis and an extensive bus system can get you around. For the other two more rural destinations, a car is also the best option — for mobility's sake.

Day Trip #1: Ottawa, the Nation's Capital

Ottawa is so Canadian. After all, it's the nation's capital. But Ottawa, which is in the province of Ontario, is completely different from Montréal and more like the rest of Canada. The difference is palpable.

Getting there

By car, Ottawa is about two hours, or 190 km (114 miles), away from Montréal. Be sure to get an early start, especially if you're visiting only for the day. From Montréal, travel west on Autoroute 40, which runs along the top of the Montréal. Stay on the 40, which goes to Hull/Ottawa and becomes the 417 after you cross into Ontario.

When you're in Ottawa proper, take exit 119, Metcalfe Street, and follow it as it twists and turns to the downtown area. After several blocks, the street ends smack in front of **Parliament Hill,** Ottawa's crown jewel and the seat of Canada's legislature.

Seeing the sights

Across from the Parliament Buildings is a tourist information center called the **Capital Infocentre,** 90 Wellington St. (☎ **800-465-1867;** www. canadascapital.gc.ca). It's open daily 8:30 a.m. to 9 p.m. from May to September, and 9 a.m. to 5 p.m. the rest of the year. The people at the center can help you round out the recommendations we provide here.

Because you're in Ottawa only for a short visit, don't feel pressured to see everything. In this section, we include the best of the Canadian capital, which makes for a full day of sightseeing. Ottawa's downtown is small, compact, and ideal for walking around. And you may be surprised by how much of the city you can cover on foot.

Ottawa's main attraction is **Parliament Hill,** 1 Wellington St. (☎ **613-239-5000,** www.parl.gc.ca), set on a bluff overlooking the Ottawa River. It is mecca for civic-minded Canadians and an interesting window into the nation's inner workings.

Downtown Ottawa

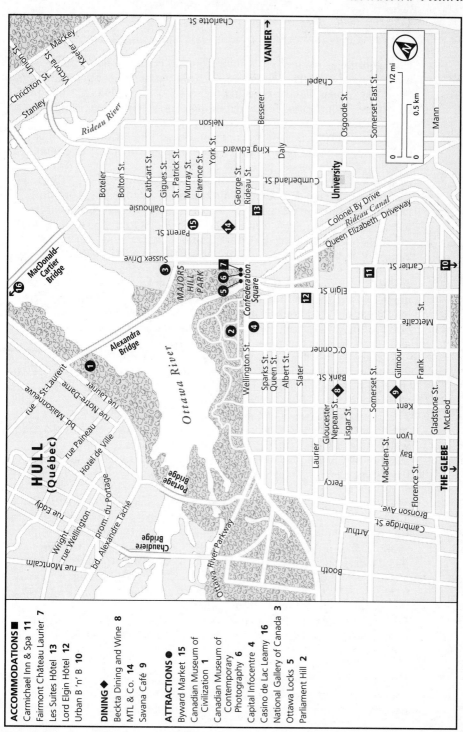

You can take a free, half-hour guided tour, which runs throughout the day. For a self-guided tour, pick up the booklet, "Discovering the Hill." Take the elevator to the top of the Peace Tower for a 360-degree view of the city and Ottawa River.

On the grounds during the summer, you find plenty going on. At 10 a.m., a Changing of the Guard ceremony with dapper and unflappable soldiers in fur hats is just like the ones in England! By night, you can watch free sound and light shows. To the left of the central Parliament Building and behind the library is a peculiar cat sanctuary. And when parliament is in session (about 137 days per year), you can attend question-and-answer periods in the public galleries of either the Senate or House of Commons.

Sparks Street runs parallel to Wellington Street and is a block south of Parliament Hill. It's a pedestrian mall with plenty of shops, boutiques, restaurants, and bars. During the summer, many Sparks Street establishments open sidewalk terraces. If you feel so inclined, a walking tour of the mall departs from the intersection of Elgin and Sparks every Saturday at 2 p.m. It lasts an hour and a half and costs C$5 (US$3.75).

Just east of Parliament Hill are the **Ottawa Locks,** which make up the north entrance of the **Rideau Canal.** The waterway, built in 1827, starts with eight flights of locks and runs all the way to Kingston on Lake Ontario. Originally built for strategic purposes and employed mainly as a trading route, the canal is now an 11-km (6-mile) parkland that runs through the city like a ribbon. In the winter, it becomes the world's longest ice rink, and office workers and students alike use it to skate to work and class.

The **Canadian Museum of Contemporary Photography,** 1 Rideau Canal (☎ **613-990-8257;** cmcp.gallery.ca), housed in a reconstructed railway tunnel, displays photos from its large permanent collection and also hosts traveling exhibitions. The museum's own collection spans from the 1960s to the present. Admission is free.

The striking **National Gallery of Canada,** 380 Sussex Dr. (☎ **613-990-1985;** www.gallery.ca), opened in 1988. The glass and granite structure was designed by Moshe Safdie, the same architect behind Montréal's Habitat '67 and the Museum of Fine Art. Light shafts and reflective panels make the most of natural light, which floods into the galleries, but in a way that's doesn't damage the art. The long, inclined walkway to the Grand Hall, an impressive landmark on its own, provides a dramatic view of the Parliament Buildings above the churning Ottawa River. The Gallery has the country's most extensive collection of Canadian art, but it also features important of works by artists from other countries and from periods throughout the ages.

Between Parliament Hill and the National Gallery and to the east of Sussex Drive is the **ByWard Market** (☎ **613-244-4410;** www.byward-market.com) area. A two-story market building, formerly a farmers' market, is at the center of this neighborhood. The surrounding streets of 19th-century brick and stone buildings are filled with trendy shops, restaurants, pubs, and bars. During the summer, vendors at all kinds of outdoor stalls hawk their wares, while street performers do their thing.

Across the Alexandra Bridge — that is, over the Ottawa River and back in Québec province — is the **Canadian Museum of Civilization,** 100 rue Laurier (☎ **800-555-5621** or 819-776-7000; www.civilization.ca), housed in a futuristic, riverfront building. The permanent exhibits celebrate Canada's aboriginal people and the evolution of this young country. Extensive artifacts are on display from native Canadian cultures; of special note is the Grand Hall, which features 43 authentic totem poles from the West Coast. Other exhibits document various aspects of Canada's history, culture, and development. Also on premise are an Imax theater and a children's museum with "hands-on" displays.

For something completely different, you can try your luck at the **Casino de Lac Leamy,** 1 bd. du Casino (☎ **800-665-2274;** www.casino-du-lac-leamy.com). Also in Québec province, it's open daily from 9 a.m. to 4 a.m. To get there from downtown Ottawa, take the Macdonald-Cartier Bridge, which becomes Highway 5, and get off at exit 3.

Where to stay

You may decide to have dinner in Ottawa, and dinner may turn into drinks. Suddenly, staying the night seems like a clever idea. Here are our choices for accommodations. All are centrally located, close to the places you're touring.

The **Fairmont Château Laurier,** 1 Rideau St. (☎ **800-441-1414** or 613-241-1414; www.fairmont.com), adjacent to the Rideau Canal and steps away from Parliament Hill, is the city's grandest hotel, in the same tradition as the Château Frontenac in Québec City and The Queen Elizabeth in Montréal. The **Lord Elgin Hotel,** 100 Elgin St. (☎ **800-267-4298** or 613-235-3333; www.lordelginhotel.ca), overlooks Confederation Park in downtown Ottawa, which is home to many seasonal events like the Jazz Festival. **Les Suites Hotel,** 130 Besserer St. (☎ **800-267-1989** or 613-232-2000; www.les-suites.com), offers a few more amenities than the average hotel room and is adjacent to Rideau Centre's 180 shops as well as the restaurants of the Byward Market area. The **Carmichael Inn & Spa,** 46 Cartier St. (☎ **613-236-4667;** www.carmichaelinn.com), is a heritage home in a quiet neighborhood, but it's still close to the action and offers spa treatments. Lastly, **Urban B 'n' B,** 160 Waverley St. (☎ **613-231-7556;** www.urbanbb.ca), offers modern rooms with shared bathrooms in a private residence near Elgin Street and the Byward Market.

Where to dine

If you're looking for a place to eat, here's the insider track. In 2003, **Beckta Dining and Wine,** 226 Nepean St. (☎ **613-238-7063**), ranked as the fourth best new restaurant in Canada in a biannual survey by *EnRoute Magazine*. It's the first Ottawa restaurant to break the top ten. Beckta serves seasonal cuisine in a modern and intimate setting. **MTL & Co.,** 47/49 William St. (☎ **613-241-6314**), seems like a fitting recommendation, given that MTL is short for Montréal, and true to its name, the restaurant becomes a lively club after dinner. On the menu are reasonably priced fusion dishes. **Savana Café,** 431 Gilmour St. (☎ **613-233-9159**), serves dishes inspired by the traditional ingredients of the Caribbean and the Pacific Rim.

Day Trip #2: The Laurentian Mountains

For the quickest and easiest day trip around Montréal, drive 45 minutes north to the Laurentian Mountains. These are rolling hills, not breathtaking peaks, but the Laurentians are impressive all the same.

Getting there

The Laurentian Highway, or Autoroute 15, takes you directly to the Laurentians and gives you the scenic route to boot. You can reach Autoroute 15 by driving north from downtown Montréal (along boulevard St-Laurent is fine) and catching Autoroute 40 West (you drive about 10 minutes until the Autoroute 15 interchange). Then follow signs to St-Jérôme. Autoroute 15 takes you through some urban sprawl for about 15 minutes, but the scenery is pretty after that.

If you have a little extra time, exit at St-Jérôme and pick up old Route 117. St-Jérôme is a small town with a quaint main street, a couple of pubs, and some gifts and craft shops. Remarkable for its charm, more so than substance. This takes you to the village of **Ste-Agathe des Monts** and through some typical older towns of the region along the way.

A good visitor information center covering the Laurentians area is in St-Jérôme: **La Maison du Tourisme des Laurentides,** 14142 rue de la Chapelle (☎ **450-436-8532;** www.laurentides.com). Take exit 39 off Autoroute 15 and follow the signs. The tourist office is in a red-roofed stone cottage. It's open daily in the summer from 8:30 a.m. to 8:30 p.m.; from 9 a.m. to 5 p.m. during the rest of the year.

Laurentian Mountains

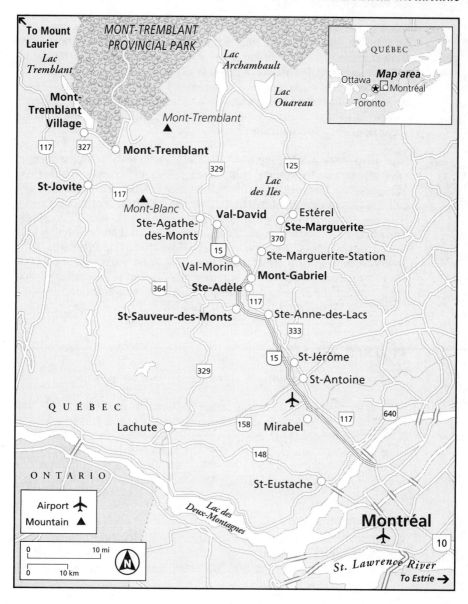

Limocar Laurentides buses leave regularly from Montréal's **Central Bus Station,** 505 bd. de Maisonneuve (☎ **888-999-3977** or 514-842-2281), with stops at Ste-Agathe, Ste-Adèle, St-Jovite, and Mont-Tremblant. For schedules, call the bus station or visit www.limocar.ca. The express bus to Ste-Adèle takes about an hour and a half; the trip to St-Jovite and Mont-Tremblant takes about two hours.

Seeing the sights

The Laurentians boast a number of interesting villages; each one can be a day trip in itself, depending on what you want to do and how much time you want to spend doing it. Driving from Montréal, your first stop is **Saint-Sauveur-des-Monts,** a popular ski resort town with lots of restaurants and street activity. In summer, the water park, **Parc Aquatique du Mont-St-Sauveur,** 350 rue St-Denis (☎ **800-363-2426;** www.montaintsauveur.com), is a popular attraction because of its wave pool and mountain water slide.

Next stop is **Ste-Adèle** (exit 67 off Route 117), a pretty village whose main street, **rue Valiquette,** is lined with cafes, galleries, and bakeries. The popular **Chantecler** ski resort here has 22 trails. For information, call the town's **Centre Municipal** at ☎ **450-229-2921.** For more down-hill skiing, continue along Route 117, and then take Route 327 to **Mont-Tremblant,** the highest peak in the Laurentians and an hour and a half drive from Montréal. The commercial center that serves the area is **St-Jovite,** whose main street, **rue Ouimet,** is lined with cafes and shops. For information on skiing and summer activities in this popular resort area, contact the **Bureau Touristique de Mont-Tremblant** on rue du Couvent in Mont-Tremblant (☎ **819-425-2434**).

Where to stay

Most of the accommodations in the Laurentians are resorts.

In Saint-Sauveur-des-Monts, the **Relais St-Denis,** 61 rue St-Denis (☎ **888-997-4766** or 450-227-4766), offers quite luxurious rooms and suites with fireplaces in a country club atmosphere, complete with a heated out-door pool and a nearby golf course. The **Manoir Saint-Sauveur,** 246 chemin du Lac-Millet (☎ **800-361-0505** or 450-227-1811), is a large resort hotel with year-round activities, including racquetball, squash, and in-house movies.

In Ste-Adèle, the **Hotel Alpine,** 1440 chemin Pierre Péladeau (☎ **877-257-4630**), offers different types of accommodations in rustic log struc-tures with meals served at communal tables. The **Chantecler** resort, 1474 chemin Chantecler (☎ **800-363-2420**), has rooms and suites, many with fireplaces and hot tubs.

Popular resorts in Mont-Tremblant include the deluxe motel **Auberge La Porte Rouge,** 1874 chemin Principale (☎ **800-665-3505** or 819-425-3505), with rooms to accommodate up to 10 people, and **Gray Rocks,** 525 chemin Principale (☎ **800-567-6767** or 819-425-2771), a family-friendly resort that offers horseback riding, boating, tennis, and golf.

Where to dine

Rue Principale in St-Sauveur-des-Monts has many restaurants. One of the best known is **Les Oliviers,** 239 rue Principale (☎ **450-227-2110**), which serves what you can probably call French country cuisine, including beef, duck, and salmon dishes.

In Ste-Adèle, **L'Eau à la Bouche,** 3003 bd. Ste-Adèle (Route 117) (☎ **450-229-2991**), serves a changing menu with seasonal fish, meats, and vegetables, plus a selection of Québec cheeses.

In St-Jovite, try **Antipasto,** 855 rue Ouimet (☎ **819-425-7580**), for Italian cuisine, including individual pizzas cooked in a brick oven. For carefully prepared traditional Québec cuisine, try **La Table Enchantée,** 600 rte 117 Nord (☎ **819-425-7113**), considered one of the best dining spots in the Laurentians area.

In Mont-Tremblant, **Aux Truffes,** 3035 rue Principale (☎ **819-681-4544**), serves upscale contemporary French cuisine.

Day Trip #3: The Eastern Townships

The **Eastern Townships** are one of Québec's best-kept tourism secrets. A beautiful landscape of rolling hills, mountains, farms, and small villages, the area has several quaint villages that are frequented mainly by Québec tourists. Much of the Townships were originally settled by British Loyalists who fled to the region during the Revolutionary War, and while 90% of the people speak French as their first language, you can see the traces of English presence everywhere. Many towns and villages have English names or names that combine the original English name with that of a Catholic saint (given by the French-speakers who later moved into the region).

For tourist information about the Eastern Townships, contact **Tourism Cantons-de-l'Est,** 20 rue Don Bosco South in Sherbooke (☎ **800-355-5755;** www.tourisme-cantons.qc.ca).

Getting there

To head to the Townships, count on two hours of driving. We suggest visiting either the small city of **Magog** (Lac Memphrémagog) or the quaint village of **North Hatley** (Lac Massawippi), which is about half an hour from Magog. Leave Montréal on the Champlain Bridge, which becomes Autoroute 10. Then follow directions toward Sherbrooke. Autoroute 10 goes directly to Magog. If you want to get there along a more scenic country road, leave the Autoroute 10 at exit 37 and follow Route 112 East. To get to North Hatley, take Autoroute 108 east from Magog for about 20 minutes.

The Eastern Townships

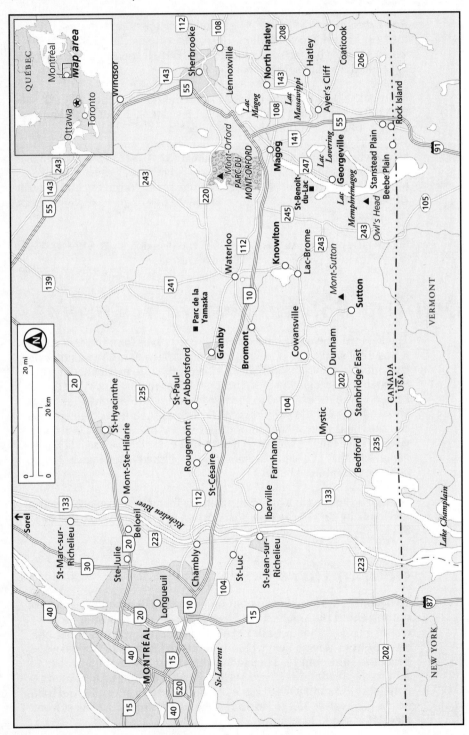

Buses for Magog and Sherbrooke leave Montréal's **Central Bus Station,** 505 bd. de Maisonneuve (☎ **888-999-3977** or 514-842-2281), roughly every two hours during the week. Call for daily schedules.

Seeing the sights

Small and mainly industrial, the city of Magog is not where you want to spend a lot of time. Head straight to the waterfront area on **Lac Memphrémagog,** with its cafes and bars. You can take a **lake cruise** aboard the **Aventure** cruise ships. Call ☎ **819-843-8068** for information or contact the **Bureau d'Information Touristique Memphrémagog** at 55 rue Cabana in Magog (☎ **800-267-2744**). Near Magog, visit the popular provincial park **Parc du Mont Orford,** which offers a golf course and 30 miles of skiing and hiking trails. To get there, take exit 115 north off the Autoroute 10. For information, call ☎ **819-843-9855.** Admission is C$3.50 (US$2.50) for adults.

North Hatley is a tiny, beautiful village on the shore of Lac Massawippi. A former resort town for rich Americans, it is now the place well-to-do Québeckers come to relax and buy paintings in the village's many art galleries. The village's main street, **rue Principale,** is also full of cute cafes, restaurants, and boutiques selling crafts and clothing. There aren't many tourist attractions here per se. Instead, people come here for the exceptional atmosphere, beautiful lakefront scenery, and all 'round New England feel. The **Gallerie Jeanine Blais,** 100 rue Principale (☎ **819-842-2784**), has lovely, fanciful folk art and **Au Gremier de Gife,** 330 chemin de la Rivière (☎ **819-842-4440**), sells painted furniture and works by local artists.

Where to stay

Lodging in Magog is neither plentiful nor very nice. If you want to stay the night, we suggest the **Relais de l'Abbaye,** 2705 chemin Gendreau (☎ **450-759-0228**), a luxurious mansion-style guesthouse with elegant rooms.

But you'll probably be happier staying in North Hatley. **Le Tricorne,** 50 chemin Gosselin (☎ **819-842-2692;** www.manoirletricorne.com), is an impeccably decorated, 125-year-old guesthouse. Rooms start at about C$125 (US$94), and some include hot tubs. If you're interested in something more luxurious, the famous **Auberge Hatley,** 325 rue Virgin (☎ **819-842-2451**), has rooms decorated with antiques and complete with hot tubs and fireplaces, and on-site is a gastronomic restaurant. **Serendipity,** 680 chemin de la Rivière (☎ **819-842-2970**), is a reasonably priced B&B with nice views.

Where to dine

The upscale inns in North Hatley offer exceptional dining choices. The **Auberge Hatley** serves fine, gourmet meals based on local ingredients like duck, venison, and bison and has a wine cellar with more than 10,000 bottles. *Table d'hôte* (complete meal) menus start at C$55 (US$40). The **Auberge Ripplecove,** 700 chemin Ripplecove (☎ 800-668-4296) has a reputation for serving creative dishes based on local delicacies, like caribou. For less expensive but still tasty food, **Pilsen,** 55 rue Principale (☎ 819-842-2971), has a pub-like atmosphere and serves quick food like nachos, burgers, and pasta. This is a great place to indulge in a large selection of locally brewed beers. Another good choice is the **Café Massawippi,** 3050 chemin Capelton (☎ 819-842-4528), for inventive but reasonably priced meals.

Part IV
Visiting Québec City

The 5th Wave   By Rich Tennant

Great curb appeal.

Château Frontenac

In this part . . .

A couple of hours downriver from Montréal is Québec City, a place that makes you feel as though you've stepped into another age. In this part, we explain where to go and what to do to get the most out of your visit. We tell you where to find the best hotels, restaurants, and attractions. We even give you a handy historical tour of Québec's Old City, so that you can see all the highlights in one afternoon.

Chapter 15

Arriving and Orienting Yourself in Québec City

- -

In This Chapter

▶ Getting to Québec City

▶ Figuring out the city's neighborhoods

▶ Traveling around the city

- -

*Y*ou're likely to spend almost all your time in Québec City in the Old City, which is divided into a fortified **Haute-Ville** (Upper City), built behind walls on a cliff overlooking the St. Lawrence River, and a **Basse-Ville** (Lower City), at the foot of the cliff running along the riverfront, to the south and east. You can easily get lost in the winding cobblestone streets in either neighborhood, but don't worry if you do. The whole point of Québec City is strolling around and soaking up the unbelievable atmosphere. This chapter explains how to get to Québec City and how to get around after you arrive.

Arriving in Québec City

No matter how you get to Canada from abroad, you have to pass through customs. See Chapter 7 for details on what to expect from the stern-faced customs agents you encounter at the border.

Getting from Jean Lesage Airport to your hotel

If you arrive in Québec City by air, you will land in the small **Jean Lesage International Airport** (500 rue Principale Sainte-Foy; ☎ 418-640-2700). No shuttles are available to downtown Québec City. A taxi ride costs a fixed rate of C$25 (US$19). If you want to rent a car, the following major agencies have desks at the airport:

✔ **Avis:** ☎ **800-879-2847** or 418-872-2861.

✔ **Budget:** ☎ **800-268-8900** or 418-872-9885.

✔ **Hertz Canada:** ☎ **800-654-3131** or 418-871-1571.

✔ **Thrifty:** ☎ **800-367-2277** or 418-877-2870.

Getting from Pierre Elliott Trudeau International Airport to your hotel

You may land at the province's main international airport, which is actually in Montréal: **Trudeau International Airport** (☎ **800-465-1213** or 514-394-7377).

You have several options to get to Québec City from Montréal's main airport:

✔ **By car:** All of Québec's major car rental companies have counters in the arrivals area of Trudeau Airport. For tips on getting the best rental deals, see Chapter 7. For telephone numbers of rental companies, see the Appendix. To get from Montréal to Québec City, follow the signs from the airport toward Autoroute 20 Est (Highway 20 East), which goes directly to Québec City. The drive takes about two and a half hours.

✔ **By bus:** Autocars Orléans Express (☎ **514-842-2281**) serves the Montréal-Québec City corridor. Express buses leave every hour on the hour from Montréal's **Central Bus Station,** located at 505 bd. de Maisonneuve Est to Québec City. The trip to takes about three hours, and a round-trip ticket costs C$57 (US$43) plus taxes. For details on how to get from Trudeau Airport to the Central Bus Station in Montréal, see Chapter 8.

✔ **By train:** Trains leave four times daily from Montréal's **Central Station** (895 rue de la Gauchetière Ouest; ☎ **514-989-2626**) to Québec City's **Gare du Palais** (450 rue Gare-du-Palais; ☎ **418-692-3940**). If you reserve five days ahead of time, a roundtrip ticket costs C$80 (US$60). The trip takes a little over three hours.

✔ **By ferry:** If you have a little time to kill and want to take the truly scenic route, a ferry (mid-May–mid-Oct) runs along the St. Lawrence River between Montréal and Québec City. The trip takes four hours. Phone **Les Dauphins du Saint-Laurent** (☎ **877-648-4499** or 514-281-8000), and see Chapter 5 for more details.

Driving to Québec City

From the Canada-United States border: From **New York City,** follow I-87 to Highway 15 to Montréal, and then pick up Autoroute 20 to

Québec City. To get into the city, take Autoroute 73 Nord (Highway 73 North) across the Pierre-Laporte Bridge (Pont Pierre-Laporte) and exit on bd. Champlain. Turn left at rue Parc des Champs-de-Batailles and follow it to Grande-Allée. When you get to Grande-Allée, turn right and head straight into the Old City.

From Boston, take I-89 to I-93 in Montpelier, Vermont, which connects with Highway 55 in Québec to link up with Autoroute 20. Follow the preceding directions.

From Montréal, you can take either Autoroute 20, which follows the south shore of the St. Lawrence River or the more scenic, less-trafficked Autoroute 40, which follows the north shore. Either way, the trip takes about two and a half hours.

Finding Information When You Arrive

Québec City has two good tourist information centers in handy locations. The main office is **Centre Infotouriste,** at 12 rue Ste-Anne, just opposite the Château Frontenac at Place d'Armes (☎ **800-363-7777** or 418-692-2608). The office is well stocked with tons of brochures and is well staffed with bilingual employees who help you find information or book hotel rooms and tours for you. The **Greater Québec Area Tourism and Convention Bureau,** near the Plains of Abraham at 835 av. Laurier (not too far from Grande-Allée) (☎ **418-649-2608**), offers the same services but tends to be a little less busy.

Québec City's Neighborhoods

Québec's Old City is really quite small, but it's so dense and packed with interesting sites, shops, museums, cafes, restaurants, and other attractions that you can spend a lot of time wandering its winding streets and still be surprised by new sites and curiosities. The only neighborhood that you'll likely want to visit outside the Old City is the Grande-Allée, a long, wide street running west of the St-Louis Gate that's lined with restaurants, boutiques, and bars. During the summer evenings, this street is hopping, and its terraces are packed with revelers.

Haute-Ville (Upper City)

This is the biggest part of the Old City, a neighborhood entirely surrounded by thick ramparts. Most of Québec City's main attractions can be found here, including the **Château Frontenac,** the **Place d'Armes,** the **Basilique Notre-Dame,** the **Québec seminary and museum,** and the **terrasse Dufferin** — a long promenade with a view of the St. Lawrence

Québec City Orientation

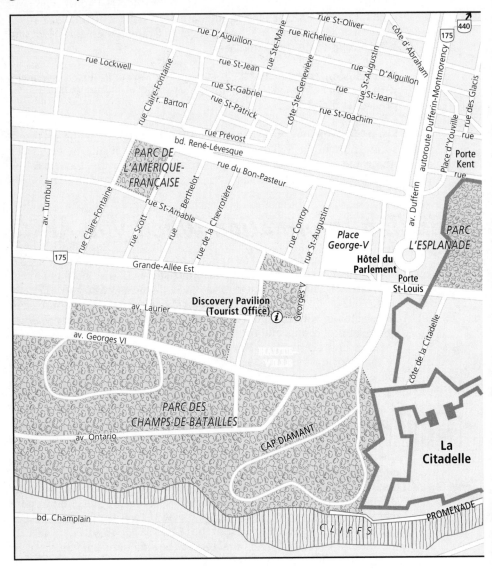

River below. Most of the buildings are at least 100 years old, some much older. The city was not built on a grid, so it can be disorienting, but don't worry; sooner or later, you'll arrive at a wall, a cliff, or a gate, and you'll be able to figure out where you are on a map.

Basse-Ville (Lower City)

Historically, this part of the city was reserved mainly for poor families that worked in the docks. Now it's pretty much a continuation of the

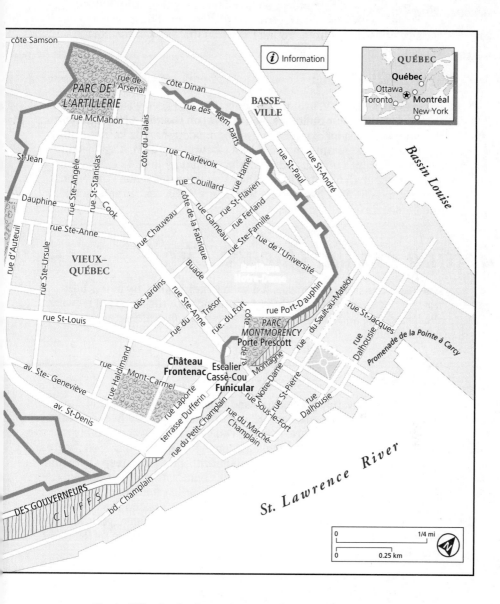

côte Samson

PARC DE L'ARTILLERIE

rue de l'Arsenal

côte Dinan

rue McMahon

rue des Remparts

BASSE–VILLE

St-Jean

côte du Palais

rue Charlevoix

rue Hamel

rue St-André

rue St-Paul

Bassin Louise

Dauphine

rue Ste-Angèle

rue St-Stanislas

Cook

rue Couillard

rue St-Flavien

côte de la Fabrique

rue Garneau

rue Ferland

rue Ste-Famille

rue de l'Université

rue d'Auteuil

rue Ste-Ursule

rue Ste-Anne

rue Chauveau

VIEUX–QUÉBEC

Buade

des Jardins

rue Ste-Anne

Trésor

rue du Fort

côte de la

rue Port-Dauphin

rue du Sault-au-Matelot

rue St-Jacques

Dalhousie

Promenade de la Pointe à Carcy

rue St-Louis

rue du Trésor

PARC MONTMORENCY

Porte Prescott

av. Ste- Geneviève

rue Haldimand

rue Mont-Carmel

Château Frontenac

Escalier Casse-Cou

Funicular

rue Notre-Dame

Montagne

rue Sous-le-Fort

rue St-Pierre

rue Dalhousie

av. St-Denis

rue Laporte

terrasse Dufferin

rue du Petit-Champlain

rue du Marché-Champlain

DES GOUVERNEURS

C L I F F S

bd. Champlain

St. Lawrence River

ⓘ Information

QUÉBEC

Québec
Ottawa
Toronto
Montréal
New York

0   1/4 mi
0   0.25 km

Haute-Ville. In the Basse-Ville, you find similar architecture, many restaurants, some small inns, and several major attractions, including the spectacular **Musée de la Civilisation** (Museum of Civilization). Rue St-Paul is a lovely strip with many art galleries and antiques stores and some very cute accommodations.

Take the elevator or the stairs down from the terrasse Dufferin or Place d'Armes, and you wind up on the delightful rue Petit Champlain, a pedestrian alley full of shops of varying quality. Don't forget to stroll along the port area. Recent development and an interest by the cruise industry has made the area more attractive and festive. You'll be in awe of the massive cruise ships from around the world that dock at the port.

Grande-Allée

If you exit the Haute-Ville at the St-Louis Gate and keep walking west past Québec's Parliament Buildings, you end up on Grande-Allée. Although this street offers a lot of hotels and accommodations, it is known mainly for it's many restaurants and bars with sidewalk terraces. It's a meeting point for the city's young, and it's lively all summer long. Keep heading west for about 15 minutes on foot and you'll reach avenue Cartier on your right — another lively street with many B&Bs, restaurants, shops, and bars.

Getting around Québec City

Québec City's small size makes it a snap to get around. By foot is best; however, at some point, you have to contend with the steep hill between the Haute-Ville and Basse-Ville. This is when the *funiculaire* (elevator) comes in handy.

By foot

If you're in reasonably good shape and have comfortable walking shoes, you can probably dispense with all motorized transport while in Québec City, especially if your hotel is in the Old City. Walking is definitely the best way to travel; the only challenge on foot is getting between the Upper and Lower Cities. To do so, you have to climb the steep stairs that join Côte de la Montagne (near the Petit Champlain) to the Dufferin Terrace. If you want, you can take the *funiculaire* (elevator) that leaves from the head of rue Petit-Champlain and also arrives on the Dufferin Terrace. In the north part of the Old City, near rue St-Jean, you can take advantage of a more gradual decline to get to the Basse-Ville by following rue Côte-du-Palais down a gentle slope to rue St-Paul.

By public transportation

We have only one exception to the rule of walking: if you're staying too far away from the Old City to make the trip in by foot. In that case, several buses run frequently into the Old City. Bus no. 7 runs up and down rue St-Jean; no. 11 runs along Grande-Allée and rue St-Louis. Both take you into the Old City, making stops all the way to Place d'Youville, just outside the walls on the north side of town. These buses pass about every ten minutes. Fares are C$2.25 (US$1.70) exact change, or you can purchase tickets at a *dépanneur* (convenience store) for C$1.90 (US$1.40).

By taxi

Taxis are plentiful in Québec City, and they're pretty easy to flag down around the big hotels and outside the gates of the Old City. Inside the Old City, you can find taxi stands at Place d'Armes and in front of the Hôtel-de-Ville (City Hall). The fares are the same as in Montréal, which can be a little expensive for short distances. The starting rate is C$2.50 (US$1.90), and then C$1.20 (US90¢) per kilometer. To call a taxi, try **Taxi Coop** (☎ 418-525-5191) or **Taxi Québec** (☎ 418-525-8123).

By car

It really makes no sense to try to get around Québec City by car. You'll have great difficulty parking on the street in the Old City, which is so compact that you can walk everywhere easily on foot. That said, if you arrive at your hotel by car, you can find plenty of places to leave it while you stroll about the city. Hotels either have parking lots or have worked out deals with parking lots nearby, and most will be able to direct where to go to find a spot. For most parking lots, expect to pay around C$10 to C$12 (US$7.50–US$9) per day. Some lots even allow you to come and go during the day at no extra charge.

By bicycle

Given how hilly and dense the Old City is, cycling isn't a very attractive option. Still, you can rent bikes for the day at several locations. Try **Cyclo Service,** 160 rue St-André in the Basse-Ville (☎ 418-692-4052) or **Vélo Passe-Sport Plein Air,** at 22 rue Côte-du-Palais, near rue St-Jean (☎ 418-692-3643). The cost is around C$20 (US$15) for 12 hours.

Chapter 16

Québec City's Best Hotels

. . . .

In This Chapter

▶ Finding the best accommodations in Québec City

▶ Reviewing runner-up choices, if the top places are booked

▶ Organizing a lists of accommodations by price and neighborhood

. . . .

*W*hen we created our list of Québec City's best places to stay, we included options in each of the city's most interesting neighborhoods, as close as possible to the cafes, shops, and attractions where you want to spend most of your time. But because Québec City is so small, accommodations can book up quickly for the high season (roughly May to October), so if you want to stay in one of our top picks for lodging, make sure you call well in advance. If you aren't able to do that, we list our runners up, in case our first picks are booked. If you need to find a room at the last minute, check out our tips in Chapter 6.

Each hotel listing in this chapter includes a $ symbol indicating the price range of the rooms. Prices included are the rack rates, the standard rate for a double room for one night, before taxes. The $ signs represent the following prices ranges:

$	Less than C$100 (US$75)
$$	C$100–C$200 (US$75–US$150)
$$$	C$200–C$300 (US$150–US$225)
$$$$	More than C$300 (US$225)

Québec City Hotels from A to Z

Auberge du Quartier
$ Grande-Allée

If you want some peace and quiet, slightly off the beaten path, this charming inn is a good choice. A 15-minute walk from Vieux-Québec, the fifteen rooms are colorful and compact — including several with exposed brick walls. Guest rooms are available with single, double, and queen beds, and

Québec City Accommodations

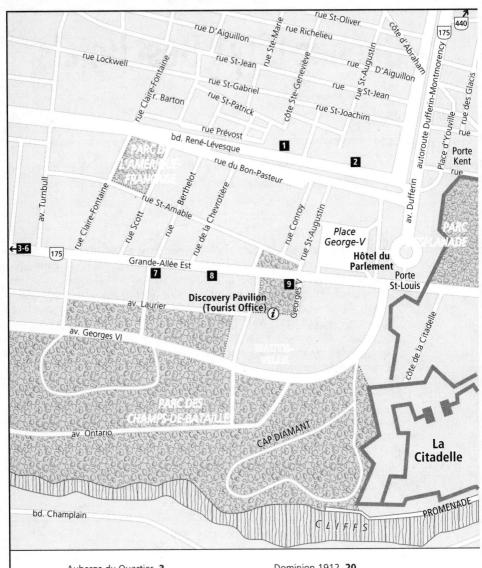

Auberge du Quartier **3**	Dominion 1912 **20**
Auberge St-Pierre **18**	Fairmont Le Château Frontenac **16**
Château Bellevue **15**	Gite Côte de la Montagne **17**
Château Cap-Diamant **12**	Hilton International Québec **2**
Château de Pierre **13**	Hôtel Belley **24**
Château Laurier **9**	Hôtel Clarendon **21**
Chez Hubert **11**	Hôtel du Vieux Québec **22**
Couettes et Café Toast **4**	Hôtel Le St-Paul **25**
Delta Québec **1**	Hôtel Loew's Le Concorde **7**

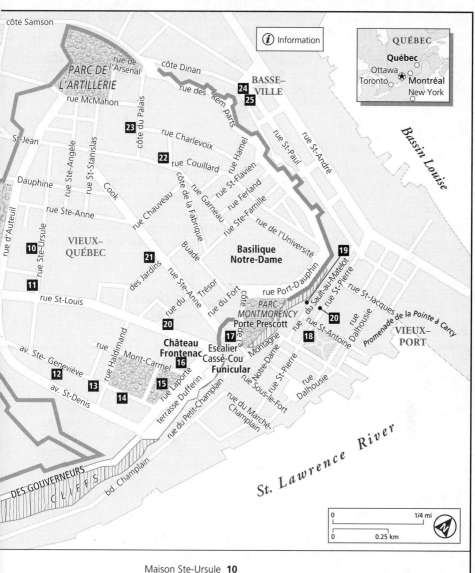

côte Samson

PARC DE L'ARTILLERIE

rue de l'Arsenal

rue McMahon

côte Dinan

rue des Remparts

24
25

BASSE–VILLE

i Information

QUÉBEC

Québec

Ottawa
Toronto   ★ **Montréal**
New York

23

St-Jean

rue Charlevoix

côte du Palais

rue Ste-Angèle

rue St-Stanislas

Cook

22 rue Couillard

rue Hamel

rue St-Flavien

rue St-Paul

rue St-André

Bassin Louise

Dauphine

rue Ste-Anne

côte de la Fabrique

rue Chauveau

rue Garneau

rue Ferland

rue Ste-Famille

rue de l'Université

rue d'Auteuil

rue Ste-Ursule

VIEUX–QUÉBEC

10

21

Buade

des Jardins

rue Ste-Anne

Trésor

côte du Fort

rue du Fort

Basilique Notre-Dame

rue Port-Dauphin

du Sault-au-Matelot

rue St-Pierre

rue St-Jacques

19

11

rue St-Louis

20

rue Port-Dauphin

PARC MONTMORENCY

Porte Prescott

Montagne

rue St-Antoine

Dalhousie

20

Promenade de la Pointe à Carcy

VIEUX–PORT

av. Ste-Genevière

rue Haldimand

Mont-Carmel

Château Frontenac

16

17

Escalier Cassè-Cou Funicular

rue Notre-Dame

rue St-Pierre

18

rue Sous-le-Fort

rue Dalhousie

12

13

av. St-Denis

14

15

rue Laporte

terrasse Dufferin

rue du Petit-Champlain

rue du Marché-Champlain

DES GOUVERNEURS

CLIFFS

bd. Champlain

St. Lawrence River

0   1/4 mi
0   0.25 km

are priced accordingly. The atmosphere is relaxing and friendly, complete with cozy arm chairs in the living room/library. Rooms don't have TVs, but there's an Internet connection available in the living room, as well as piles of Québec literature to leaf through.

170 Grande-Allée Ouest. ☎ *800-782-9441 or 418-525-9726. Fax: 418-521-4891. Internet:* www.quebecweb.com/ADQ. *Parking: C$10 (US$7.50). Rates: C$80–C$100 (US$60–US$75). AE, DISC, MC, V.*

Auberge St-Pierre
$$–$$$$ Basse-Ville

Just five years old, this hotel in the heart of the Basse-Ville does an almost magical job of looking and feeling antique, from the distressed painted furniture to deliberately scratched hardwood floors, high ceilings, exposed brick-and-stone walls, and old-fashioned hot-water radiators. But the rooms are utterly modern in term of amenities and convenience; the spacious bathrooms, for example, are generously equipped, right down to the built-in hairdryers. One luxurious suite has a hot tub and king-size bed.

79 rue St-Pierre. ☎ *888-268-1017 or 418-694-7981. Fax: 418-694-0406. Valet parking: C$13 (US$9.75). Rates: C$109–C$359 (US$82–US$269), doubles and suites. Rates include breakfast. AE, DC, DISC, MC, V.*

Château Bellevue
$$–$$$ Haute-Ville

At first sight, you may mistake this small hotel for one of the oodles of B&Bs and guesthouses that surround it, all facing the peaceful Jardin des Gouverneurs park. Château Bellevue actually has 58 rooms, small but not overly quaint, but quiet and equipped with basic amenities like phones and cable TV. Unlike many accommodations in the Old City, this place has an elevator, so you have no steep stairs to climb. The staff is very helpful. Some of the pricier rooms face the park, and in winter they have a view of the St. Lawrence River.

16 rue Laporte. ☎ *800-463-2573 or 418-692-2573. Fax: 418-692-4876. Parking: Free. Rates: C$119–C$219 (US$89–US$164) doubles. Rates include breakfast off-season only. AE, DC, DISC, MC, V.*

Château Cap-Diamant
$$ Haute-Ville

The idyllic enclosed garden behind this Victorian guest house, with its crumbling rock walls, flower-filled porch, and fountain, is almost worth the price of a room itself. Each room in this quaint inn is different. All are decorated with antiques, and the place feels something like a work in progress. Bathrooms are tiny. Although most rooms are accessible by steep narrow stairs, there's a small elevator to lift luggage to the upper floors. Whew! Rooms have cable TV, and Internet access is available in the reception area. The owners are inviting and helpful. Ask for a room overlooking the rooftops of the Old City.

39 av. Ste-Geneviève. ☎ *418-694-0313. Parking: C$10 (US$7.50). Rates: C$125–C$155 (US$94–US$124). MC, V. No phones.*

Château de Pierre
$$ Haute-Ville

A European-style inn on a quiet, elegant street packed with small B&B-style hotels, the Château de Pierre distinguishes itself in the details: polished banisters, pretty wallpaper, a chandelier in the reception area, and a small patio for summer lounging. The owners want you to take your time here, relax, and stay in bed late. All 15 rooms are nonsmoking, and most have bath tubs. The only drawback of this place is very steep staircases that you have to climb to get to most of the rooms.

17 rue Ste-Geneviève. ☎ *418-694-0429. Fax: 418-694-0153. Parking: C$10 (US$7.50). Rates: C$110–C$130 (US$83–US$98) doubles. Rates include continental breakfast. AE, DC, MC, V.*

Château Laurier
$$–$$$$ Grande-Allée

Facing the elegant Place George V, this recently renovated, 154-room hotel keeps you in European-style comfort while putting you just a few minutes walk from Vieux-Québec. The main reception area features a grand piano and sumptuous leather couches. Some rooms have working fireplaces, CD players, king beds, and Jacuzzis. Basic rooms are spacious and tastefully appointed. It's a family-owned establishment, but it feels like an upscale chain hotel. The hotel caters to tour groups, which yields a bustling atmosphere, but can also be a bit noisy. Ask for a room in the new wing (they're bigger) and facing the park.

1220 place George V. ☎ *800-463-4453 or 418-522-8108. Fax: 418-524-8786. Parking: Free valet parking. Rates: C$129–C$289 (US$97–US$217) double and suites. AE, DC, DISC, MC, V.*

Chez Hubert
$ Haute-Ville

This small B&B feels something like a nicely worn-in doll house, with its winding staircase and brightly painted, eclectic decor. It offers only three rooms, but each is large and handsomely renovated, with wood floors and lovely painted antique furniture. You'll find plenty of comfortable space for relaxing, but only one bathroom, and no TV or telephones in the rooms (both are available in the living room downstairs). Due to the presence of the family dog, no other animals are allowed. Call well ahead to reserve a room.

66 rue Ste-Ursule. ☎ *418-692-0958. Parking: Free. Rates: C$85 (US$64). Rates include breakfast. Cash or travelers' cheques only.*

Delta Québec

$$ **Boulevard René-Levesque**

This upscale, well-located hotel delivers comfortable rooms with all the trimmings — including a heated outdoor pool. Surprisingly easy to miss, it is actually connected to the Centre des Congrès, Québec City's convention center. The reception area is two floors up from the front entrance, and the maze of escalators and mezzanines are a little confusing, but you get the hang of it. Spacious, rustic-style rooms with pine furniture come with small desks equipped with ergonomic chairs and Internet connections. You're about a ten-minute walk from the Parliament Buildings and Vieux-Québec, making this a good choice for business or pleasure.

690 bd. René-Levesque Est. ☎ *888-884-7777 or 418-647-1717. Fax: 418-647-2146. Internet:* www.deltaquebec.com. *Parking: C$19 (US$14.25). Rates: C$139–C$170 (US$104–US$128) double and suites. AE, DC, MC, V. Wheelchair accessible.*

Fairmont Le Château Frontenac

$$$$ **Haute-Ville**

A tourist attraction in itself, the 100-year-old Château Frontenac is definitely the place to stay if you want the full Vieux-Québec experience (and pay for the priviledge, of course). Perched on the terrasse Dufferin, it looks like a castle from the outside and feels like one on the inside — from the elaborate wood paneling of the reception area to the parking valets dressed in period costumes. The 618 rooms vary enormously, with everything from luxurious suites to standard, good-size rooms that are actually decent value for the money. Prices vary a lot depending on season and availability, and you get the best rates by far in package deals. There's plenty to keep kids amused, from the pool to kids programs and a video arcade.

1 rue des Carriéres. ☎ *800-828-7447 or 418-692-3861. Fax: 418-692-1751. Internet:* www.fairmont.com. *Parking: Valet C$20 (US$15). Rates: C$409–C$759 (US$306– US$569), doubles. Rates include breakfast. AE, DC, DISC, MC, V.*

Hilton International Québec

$$–$$$ **Boulevard René-Levesque**

In addition to all the comfort and pampering you expect from the name, Québec City's Hilton offers a simply amazing view of Vieux-Québec. In fact, you're probably better off staying here and looking at the stately Château Frontenac, than staying in the Frontenac itself. All the rooms are spacious and offer a view of the Old City. This Hilton is especially kid friendly, with gifts, special kids programs, and discount coupons for the hotel's restaurant, where, among other things, you can indulge in an all-you-can-eat lobster dinner. Added amenities include a health center with trainers, a heated outdoor pool open year round, and high-speed Internet connections in every room. Plus, it's just a five-minute walk from the walls of Vieux-Québec and some 20 nearby gastronomic restaurants. Good rates are available off season.

1100 bd. René-Levesque Est. ☎ *800-445-8667 or 514-647-2411. Fax: 418-647-6488. Internet:* www.hilton.com. *Parking: C$16.95 (US$13). Rates: C$93–C$299 (US$70–US$224) double and suites. Rates include breakfast. AE, DC, DISC, MC, V. Some wheelchair-accessible rooms.*

Hôtel Belley
$–$$ Basse-Ville

This is a fun and funky place to stay if you're looking for reasonably priced accommodations within walking distance of the art galleries and antiques stores along rue St-Paul. The Hôtel Belley has eight bright, if sparsely decorated, rooms; some with added touches such as exposed beams and brick walls and skylights. All rooms are nonsmoking. Bathrooms are extremely compact. Several rooms have extra pullout beds for kids, and one family-size room has a queen and two single beds. Light meals are available at all hours in the small tavern on the first floor of the hotel.

249 rue St-Paul. ☎ *418-692-1694. Fax: 418-692-1696. Internet:* www.oricom.ca/ belley. *Parking: Available nearby for C$7–C$11/day (US$5–US$8/day). Rates: C$70–C$125 (US$53–US$94). AE, MC, V.*

Hôtel Clarendon
$–$$$ Haute-Ville

This elegant, well-maintained Art Deco–style hotel is one of the oldest hotels in Vieux-Québec and has even maintained its original, wicket-style reception desk. Located in the heart of the Haute-Ville, it couldn't be better situated, and you'll definitely feel as though you've been transported back in time. Rooms are rather dark and claustrophobic, but bathrooms are modern. There's a lively pub, known for its jazz evenings, right off the reception area. The hotel's restaurant, Le Charles Baillargé, offers excellent French food. Facials, body scrubs, and massage are available on location. Nonsmoking rooms.

57 rue Ste-Anne. ☎ *888-554-6001 or 418-692-4652. Fax: 418-692-4652. Parking: C$12 (US$9) in public parking lot. Rates: C$99–C$289 (US$74–US$217) double. AE, DC, DISC, MC, V.*

Hôtel du Vieux-Québec

$$–$$$ **Haute-Ville**

Housed in a century-old brick manor, the Hôtel du Vieux-Québec offers a cool, comfortable ambience, including spacious rooms and a cozy living room, where you can rest after a busy day of sightseeing. This place is popular with families because many of the doubles have extra sofas. Extra guests stay for C$15 (US$11) per day. Kids stay for free in the winter, and significant rate reductions are available off-season. The staff is friendly and helpful. The hotel is close to shopping, nightspots, and restaurants. Ask for one of the 24 recently renovated rooms.

1190 rue St-Jean. ☎ *800-361-7787 or 418-692-1850. Fax: 418-692-5637. Internet:* www.hvq.com. *Parking: Available at the Hotel de Ville (City Hall) C$10 (US$7.50). Rates: C$135–C$255 (US$101–US$191). AE, DC, MC, V.*

Hôtel Loew's Le Concorde

$$–$$$$ **Grande-Allée**

A large, upscale hotel, Loew's is smack in the middle of the action on Grande-Allée and a ten-minute stroll through a lively neighborhood to the gates of Vieux-Québec. Rooms on the side of the hotel facing the Old City have a remarkable view. The lobby is a little worn, with threadbare furniture, but the rooms are spacious and classic feeling and include good-size bathrooms with marble counters. The hotel has a gym and a pool. A revolving restaurant at the top, L'Astral, serves excellent French food while offering a panoramic view of the city. Meanwhile, you're only an elevator ride away from cafes and restaurants galore down below on Grande-Allée. Special rates for kids.

1225 Place Montcalm. ☎ *800-463-5256 or 418-647-2222. Fax: 418-647-4710. Internet:* www.loewshotels.com. *Parking: $17 (US$13). Rates: C$145–C$380 (US$109–US$285) double and suites. Rates include breakfast. AE, DC, DISC, MC, V.*

Le Krieghoff B&B

$ **Avenue Cartier**

This clean and convenient B&B is perched above the boutiques, restaurants, and bars on lively avenue Cartier. The five rooms are surprisingly big and airy, although basic, and not all have bathrooms attached. A living area on the first floor has a microwave, a fridge for guests's use, telephone and TV, a big comfy couch, and a small balcony that looks over avenue Cartier. The only drawbacks include two flights of stairs to climb to the rooms and slightly indifferent service. Breakfast is served in the cafe downstairs, where decent food and coffee are served at reasonable prices all day.

1091 av. Cartier. ☎ *418-522-3711. Fax: 418-647-1429. Internet:* www.cafe krieghoff.qc.cq. *Parking: Free. Rates: C$75–C$85 (US$56–US$64). MC, V.*

Le Priori

$–$$ Basse-Ville

Sleek and modern, this 26-room hotel, built inside an old building in the Basse-Ville, is a design buff's dream come true. It's reasonably priced and very conveniently located near the rue St-Paul strip of art galleries. Rooms are a little dark and on the small side, but the minimalist decor makes them seem spacious enough. All the comforts are there, including queen-size beds with down comforters. Suites have nice extras, including wood-burning fireplaces, kitchens, and Jacuzzis. The view is, unfortunately, restricted to neighboring rooftops. All rooms have Internet connection. Le Priori welcomes a mix of straight and gay guests.

15 rue Sault-au-Matelot (corner rue St-Antoine). ☎ **800-351-3992** *or 418-692-3992. Fax: 418-692-0883. Internet:* www.hotellepriori.com. *Parking: Public lot nearby for C$12 (US$9). Rates: C$99–C$169 (US$75–US$127). Rates include full breakfast. AE, DC, DISC, MC, V.*

Maison Ste-Ursule

$ Haute-Ville

This popular guest house has a distinct youth hostel feel to it, with its peeling wallpaper and slightly bohemian clientele, but it offers good accommodations at an excellent price in an even better location on a quiet street in Vieux-Québec. The second oldest house on the street, built in 1739, it boasts stone walls and a lovely, leafy sitting garden out back. Breakfast is not available in the hotel but is easy to find in a close proximity. Several smoking rooms are available. Parking is not included but is available nearby.

40 rue Ste-Ursule. ☎ **418-694-9794.** *Fax: 418-694-0875. Internet:* www.quebec web.com/maisonsteursule. *Rates: C$49–C$89 (US$37–US$67) single and double. AE, MC, V.*

Manoir Lafayette

$$ Grande-Allée

The small, somewhat luxurious Manoir Lafayette puts you very close to Vieux-Québec while affording you some room to breathe. You get more of a big hotel feeling here than in the many small inns along the Grande-Allée. The elegant reception area is decorated with nice antiques, while rooms are of a decent size, are modern, and offer queen or double beds.

661 Grande-Allée Est. ☎ **800-363-8203** *or 418-522-2652. Fax: 418-522-4400. Parking: Free. Rates: C$149–C$189 (US$112–US$142). Rates include breakfast. AE, DC, DISC, MC, V.*

Manoir Victoria

$$–$$$$ Haute-Ville

The formal lobby of this small hotel, with its fireplaces, antique armchairs, and elegant dining room done up in dark burgundy and blue, projects an Old World feel. The 145 rooms are classic in style, but modern and spacious, with two double beds. The hotel offers all the perks and services you'd expect in a larger hotel, including valet parking, an indoor pool, sauna and fitness center, Internet lounge, and even baby-sitting. This end of the Haute-Ville is convenient, with restaurants of all types for all budgets, and lots of shopping on nearby rue St-Jean. In the low season, it's popular among the corporate crowd.

44 Côte-du-Palais. ☎ *418-692-1030. Fax. 418-692-3822. Internet:* www.manoir-victoria.com. *Parking: C$15 (US$11). Rates: C$149–C$600 (US$112–US$450), doubles and suites. AE, DC, DISC, MC, V.*

Relais Charles-Alexandre

$$ Grande-Allée

A cool, peaceful, and meticulously kept inn close to the Plains of Abraham, this is one of the best deals along the Grand-Allée and a regular hangout for vacationing New Englanders — and it's just a ten-minute walk to the Old City. The 24 guest rooms are bright, spacious, and recently renovated, with polished wood floors and flowery, matching curtains and bedspreads. Rooms are equipped with small desks and TVs and have queen or twin beds; bathrooms have showers or baths. The staff is helpful and friendly.

Grand-Allée Est. ☎ *418-523-1220. Fax: 418-523-9556. Parking: C$8 (US$6). Rates C$115–C$125 (US$79–US$80). Rates include continental breakfast. AE, MC, V.*

Runner-up Hotels

Dominion 1912

$$$–$$$$ Basse-Ville   A particularly nicely renovated place, this rather luxurious hotel has big rooms with queen- or king-size beds and down-filled comforters. *126 rue St-Pierre.* ☎ *888-883-5253 or 418-689-2224. Fax: 418-692-4403. Internet:* www.hoteldominion.com.

Couettes et Café Toast

$ Avenue Cartier   One of the more convenient and tastefully decorated B&B options in a quiet part of the city, but not too far from the action on Grande-Allée. 1020 av. Cartier. ☎ *418-523-9365. Fax: 418-523-6706. Internet:* www.quebecweb.com/toast&French.

Hôtel Le St-Paul

$$ Basse-Ville A luxurious place with exposed brick walls and warm, intimate rooms. 229 rue St-Paul. ☎ *888-794-4414* or *418-694-4414. Fax: 418-694-0889. Internet:* www.lesaintpaul.qc.ca.

Gite Côte de la Montagne

$$–$$$$ Haute-Ville Spacious rooms with view on the St. Lawrence River, located in a luxuriously renovated house built in 1722. 54 côte de la Montagne. ☎ *877-778-8977* or *418-266-2165. Fax: 418-266-1535 Internet:* www.quebecweb.com/gitecotedelamontagne.

Manoir-sur-le-Cap

$$ Haute-Ville A totally renovated inn near the Jardin des Gouverneurs park with exposed brick walls and wood floors. 9 rue Ste-Geneviève. ☎ *418-694-1987. Fax: 418-627-7405. Internet:* www.manoir-sur-le-cap.com.

Index of Accommodations by Neighborhood

Vieux-Québec/Haute-Ville
Château Bellevue ($–$$)
Château Cap-Diamant ($$)
Château de Pierre ($$)
Chez Hubert ($)
Fairmont Le Château Frontenac ($$–$$$$)
Gite Côte de la Montagne ($$–$$$$)
Hôtel Clarendon ($–$$$)
Hôtel du Vieux-Québec ($$–$$$)
Maison Ste-Ursule ($)
Manoir-sur-le-Cap ($$)
Manoir Victoria ($$–$$$$)

Vieux-Québec/Basse-Ville
Auberge St-Pierre ($$–$$$$)
Dominion 1912 ($$$–$$$$)
Hôtel Belley ($–$$)

Hôtel Le St-Paul ($$)
Le Priori ($–$$)

Grande-Allée
Auberge du Quartier ($)
Château Laurier ($$–$$$$)
Hôtel Loew's Le Concorde ($$–$$$$)
Manoir Lafayette ($$)
Relais Charles-Alexandre ($$)

Boulevard René-Levesque
Delta Québec ($$)
Hilton International Québec ($$–$$$)

Avenue Cartier
Couettes et Café Toast ($)
Le Krieghoff B&B ($)

Index of Accommodations by Price

$$$$

Auberge St-Pierre (Basse-Ville)
Château Laurier (Grande-Allée)
Dominion 1912 (Basse-Ville)
Fairmont Le Château Frontenac
 (Haute-Ville)
Hôtel Loew's Le Concorde
 (Grande-Allée)

$$$

Gite Côte de la Montagne (Haute-Ville)
Hilton International Québec (boule-
 vard René-Levesque)
Hôtel Clarendon (Haute-Ville)
Hôtel du Vieux-Québec (Haute-Ville)
Manoir Victoria (Haute-Ville)

$$

Château Bellevue (Haute-Ville)
Château Cap-Diamant (Haute-Ville)

Château de Pierre (Haute-Ville)
Delta Québec (boulevard
 René-Levesque)
Hôtel Belley (Basse-Ville)
Hôtel Le St-Paul (Basse-Ville)
Le Priori (Basse-Ville)
Manoir Lafayette (Grande-Allée)
Manoir-sur-le-Cap (Haute-Ville)
Relais Charles-Alexandre
 (Grande-Allée)

$

Auberge du Quartier (Grande-Allée)
Chez Hubert (Haute-Ville)
Couettes et Café Toast (avenue
 Cartier)
Le Krieghoff B&B (avenue Cartier)
Maison Ste-Ursule (Haute-Ville)

Chapter 17

Dining and Snacking in Québec City

. . . .

In This Chapter

▶ Getting to know the local dining scene

▶ Discovering Québec City's best restaurants

▶ Finding great snacks and light meals

. . . .

French, French, and more French. That's what you can expect to eat in the heart of historic New France — and, fortunately, Québec City has plenty of great French restaurants. But if you're not a fan of frogs' legs, don't worry: Québeckers are enthusiastic about all categories of culinary delights. You can find everything to satisfy your palate, from sushi to pizza and pasta.

You can find great places to eat all over the city, but in this chapter, we give you the best choices in and around the Old City and Grande-Allée. We just figure that's where you'll probably be when you get hungry.

What's Hot Now

Where restaurants are concerned, Québec City has two faces. On the one hand, the city caters to tourists looking for a trip back in history, so a lot of restaurants serve traditional French and Québec food. Don't think traditional means bland or boring, though. Québeckers typically serve both their homegrown fare and other, French-inspired meals with panache.

On the other hand, Québeckers are pretty cutting edge about their food. The Old City isn't overflowing with ethnic eateries, but you can find interesting Italian and Asian-inspired restaurants, as well as sushi, particularly along Grande-Allée, where everything gets a little more modern.

Québec City Dining and Snacking

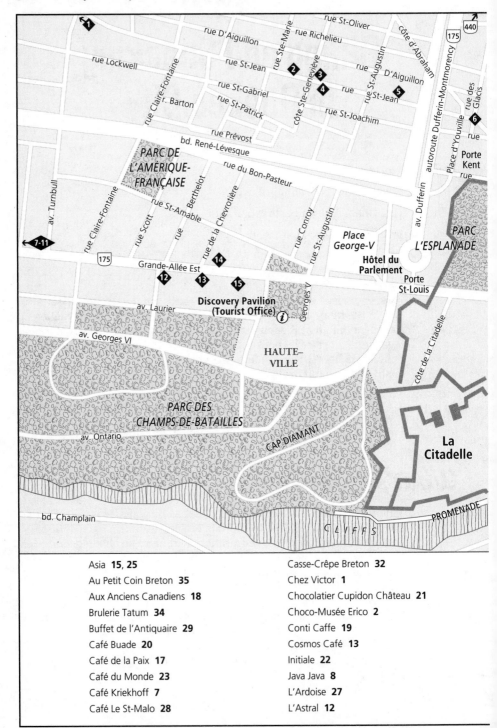

Asia **15, 25**	Casse-Crêpe Breton **32**
Au Petit Coin Breton **35**	Chez Victor **1**
Aux Anciens Canadiens **18**	Chocolatier Cupidon Château **21**
Brulerie Tatum **34**	Choco-Musée Erico **2**
Buffet de l'Antiquaire **29**	Conti Caffe **19**
Café Buade **20**	Cosmos Café **13**
Café de la Paix **17**	Initiale **22**
Café du Monde **23**	Java Java **8**
Café Kriekhoff **7**	L'Ardoise **27**
Café Le St-Malo **28**	L'Astral **12**

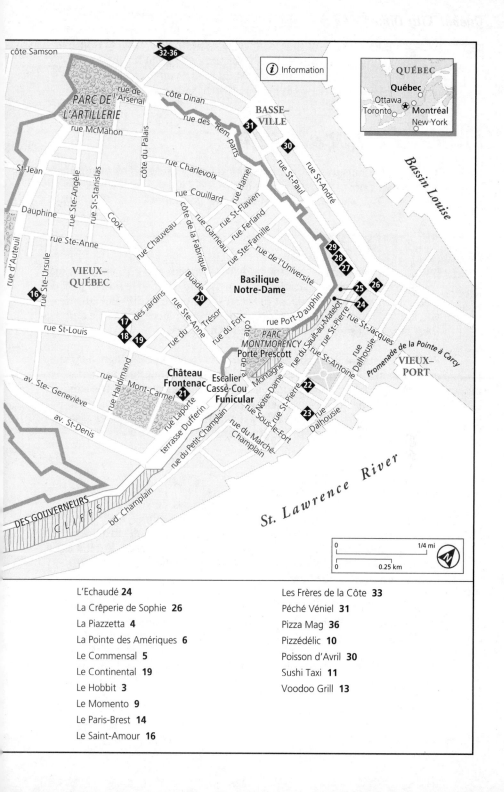

Our advice for getting the most out of eating in this city? See our recommendations in this chapter and treat eating like a tourist activity on par with taking a tour of the Old City or spending a couple of hours in the Musée de la Civilisation. Take your time and go in for the experience, not just to fill your stomach. At its best, food is as close as you'll find to an art form here — at least in North America.

Where the Locals Eat

If you think locals avoid Québec City's touristy areas, think again. Many of the city's finest restaurants are in the Old City and on the Grande-Allée, and locals come here to indulge in a good meal.

The Old City

Both the Upper and Lower Cities are full of quaint and charming eating spots that serve some variation of French food, from cafe fare to bistro meals and formal dining. Most of these serve quite traditional cuisine — you know, French onion soup; crêpes (in crêpe places); mussels and fries; steak frites; and lamb, pork, and fish dishes.

Prices at restaurants in the Old City aren't astronomically high, as you may have suspected, but you can save money by shopping around a little. Almost all restaurants in the Old City display menus in the window with prices. Check them out before you enter. Many offer a complete meal menu (table d'hôte), and they're usually a good deal. Many also offer a special lunch menu, and these are usually a *very* good deal.

Grande-Allée

As you step outside the Porte St-Louis and head down Grande-Allée, the restaurants get a little more modern. In the summer, after just a five-minute walk outside the gate, you see a broad boulevard lined with rows of tables on each side. It looks like one huge terrace, but it's actually the combined effect of patios of dozens of different restaurants, crammed together for blocks.

You can find just about every type of food here, from fine French dining to traditional Québec cooking, plus Italian restaurants, burger joints, bagel and sandwich spots, sushi restaurants, pizzerias, and seafood and steak places. Stroll along and read the menus, which are usually displayed near the sidewalk. Or just cut to the chase and head to the places we recommend in this chapter.

Québec City's Best Restaurants

In this section, you find our top choices for dining in Québec City.

The dollar sign ratings represent the price of one dinner (appetizer, entrée, and dessert), including drinks and tip, and correspond with the following price ranges:

$	Less than C$10 (US$7.50)
$$	C$10–C$20 (US$7.50–US$15)
$$$	C$20–C$30 (US$15–US$22.50)
$$$$	More than C$30 (US$22.50 or higher)

You can cut your dining costs in a variety of ways. We explain these techniques in Chapter 10, and a lot of them apply to Québec City, as well.

In the heady tourist atmosphere of Québec City at high season, the best restaurants fill up quickly. Make your dinner reservations at least in the afternoon of the same day, and preferably the night before. In the off-season (Oct–Apr) — when the tourist frenzy in Québec City cedes to an atmosphere of barely discernable activity in the streets — you can get a table in most establishments on the spot. And they'll be happy to see you.

Asia

$$–$$$ Grande-Allée   ASIAN

This extremely popular restaurant is a great place to turn if you're getting tired of French food (not likely, but it happens). Asia offers a wide variety of dishes with Thai, Vietnamese, and Indochinese influences. Its specialty is grilled meats, but the restaurant also offers seafood plates, an excellent red curry chicken, and marinated shrimp and sautéed pork, plus Thai soup and pad Thai. Asia has a second location in the Basse-Ville.

585 Grande-Allée Est. ☎ *418-522-0818. Basse-Ville location: 89 rue Sault-au-Matelot (*☎ *418-692-3799). Reservations recommended. Table d'hôte: C$23–C$25 (US$17–US$19). AE, DC, MC, V. Open: Lunch and dinner daily.*

Aux Anciens Canadiens

$$$$ Haute-Ville   QUEBEC

This restaurant brings historic Québec all together. It's housed in the oldest private dwelling in the Haute-Ville, the Maison Jacquet, built in 1690. Aux Anciens Canadiens is named after one of its early owners' novels. It translates into Canadians of Old. The food is authentic Québec cuisine, from old standards like pork and beans, ham, *tourtière* (meat pie), caribou, and blueberry pie to more recently discovered delicacies like duck from the Eastern Townships (see Chapter 14). The servers are dressed in period costumes to complete the effect. If the price makes you hesitate, try it out at lunch, when the price of the *table d'hôte* is quite reasonable.

34 rue St-Louis (corner rue Haldimand). ☎ *418-692-1627. Reservations recommended. Main courses: C$28–C$54 (US$21–US$40). AE, DC, MC, V. Open: Lunch and dinner daily.*

Buffet de l'Antiquaire

$–$$ Basse-Ville   QUEBEC

Strolling by the antiques shops along rue St-Paul, you may not even notice this closet-sized restaurant at first. It's worth a stop, though. This is where locals go to eat authentic Québec specialties like *poutine* (fries with gravy and cheese curd) and *fèves au lard* (Québec's version of pork and beans: all lard, no meat). Meat dishes, like steak frites, or lighter meals, such as soup, sandwiches, and salads, are also on the menu. This place is definitely off the tourist track — while being right in the middle of the action — plus it's cheap.

95 rue St-Paul (near rue Sault-au-Matelot). ☎ *418-692-2661. Main course: Under C$12 (US$9). AE, MC, V. Open: Lunch and dinner daily.*

Café de la Paix

$$$$ Haute-Ville   FRENCH

It looks small and unpresuming from the street, but if you want high-quality, classic French cooking in a totally classic setting, this is the place. You'll find frogs' legs, as well as beef sirloin, Chateaubriand, rabbit, scallops, steak tartre, lobster, duck, and (need we say it?) French onion soup. The atmosphere is dark and cozy. Service is not genteel, but the career waiters — mostly surly older men — do know their stuff. You feel like you're in France.

44 rue des Jardins (between Donnacona and rue St-Louis). ☎ *418-692-1430. Reservations recommended. Main courses: C$22–C$40 (US$17–US$30). AE, MC, V. Open: Lunch and dinner daily.*

Café du Monde

$$–$$$$ Basse-Ville   FRENCH BISTRO

This legendary Québec City bistro recently moved from its small, Parisian-style digs on rue Dalhousie to a big, new, glamorous location in the *términal des croisières* (cruise liner terminal) facing the port. The two walls facing the river are made entirely of glass, so the riverview is exceptional. And, we're happy to say, the food is as good as ever. Famous for *brasserie* fare like mussels, steak frites, sausage, and duck confit, Café du Monde also serves up sandwiches, salads, and seafood selections. Service is friendly, but waiters don't have time to linger at your table. Reservations are not taken for the terrace (with river views), so get there early if you want to eat outside.

84 rue Dalhousie (near the cruise liner terminal on the Old Port). ☎ *418-692-4455. Reservations required; not accepted for the terrace. Main courses: C$12–C$19 (US$8.65–US$12). AE, DC, MC, V. Open: Lunch and dinner daily, brunch Sat–Sun, 9:30 a.m.–2 p.m.*

Casse-Crêpe Breton
$–$$ Haute-Ville   CRÊPES

This little place on rue St-Jean is extremely popular, both with locals and tourists, and you almost always encounter a line at lunchtime. It's worth the short wait. The crêpes are perfect and very filling, and you can have them as main courses, dessert, or both. A long list of potential main course fillings includes ham, cheese, mushrooms, asparagus, eggs, and more, and dessert options range from chocolate to fruit to plain sugar. You can watch them being prepared in the open kitchen. Service is friendly but don't dawdle: Other people are waiting for your seat!

1136 rue St-Jean (near rue Garneau). ☎ *418-692-0438. Reservations not accepted. Main courses: Under C$6 (US$4.50). MC, V. Open: Daily 7 a.m.–1 a.m.*

Conti Caffe
$$–$$$ Haute-Ville   ITALIAN

With its stone walls and fashionable modern decor, this new Italian bistro definitely stands out among the more traditional eateries on rue St-Louis. It's a great spot for lunch — you can have a three-course meal here with coffee for C$10 (US$7.50). At night, the menu gets a little more sophisticated, with additions like veal medallions, beef sirloin, and even escargot to the pasta and pizza selections. Pizza is of the thin crust variety, with imaginative toppings.

26 rue St-Louis (next to its owner, Le Continental Restaurant, which has the same address). ☎ *418-694-9995. Main courses: C$10–C$28 (US$7.50–US$21). AE, DC, MC, V. Open: Lunch and dinner daily.*

Initiale
$$$$ Basse-Ville   FRENCH

This is *the* place to go in Québec City for fine French cuisine in an elegant, rather formal setting. Located in a former bank building, its decor is classical and modern, with high ceilings and decorative moldings. Like most skilled, up-to-the-minute chefs these days, Yvan Lebrun focuses on local, seasonal ingredients. Plates range from French classics such as grilled salmon, lamb, lobster, and filet mignon to slightly more adventuresome dishes like foie gras and pigeon. Give the Québec cheeses a try between your main course and dessert. Expect service to be attentive and none too quick. And the point here is savoring, not saving.

54 rue St-Pierre (corner Côte de la Montagne). ☎ *418-694-1818. Reservations recommended. Main courses: C$14–C$39 (US$10–US$28). AE DC, MC, V. Open: Lunch Mon–Fri and dinner daily.*

L'Ardoise

$$–$$$ **Basse-Ville**   **FRENCH BISTRO**

The dishes served in French bistros are what the French consider comfort food. That's what you'll get at L'Ardoise, which caters equally to locals and tourists with its welcoming casual atmosphere and hearty dishes. Specialties include mussels and fries — with seconds of mussels for free — grilled blood sausage, veal liver, rib steak, and fish selections. Fish lovers with an appetite should try the Royale de la mer (Royal Sea) dish of salmon, shrimp, mussels, and scallops in a rich sauce. This is a nice place to hang out and sip an after-dinner espresso.

71 rue St-Paul (near rue des Navigateurs). ☎ *418-694-0213. Reservations recommended for dinner. Main courses: C$12–C$17 (US$8.65–US$12). AE, DC, MC, V. Open: Lunch Mon–Fri, dinner daily, brunch Sat–Sun.*

L'Astral

$$$–$$$$ **Grande-Allée**   **FRENCH**

With a capacity for a thousand guests, this rotating restaurant on top of the Loew's hotel on the Grande-Allée is obviously not the place to come for intimacy. But the view is as good as it gets, stretching dozens of miles across the Plains of Abraham and the Old City all the way to the Laurentian Mountains. For such a huge place, the food is, surprisingly, very good — a mix of mainly French-based plates with Asian and Cajun touches. Prices are reasonable and if you calculate the view, the whole experience is pretty easy on your wallet. Sunday brunches here are quite lavish. Just make sure the weather is clear before you go.

1225 cours du Général-de-Montcalm (corner Grande-Allée). ☎ *418-647-2222. Reservations recommended. Main courses: C$20–C$44 (US$15–US$33). AE, DC, DISC, MC, V. Open: Lunch, Mon–Sat, dinner daily, Sun brunch.*

L'Echaudé

$$–$$$ **Basse-Ville**   **FRENCH BISTRO**

This is one of the slicker French bistros in the Basse-Ville, with its checker-tiled floor, zinc bar, and Art Deco decor. The food, however, is very good and reasonably priced. Specialties include grilled meats, fishes, bouillabaisse seafood stew, fish selections, steak and salmon tartare, steak frites, and ravioli. Drinkwise, L'Echaudé distinguishes itself by carrying 24 brands of beer and 125 different wines, including 10 wines by the glass.

73 rue du Sault-au-Matelot (near rue St-Paul). ☎ *418-692-1229. Reservations recommended. Main courses: C$15–C$29 (US$11–US$22). AE, DC, MC, V. Open: Lunch Mon–Fri and Sun, dinner daily.*

Le Continental

$$$$ Haute-Ville   CONTINENTAL

One of the oldest restaurants in Québec City, Le Continental has been a hangout for Québec's political class for the last five decades. Don't expect any great surprises, and you won't be disappointed — you get a classic menu with an atmosphere to match. Plates range from crab in hollandaise sauce to steak tartare and duck à l'orange. Waiters are attentive, courteous, and discreet — as they should be when they spend their days inadvertently listening in on gossip among Québec's political elite.

26 rue St-Louis. ☎ *418-694-9995. Reservations recommended. Main courses: C$33–C$41 (US$25–US$31). AE, DC, MC, V. Open: Lunch Mon–Fri, dinner daily.*

Le Momento

$$–$$$$ Grande-Allée   CONTEMPORARY ITALIAN

This modern-feeling restaurant has a trattoria feel and offers sophisticated Italian cooking with a emphasis on fresh ingredients — definitely not one of those places serving huge portions of pasta with stick-to-your-ribs meat sauce. Instead, you choose from eight California-style thin-crust pizzas with dressing like marinated chicken and sun-dried tomatoes; pasta selections with savory and interesting sauces; and heartier plates like osso buco and lamb dishes.

1144 av. Cartier (corner rue Aberdeen). ☎ *418-647-1313. Reservations recommended for dinner. Main courses: C$15–C$21 (US$11–US$16). AE, DC, MC, V. Open: Lunch Mon–Fri, dinner daily. Wheelchair accessible.*

Le Paris-Brest

$$$–$$$$ Grande-Allée   CONTEMPORARY FRENCH

Considered one of the best tables in Québec City, this fashionable restaurant offers French food with modern flair. The menu includes fancy items such as Dijon rib of beef and milk veal with Brie cheese, but it also includes higher-brow French classics, like lamb cutlets, scallops, steak tartare, and sweetbreads. Lighter selections include pasta dishes with seafood. Atmosphere is fairly informal, but neat.

590 Grande-Allée Est (corner rue de la Chevrotière). ☎ *418-529-2243. Reservations recommended. Main courses: C$26–C$30 (US$19–US$22). AE, DC, MC, V. Open: Lunch Mon–Fri, dinner daily.*

Le Saint-Amour

$$$$ **Haute-Ville** **CONTEMPORARY FRENCH**

Tucked in among the many B&Bs along rue Ste-Ursule, Le Saint-Amour offers a truly gastronomic experience. The decor is elegant and romantic, with lace curtains, flickering candles, and a glass roof for star-gazing lovers. Award-winning chef Jean-Luc Boulay presents delicacies with a regional flavor, like lobster from Québec's Gaspé area, caribou steak, and duck from the Eastern Townships (discussed in Chapter 14), and tops it off with selections like foie gras, served with fig compote and caviar. Expect the meal to move slowly — the waiters assume you want to take your time. If you're in a hurry, let them know.

48 rue Ste-Ursule. ☎ *418-694-0667. Reservations recommended. Main courses: C$24–C$34 (US$18–US$25). AE, DC, MC, V. Open: Lunch Mon–Fri, dinner daily.*

Les Frères de la Côte

$$ **Haute-Ville** **ITALIAN**

This lively pizzeria-cafe on rue St-Jean is a favorites of locals and a great place to bring kids. With 17 kinds of pizza — cooked in wood-burning ovens — plus pasta dishes and platters of meat and fish brochettes, you're sure to find something for even the pickiest pint-sized eater. The music is loud practically all the time, but the high spirits that reign here are infectious. Also open for Sunday brunch.

1190 rue St-Jean. ☎ *418-692-5445. Reservations recommended. Main courses: C$13–C$14 (US$10–US$11). AE, DC, MC, V. Open: Lunch and dinner daily, Sun brunch.*

Péché Véniel

$$–$$$ **Basse-Ville** **FRENCH BISTRO**

For good food in a warm and inviting atmosphere, this informal little corner bistro off rue St-Paul is hard to beat. The menu consists of classic French *brasserie* food like steak frites and mussels, and some traditional Québec cuisine, including smoked meat sandwiches and a very filling and satisfying version of Québec's famous Lac St-Jean meat pie. Lunch specials (around C$10/US$7.50) include soup, a main course, dessert, and coffee and are an excellent deal. Service is just what it should be. A nice place for a leisurely lunch that won't break the bank.

233 rue St-Paul. ☎ *418-692-5642. Main courses: C$10–C$15 (US$7.50–US$11). Reservations recommended. AE, DC, MC, V. Open: Lunch and dinner daily.*

Poisson d'Avril

$$$–$$$$ Basse-Ville   SEAFOOD

One of the few seafood restaurants in Québec City, the decor is straight out of Cape Cod: nautical motifs, hanging model ships, and marine prints. The expansive menu includes starters of mussels, crab, and smoked salmon, escargot, oysters, and fish soup. Main courses include combo plates with scallops and seasonal fish. The restaurant also serves mussels and shrimp; straightforward salmon, cod, and tuna plates; southern French bouillabaisse; and, of course, lobster. Prices are probably comparable to what you'd pay in Cape Cod, too: not cheap, but not outrageous.

115 quai Saint-André (in the Old Port, near rue St-Thomas). ☎ *418-692-1010. Reservations recommended. Main courses: C$17–C$30 (US$13–US$23). AE, DC, MC. V. Open: Lunch and dinner daily.*

Sushi Taxi

$$–$$$ Grande-Allée   SUSHI

Québec City is not exactly a sushi town, but this small chain has garnered a loyal following of locals for its good, reasonably price offerings. The avenue Cartier restaurant recently expanded to add some atmosphere to the menu with 30 tables (30 more on the terrace in the summer) in a Zen-like decor. If you're unfamiliar with the art of eating raw fish, Sushi Taxi has a Discovery Plate with a bit of maki, nigiri, temaki, and sashimi.

813 av. Cartier. ☎ *418-529-0068. Table d'hôte: Lunch C$15 (US$11), dinner C$26 (US$20). AE, MC, V. Open: Lunch Mon–Fri, dinner daily.*

Voodoo Grill

$$–$$$$ Grande-Allée   ASIAN/FRENCH

Quite a hot spot on Grande-Allée, this restaurant adds a bar atmosphere to its lounge decor, which results in a restaurant with a post-modern Middle Eastern decor with African and designer influences. The menu is as variously inspired, with everything from Singapore chicken and Bankok soup to Volcano steak, with plenty of grilled fish selections and some sushi tossed in for good measure. Although the concept may sound a little unfocused, the food is surprisingly good, well prepared, and beautifully presented. Just be ready for some entertainment of dubious quality and mysterious origin — like belly dancers — and count on loud music. Servers were evidently hired more for looks than skill, but they do the job.

575 Grande-Allée Est. ☎ *418-647-2000. Reservations recommended. Main courses: C$16–C$30 (US$12–US$22). AE, DC, MC, V. Open: Dinner daily.*

Index of restaurants by neighborhood

Grande-Allée

Asia (Asian, $$–$$$)

L'Astral (French, $$$–$$$$)

Le Momento (Contemporary Italian, $$–$$$$)

Le Paris-Brest (Contemporary French, $$$–$$$$)

Sushi Taxi (Sushi, $$–$$$$)

Voodoo Grill (Asian/French, $$–$$$$)

Basse-Ville

Asia (Asian, $$–$$$)

Buffet de l'Antiquaire (Québec, $–$$)

Café du Monde (French Bistro, $$–$$$$)

Initiale (French, $$$$)

L'Ardoise (French Bistro, $$–$$$$)

L'Echaudé (French Bistro, $$–$$$$)

Péché Véniel (French Bistro, $$–$$$)

Poisson d'Avril (Seafood, $$$–$$$$)

Haute-Ville

Aux Anciens Canadiens (Québec, $$$$)

Café de la Paix (French, $$$$)

Casse-Crêpe Breton (Crêpes, $–$$)

Conti Caffé (Italian, $$–$$$)

Le Continental (Continental)

Le Saint-Amour (Contemporary French, $$$$)

Les Frères de la Côte (Italian, $$)

Index of restaurants by cuisine

Asian

Asia (Haute-Ville, Basse-Ville, $$–$$$)

Voodoo Grill (Grande-Allée, $$–$$$$)

Contemporary French

Le Paris-Brest (Grande-Allée, $$$–$$$$)

Le Saint-Amour (Haute-Ville, $$$$)

Contemporary Italian

Le Momento (Grande-Allée, $$–$$$$)

Continental

Le Continental (Haute-Ville, $$$$)

Crêpes

Casse-Crêpe Breton (Haute-Ville, $–$$)

French

Café de la Paix (Haute-Ville, $$$$)

Initiale (Basse-Ville, $$$$)

L'Astral (Grande-Allée, $$$–$$$$)

French Bistro

Café de Monde (Basse-Ville, $$–$$$$)

L'Ardoise (Basse-Ville, $$–$$$$)

L'Echaudé (Basse-Ville, $$–$$$$)

Péché Véniel (Basse-Ville, $$–$$$)

Québec

Aux Anciens Canadiens ($$$$)

Buffet de l'Antiquaire ($–$$)

Sushi

Sushi Taxi (Grande-Allée, $$–$$$)

Italian

Conti Caffé (Haute-Ville, $$–$$$)

Frères de la Côte (Haute-Ville, $$)

Seafood

Poisson d'Avril (Basse-Ville, $$$–$$$$)

Index of restaurants by price

$

Casse-Crêpe Breton (Haute-Ville, Crêpes)
Buffet de l'Antiquaire (Basse-Ville, Québec)

$$

Café Conti (Haute-Ville, Italian)
Frères de la Côte (Haute-Ville, Italian)
Péché Véniel (Basse-Ville, French Bistro

$$$

Asia (Haute-Ville, Basse-Ville, Asian)
Café du Monde (Basse-Ville, French Bistro)
L'Ardoise (Basse-Ville, French Bistro)
L'Echaudé (Basse-Ville, French Bistro)

Le Momento (Grande-Allée, Contemporary Italian)
Poisson d'Avril (Basse-Ville, Seafood)
Sushi Taxi (Grande-Allée, Sushi)
Voodoo Grill (Asian/French, Grande-Allée)

$$$$

Aux Anciens Canadiens (Haute-Ville, Québec)
Café de la Paix (Haute-Ville, French)
Initiale (Basse-Ville, French)
L'Astral (Grande-Allée, French)
Le Continental (Continental)
Le Paris-Brest (Grande-Allée, Contemporary French)
Le Saint-Amour (Haute-Ville, Contemporary French)

Québec City's Best Snacks

As a tourist town, Québec City is loaded with eating opportunities of all types and qualities. You're more likely to feel the anxiety over the abundance — rather than a lack — of eating options packed into this small area. The following sections list snacks and light food and should help you narrow the field when you want to grab a coffee, a sweet, or a bite to eat.

Cafes for coffee and more

Cafes aren't just for coffee, although you can usually get an excellent cup of joe at the following recommended places. You can often get light meals at these cafes, too, including soups, salads, and sandwiches.

- **Brulerie Tatum,** 1084 rue St-Jean (☎ 418-692-3900), specializes in its own roasts of coffee and serves tasty snacks like *croque monsieurs* (a toasted roll with ham, tomato, and cheese).

- **Café Buade,** 31 rue de Buade (☎ 418-692-3909), serves coffee and lighter meals like pizza and pasta in a classic French cafe atmosphere.

- **Café Kriekhoff,** 1091 av. Cartier (☎ 418-521-3711), serves light tasty meals including salads, quiche, and soup in a down-to-earth, French-style cafe. In summer, a covered terrace offers pleasant street views.

- **Café Le St-Malo,** 75 rue St-Paul (☎ 418-692-2004), with its charming sidewalk terrace and nautical decor, is a great place for a drink and a light bite.

- **Le Hobbit,** 700 rue St-Jean (☎ 418-647-2677), has a cafe on the first floor that serves coffee, while meals are served on the second floor.

- **Java Java,** 1112 av. Cartier (☎ 418-522-5282), is a fun place for coffee or snacks like panini sandwiches or burger and fries.

Pizza and burgers

Québec is even less of a burger town than Montréal, so we have only two good burger joints to recommend, but they really are great, despite being members of a rare species. If you're looking for a quick meal, you'll find more choices in the pizza category.

- **Chez Victor,** 143 rue St-Jean (☎ 418-529-7702), comes up with new and imaginative types of burgers every day.

- **Cosmos Café,** 575 Grande-Allée Est (☎ 418-640-0606), right in the thick of the Grande-Allée action, serves respectable burgers and very good breakfasts.

- **La Piazzetta,** 707 rue St-Jean (☎ 418-529-7489), a Québec chain, was one of the forerunners in the local trend toward European-style pizza. Pizzas have interesting toppings and very thin crusts.

- **Pizzédélic,** 1145 av. Cartier (☎ 418-523-7171), puts a psychedelic spin on the thin-pizza concept, offering one-serving pizzas with original toppings. Salads are great.

- **Pizza Mag,** 363 rue St-Paul (☎ 418-692-1910), offers 20 different types of more traditional, thick-crust pizza, some with unusual toppings like leeks, escargots, and smoked fish.

- **La Pointe des Amériques,** 964 rue St-Jean (☎ 418-694-1199), serves gourmet pizza, with all the combinations of toppings you can imagine.

For chocolate lovers

If you have a hankering for something tastier than the convenience-story quality of your favorite brown substance, you have two excellent places to go for chocolate in the Old City. You can find French, Belgian, and Swiss varieties at **Chocolatier Cupidon Château,** 1 rue des Carrières (behind the Château Frontenac; ☎ **418-692-3340**). At **Choco-Musée Erico,** 634 rue St-Jean (☎ **418-524-2122**), high-quality chocolate comes in some very interesting forms.

All crêpes, all the time

It's hard to imagine visiting Québec City without eating crêpes at least once. They are a great option for lunch, because they are cheap and relatively quick. And no worries — you can really fill up on them, especially if you order them for your main course and dessert. We give you our top choices in this section, but honestly, crêpes are pretty hard to screw up (unless you order them in a place that doesn't specialize in them). They are just stuffed pancakes, after all.

Our first choice is the **Casse-Crêpe Breton,** 1136 rue St-Jean (☎ **418-692-0438**), both for its bustling atmosphere and delicious fresh dishes. In the (very likely) event that it is full, try **Au Petit Coin Breton,** just down the street at 1029 rue St-Jean (☎ **418-694-0758**). The crêpes are just as good, although the atmosphere is not as fun. In the Basse-Ville, **La Créperie de Sophie,** 48 rue St-Paul (☎ **418-694-9595**) is a good choice, although more reputed for presentation than actual taste.

A vegetarian outpost

Vegetarians are not exactly in the promised land in this town of blood sausage and veal scallops. There is really only one restaurant in the Old City that caters exclusively to vegetarians. **Le Commensal,** 860 rue St-Jean (☎ **418-647-3733**), serves excellent buffet-style vegetarian food that is sold by weight.

Chapter 18

Exploring Québec City

● ●

In This Chapter

▶ Exploring Québec City's best attractions

▶ Seeing the city by guided tour

▶ Discovering Québec City's historical highlights

● ●

*Q*uébec City's most interesting attractions are conveniently packed
together in an area that you could probably cross by foot in half
an hour if you walked straight without stopping. Of course, you have
many, many reasons to stop, so you're likely to linger a bit longer than
30 minutes. Half a day will give you a good overall impression, but several days still won't be enough to see absolutely everything. In this
chapter, you find the top sights you want to try to hit.

Exploring Québec City's Top Sights from A o Z

There's plenty to do in Québec City. The past comes alive here because
many of the attractions recount the history of this fortified city — the
only one in North America.

Basilique Notre-Dame-de-Québec
Haute-Ville

The site of the oldest Christian parish north of Mexico, Québec City's
founder Samuel de Champlain originally chose this spot for a chapel back
in 1633. Over the centuries, the Basilique Notre-Dame was built, torn
down, burned, and expanded into roughly its present, neo-baroque style
in the 1920s. The light inside is quite inspiring, combining the effects of
candlelight and two floors of stain-glassed windows depicting scenes of
evangelists, arch angels, saints, and the Virgin Mary. Opinions are mixed
about *Feux Sacrés* (Sacred Fire), a 30-minute light and sound show on five
centuries of Québec history that plays outside the basilica during the
summer. Some say it's impressive; others say it's tacky. You be the judge.

Québec City Attractions

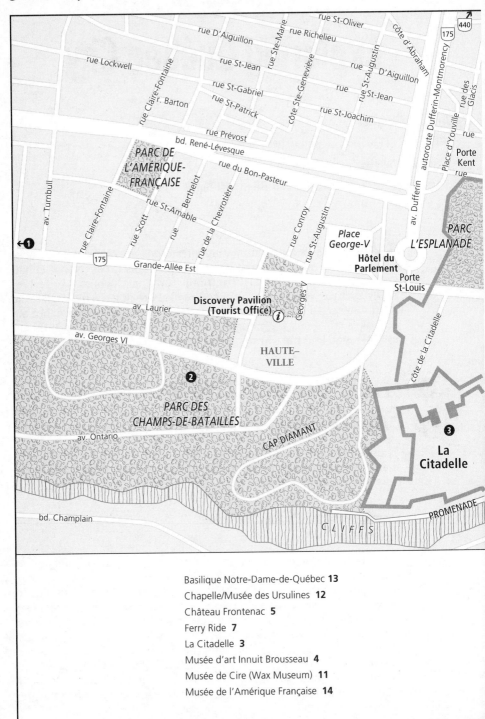

Basilique Notre-Dame-de-Québec **13**

Chapelle/Musée des Ursulines **12**

Château Frontenac **5**

Ferry Ride **7**

La Citadelle **3**

Musée d'art Innuit Brousseau **4**

Musée de Cire (Wax Museum) **11**

Musée de l'Amérique Française **14**

Musée de la Civilisation **9**

Musée du Fort **10**

Musée du Québec **1**

Parc des Champs de Bataille **2**

Place de l'Artillerie **15**

Place Royale **8**

Terrasse Dufferin **6**

20 rue Buade (at corner of côte de la Fabrique). ☎ *418-694-0665. Admission to basilica and guide tours: free. Basilique open: Daily 7:30 a.m.–4:30 p.m. Feux Sacrés admission: C$7.50 (US$5.50) adults; C$5 (US$3.75) seniors, students, children 6 and older; children under 6 free. May–Oct, hourly from 3:30–8:30 p.m.*

Chapelle/Musée des Ursulines
Haute-Ville

The French nun Marie de l'Incarnation founded the Ursulines order in Québec when she arrived in 1630; the convent was built in 1642. The chapel came much later, in 1902, but much of what you see in the interior dates to 1732. The museum and chapel interior are packed with artifacts, including Louis XIII furniture, a painting that was removed from Paris during the French Revolution, and altar cloths and church robes that the Ursulines nuns wove with gold thread. General Montcalm, who led the French troops when they lost Québec to the English in 1759, was originally buried here.

12 rue Donnacona (corner rue des Jardins). ☎ *418-692-0694. Admission: Chapel free; Museum C$5 (US$3.75) adults, C$4 (US$3) seniors, C$3 (US$2.25) students, C$2 (US$1.50) children 12–16, children under 11 free. Open: Tues–Sat, 10 a.m.–noon and 1–5 p.m., Sun 1–5 p.m. Hours vary seasonally.*

Château Frontenac
Haute-Ville

If one piece of architecture symbolizes Québec City, this is it. In Chapter 16, we recommended that you stay at this castle-like hotel, but in case you can't afford to actually spend the night, take a few minutes to wander inside. You can't really miss it. Just look for the pointy, green, copper roof rising above the cliff overlooking the St. Lawrence River. The château was built by the Canadian Pacific Railway in the early 1890s, and although it was inspired by the châteaux of the Loire Valley in France, it was designed by an American architect, Bruce Price. The inside is truly regal, with wood paneling, imposing antiques, and dainty boutiques surrounding the reception area. Guided 50-minute tours are given from May to October.

1 rue des Carrières (facing the terrasse Dufferin). ☎ *418-692-3861. Admission: Free for a peek; tours: C$6.50 (US$5) adults, C$5.50 (US$4) seniors, and C$3.75 (US$3) children 6–16, free for kids under 6. Tours daily on the hour, 10 a.m.–6 p.m. Mon–Fri, 1–5 p.m. Sat–Sun. Reservations required; call* ☎ *418-691-2166.*

La Citadelle
Grande-Allée

Much of Québec City's history is dominated by the battles various empires waged to get control of this prime trading port on the St. Lawrence River.

La Citadelle gives you a taste of the stormy military past — even though it was never actually used during a war. Still, you get an idea of the stakes of a possible enemy attack when you visit this star-shaped fortress comprising 25 separate buildings. First built by the French in the late 1700s, then rebuilt by the English in the 1830s, La Citadelle now houses a French Canadian regiment of the Canadian army. Notable features include a powder house and a prison. The guided tour is a little dry and perhaps better suited to military history buffs, but the changing of the guards, usually once a day, is pretty cool.

1 côte de la Citadelle (enter off rue St-Louis, leaving the St-Louis Gate in the direction of Grande-Allée). ☎ 418-694-2815. Internet: www.lacitadelle.qc.ca. *Admission: C$6 (US$4.50) adults, C$5 (US$4) seniors, C$3 (U$2.25) children 7–17, free for persons with disabilities and children under 7. Open: Daily 9 a.m.– 6 p.m. July 1–Labour Day; hours vary off-season. Guided tours leave on the hour.*

Musée d'art Inuit Brousseau
Haute-Ville

If you find yourself tired of the full-French experience in Québec City, this is an excellent, though less-known museum that explores another facet of Canadian history. Inuit art, such paintings and soapstone carvings, became very popular in Canada in the 1960s and '70s. This museum highlights the most famous artists in the communities. Started by renowned collector Raymond Brousseau (and located just off his gallery on rue St-Louis), the museum contains some mind-boggling sculptures — some for sale, some just for show, but you'll be moved all the same.

39 rue St-Louis. ☎ 418-694-1828. Admission: C$6 (US$4.50) adults, C$4 (US$3) seniors and students 13 and older, free for children 12 and under with adult. Open: Daily 9:30 a.m.–5 p.m.

Musée de l'Amérique Française
Haute-Ville

Housed in a former seminary built in 1663, this museum is an excellent place to get a French perspective on history. The museum is dedicated to showing the evolution of French culture and civilization in North America through the history of all seven French communities in the New World. The five floors of the museum contain 450,000 artifacts in all — everything from silverware and scientific instruments to paintings, engravings, parchments, old and rare books, and even the first Egyptian mummy to be brought to North America. Descriptions are in both English and French.

2 côte de la Fabrique. ☎ 418-692-2843. Admission: C$4 (US$3) adults, C$3 (US$2.25) seniors and students over 16, C$1 (US75¢) children under 12. Open: Late June– Labour Day daily 9:30 a.m.–5 p.m.; Sept–mid-June Tues–Sun 10 a.m.–5 p.m. Guided tours available. Call for information.

Musée de la Civilisation
Basse-Ville

If you have time for only one major museum outing, this is the place. It won't teach you the most about the specific history of Québec City, but the permanent exhibits on daily life in the history of the province of Québec (called *Memoires,* or Memories) and on Canada's First Nations (called *Nous, les Premiéres Nations*) are totally captivating. While light on written explanations, the exhibits have objects displayed beautifully and sensibly. They draw visitors in and satisfy all their senses (except maybe smell), while doing a good job of illustrating two distinct cultures. Plan on spending about two hours here. An added bonus: On the second floor, there's a lovely, bright, and modern visitors lounge with computers where you can check your e-mail for free.

85 rue Dalhousie (corner of rue St-Antoine). ☎ *418-643-2158. Admission C$7 (US$5.25) adults, C$6 (US$4.50) seniors, C$4 (US$3) students over 16, C$2 (US$1.50) children 12–16, free for children under 12. Open: Late June–Labour Day daily 9:30 a.m.–6:30 p.m. Sept–June, Tues–Sun 10 a.m.–5 p.m.*

Parc des Champs-de-Bataille
Grande-Allée

If the Château Frontenac stands as a symbol of Québec City, this park is the symbol of tension between Canada's English and French populations. Québec's Battlefield Park is where General Montcalm led the French against General Wolfe and the English in the famous battle of the Plains of Abraham in 1759 (the English won; both generals died). While it's famous for a battle, the 108-hectare (267-acre) park is actually a rather idyllic place to stroll (with some 5,000 trees), not too far from the Grande-Allée. Locals like to cross-country ski here in the winter and rollerblade and bike in the summer. Summer also brings theater and musical performances. The park's **Maison de la Découverte** (Discovery Pavilion) explains the significance of the Plains of Abraham to Québec.

Discovery Pavilion, 835 av. Laurier. ☎ *418-648-4071. Internet:* www.ccbn-nbc. gc.ca. *Admission: Free. Park open 24 hours; Discovery Pavilion open: daily 9 a.m.–5 p.m.*

Place-Royale
Basse-Ville

This quaint cobblestone square, located on the spot where Champlain founded Québec in 1608, feels like a microcosm of Vieux-Québec. Right at the bottom of the Breakneck stairs, Place-Royale is dominated by the Notre-Dame-des-Victoires church, the oldest church in Canada built in

1688, which is small and rather plain but contains some lovely paintings and a large model boat suspended from the ceiling. This was a town marketplace during the seventeenth and eighteenth centuries. Now you can see a bust of French King Louis XIV, a copy of the original bust erected in 1686. All the buildings around the square have been restored, and you can souvenir shop to your heart's content in this part of the Basse-Ville. The **Centre d'Interpretation de Place-Royale** (Interpretation Center) explains the history of the square.

Centre d'Interpretation de Place-Royale, 27 rue Notre-Dame (walk down the Breakneck stairs and take côte de la Montagne to rue Notre-Dame). ☎ **418-646-3167.** *Admission: C$3 (US$2.25) adults, C$2.50 (US$2) seniors, C$2 (US$1.50) students 17 and older, C$1 (US75¢) children 12–16, children under 12 free. Open: Late June–Labour Day, daily 9:30 a.m.–5 p.m.; Labour Day–late June Tues–Sat. 10 a.m.–5 p.m.*

Musée du Québec
Grande-Allée

Not too far from the Parc Champs-de-Bataille, this museum houses the largest collection of Québec art in North America, including over 23,000 pieces dating from the 18th century to the present. Eight galleries are spread over three buildings. The Great Hall has a reception area and attached auditorium. The Gérard Morrisset Pavillon houses permanent exhibits, including works from the early colonial period, African masks and carvings and musical instruments. The Baillargé Pavillon, a former prison built in 1867, holds temporary exhibits.

1 av. Wolfe-Montcalm (near Place George V). ☎ **418-643-2150.** *Internet:* www. mdq.org. *Admission: permanent collection, free; special exhibitions, C$10 (US$7.50) adults, C$9 (US$6.75) seniors, C$5 (US$3.75) students, C$3 (US$2.25) children 12–16, children under 12 free. Open: June 1–Labour Day, daily 10 a.m.–5 p.m., Wed. till 9 p.m., Closed Mon Sept–May.*

Index of top sights by neighborhood

Grande-Allée
La Citadelle
Musée du Québec
Parc des Champs-de-Bataille

Basse-Ville
Musée de la Civilisation
Place-Royale

Haute-Ville
Chapelle/Musée des Ursulines
Château Frontenac
Musée d'art Innuit Brousseau
Musée de l'Amérique Française
Basilique Notre-Dame

Index of top sights by type

Churches and Historic Buildings

Château Frontenac
Fortifications
La Citadelle
Basilique Notre-Dame

Museums

Chapelle/Musée des Ursulines
Musée d'art Inuit Brousseau

Musée de la Civilisation
Musée de l'Amérique Française
Musée du Québec

Parks and Squares

Parc des Champs-de-Bataille
Place-Royale

Finding More Cool Things to See and Do

In this section, you find suggestions for following a specific interest, whether you want to keep the kids entertained; get your fill of wars, battles, and armory; make your teenagers happy; stroll some lovely streets; or take a tour.

Kid-pleasing places

Kids are sure to be enchanted by Québec City, whether it's the fairy-tale-castle effect of the Château Frontenac or the real (but not in use!) canons and armory scattered around the city. The best museum for kids is the **Musée de la Civilisation,** which has great exhibits plus loads of room to run around. Following are a few other suggestions for entertaining children.

Ferry Ride
Old Port

Not very expensive, but usually a thrill for the little ones, you can cross the river from Québec City over to Lévis in about ten minutes. The view of Québec City from the river is quite spectacular, especially at night. There's not much to do in Lévis, but take a stroll around, anyway. The ferry leaves close to Place-Royale. Buy tickets at the Société des Traversiers du Québec building, right on the port.

Société des Traversiers du Québec, 10 rue des Traversiers. ☎ **418-644-3704.** *Tickets: C$2.50 (US$2) adults, C$2.25 (US$1.75) seniors, C$1.75 (US$1.25) children 5–11, free for children under 5. Departs from Québec three or four times per hour.*

Musée de Cire (Wax Museum)
Haute-Ville

Pop in to this seventeenth-century house to see wax renditions of major personalities in Québec history. There are 60 individuals in all, in 16 settings. From pop stars to military heroes, you get your fill of tackiness, and then some.

22 rue Ste-Anne. ☎ *418-692-2289. Admission: C$3 (US$2.25) adults, C$2 (US$1.50) seniors and students, children under 12 free with adult. Open: May–Oct daily 9 a.m.–10 p.m., rest of year daily 9 a.m.–5 p.m.*

Terrasse Dufferin
Haute-Ville

Head straight to this square looking out onto the St. Lawrence River for a kind of one-stop children's entertainment package. Within a short walking distance (even shorter running distance), you have **coin-operated telescopes** for a look across the river. In the summer, **street entertainers** abound, from living "statues" to mimes to musicians playing wine glasses. If you want to burn off some serious steam, try tackling the Breakneck stairs, leading down to the Basse-Ville. For a real thrill, take the kids to nearby Place d'Armes and pick up a **horse-drawn carriage ride** (C$60/US$45 for a 35-minute ride).

For military history buffs

Kids aren't the only ones fascinated by epic battles. If you like stories about warfare, this section gives you few places to find them.

Musée du Fort

For explanations of sieges and battles fought in Québec City, this small museum just off Place d'Armes is hard to beat. Battles are retold using sound and light, in both English and French.

10 rue Ste-Anne. ☎ *418-692-1759. Admission C$6.75 (US$5) adults, C$5.25 (US$4) seniors, C$4 (US$3) students. Open: July–August daily, 10 a.m.–5 p.m. Open: Apr–Oct daily 10 a.m.–5 p.m. (until 7 p.m. June–mid-Sept), rest of year daily noon–4 p.m.*

Place de l'Artillerie

Near the Porte St-Jean, this enormous military installation was the French military headquarters starting in 1747. Later, it housed the British garrison, and then became a munitions factory, which was in use until 1964. Now it serves as an interpretative center. Don't miss the scale model of Québec City, showing what the city looked like in the 1800s.

2 rue d'Auteuil (near St-Jean Gate) ☎ **418-648-4205**. *Admission C$4 (US$3) adults, C$3.50 (US$2.65) seniors and students over 17, C$2.75 (US$2.05) children 6–16, children under 6 free. Open: Apr–Oct, Wed–Sun 10 a.m.–5 p.m., also open Mon and Tues May 12–Oct 12.*

Fortifications de Québec

If the wall around Québec City — built to protect the city from marauding invaders — is still standing, it's because it was restored and remains a protected site. You can walk the complete three-mile circuit starting at the kiosk of terrasse Dufferin or take a 90-minute tour and discover the wall's history.

Tour tickets available at kiosk at terrasse Dufferin. ☎ **418-648-7016**. *Tour: C$10 (US$7.50) for adults, C$7.50 (US$5.50) for kids.*

Teen-tempting areas

Québec City is a popular destination for school trips, especially for the early teen demographic. If you happen to find yourself accompanied by members of that select group, this section tells you where you can take them.

Rue St-Jean

This street has shops galore. The busy commercial street on the north end of the Haute-Ville has souvenir boutiques, clothes stores, inexpensive cafes, book and CD shops, and plenty of action to keep your teenagers engrossed for hours.

Place-Royale

Perhaps your teenager isn't that interested in the history of early French colonialism. Not a problem. This little area has plenty of distractions for them, including cute boutiques and even cuter cafes. They'll go nuts. Just make sure they each have a map.

The best strolling streets

There's really no such thing as just "strolling around" Québec City. Vieux-Québec is so packed with things to see and do, you're sure to get sidetracked. But whether you have some specific purchases in mind or just want to stretch your legs, the walking suggestions in this section should do the trick.

Le Petit Champlain
Basse-Ville

This narrow pedestrian alley tucked into the base of the cliffs right below the Château Frontenac gets As for atmosphere. One of the oldest streets in Québec City, opened in 1685, Le Petit Champlain originally housed artists, and then became the home of poor Irish immigrants in the 1800s. These days, it's packed with quaint, mostly high-quality souvenir shops, cafes, and restaurants. It's a good place to pick up items such as jewelry made by Québec designers, unique toys, clothing, and French kitchen implements. Take the Breakneck stairs, and then keep following côte de la Montagne down the hill. You hit another set of stairs, and Le Petit Champlain starts at the bottom of them.

Rue St-Paul
Basse-Ville

Slightly off the beaten track — off the beaten *tourist* track, anyway — this street running parallel to the Bassin Louise has an authentic port feel to it. It's also packed with antiques shops, has a number of good art galleries, and boasts quiet little eateries where you can have a leisurely drink or coffee. Take côte du Palais (just off rue St-Jean) and walk down past the city wall and down rue des Vaisseaux-du-Roi and you'll hit rue St-Paul. Turn right.

Promenade de la Pointe à Carcy
Old Port

The cruise ship business in Québec City's port has really taken off over the last decade, and the port area has benefited from the increased activity. Unlike in Montréal, though, there is no commercial street running along Québec City's port (rue Dalhousie is the closest one). Instead, city authorities have transformed this area into a kind of urban park, with a bike trail, fountains, and scrupulous security guards who make sure tourists don't get too close to the edge. It's a great place to park yourself on a bench and read or just wander around gazing at the river traffic.

Rue du Trésor
Haute-Ville

This little street runs between rue St-Louis and rue de Buade and is a veritable outdoor art market, with artists lined up the whole length of the street selling paintings, sketches, and engravings of various styles and qualities. More for shopping than walking, it's still worth checking out, just for the atmosphere. Head here if you want your caricature drawn.

Seeing Québec City by guided tour

If you're short on time, a guided tour is a good option for seeing a lot of Québec City with minimum effort. Walking is our first choice and should be yours, but you can also get around by bus tours, horse-drawn carriages, or even river cruises. This section gives you our recommendations.

Walking tours

Walking is the best way to see the nooks and crannies of Québec City — and there are many of them. With a walking tour, you get history, hear insider info, and have areas of interest pointed out to you that you probably wouldn't normally notice on your own. Most walking tours leave from the terrasse Dufferin. The best idea is to see what's being offered at the nearby **Centre Infotouriste** at 12 rue Ste-Anne just opposite the Château Frontenac at Place d'Armes (☎ **800-363-7777** or 418-692-2608). Or call the **Association des guides touristiques de Québec (☎ 418-624-2581**), which provides guides for any length of time, on foot, or in your car or theirs. Here are our favorite tours:

- ✔ **Paul Gaston L'Anglais (☎ 418-592-3422**; e-mail: langlaispaul@yahoo.com) is an archeologist who offers thematic walking tours of the city on topics like "Beer Brewing," "Cemeteries of Old Québec," "Women's Struggle to Get the Vote," and more. Tours cost between C$8 and C$12 (US$6–US$9) per person and last two hours.

- ✔ **La Compagnie des Six Associés (☎ 418-802-6665**) also offers thematic tours. "Vice and Drunkenness," explaining the underside of the history of Québec, is a popular one. Book tours at the main tourist office opposite Place d'Armes. Tours cost C$12 to C$15 (US$9–US$11) per person.

- ✔ At the main tourist information office, you can also rent a **CD Tour** (☎ 418-645-1115) for C$10 (US$7.50) or C$15 (US$11) for two. These portable audio tours, in which historical figures explain the sites, lets you stop where you please and tour at your leisure.

- ✔ The **Centre d'Initiation aux Fortifications de Québec (☎ 418-648-7016**) offers "Québec: Fortified City" tours starting from the terrasse Dufferin. Tours last about 90 minutes and cost C$10 (US$7.50).

Bus tours

If you're not up to walking, or if it's extremely hot (or cold) and you want to escape the elements (while not missing the sites), bus tours are a good solution. Two good companies offer tours year-round:

✔ **Les Tours du Vieux-Québec** (☎ 800-267-8687 or 418-664-0460) offers guided tours in small comfortable buses, both inside the city and in surrounding areas like Île d'Orléans. Québec City tours last about 2 hours and cost C$26 (US$20) per person.

✔ **Grayline Québec** (☎ 888-558-7668 or 418-694-9226) offers more luxurious tours in bigger buses, both of the city and the surrounding area. Tours last about 2 hours and cost C$26 (US$20) per person.

Horse-drawn carriage tours

Get a tour of Québec City the old-fashioned way and experience not only the sights and sounds but also the smells of yesteryear. You can visit Vieux-Québec by *calèche* all year round. Rides cost C$60 (US$45) for 35 minutes. You can pick one up on the fly at **Place d'Armes** or call **Calèches du Vieux-Québec** at ☎ 418-683-9222 or 418-624-3062.

River cruises

You won't get the most out of seeing Québec City by boat, but if you like cruises, **Croisières AML** (☎ 800-563-4463 or 418-692-1159) offers 90-minute cruises aboard a renovated 1930s ferry, departing three times daily from Quai Chouinard, 10 rue Dalhousie, near Place-Royale in the Lower Town. The show comes with bilingual guides, and full dining facilities and a bar are right on the boat. Evening cruises last 2½ hours with dining and dancing included. Prices for day cruises start at C$24 (US$18) for adults, C$22 (US$17) for seniors, and C$10 (US$7.50) for kids, and go up in the evening. You can buy tickets at the kiosk on terrasse Dufferin.

Hitting the Historical Highlights of Vieux-Québec

Québec City *is* history. Step through any gate leading in to the Old City, and you see that for yourself. The walking tours in the following sections stop at some of the top historical sites and show you some other nice things to see (and eat) along the way. You can wander along the itinerary at your own leisure or do the whole thing backward, if you like. Some sights are bound to interest you more than others, so pick and choose as you go along.

Start by entering Vieux-Québec at the **Porte St-Louis,** which you reach either by walking along the Grande-Allée or by turning left onto rue St-Louis from avenue Honoré-Mercier. The gate was designed to bring to mind medieval castles and horsemen, but it's actually Victorian, the work of an Irish architect that was completed in 1878.

A few steps inside the gate, on your left, is the **Fortifications of Québec National Historical Site,** where you can learn about the history of the wall that surrounds the Old City. The wall, originally wooden, was first erected by the French in 1693. The same French started working on the stone wall in 1745, but they had to hand the job over to the English when the Brits conquered the city in 1759.

Continue along rue St-Louis until your reach rue du Parloir, turn left and you'll see the **museum and the monastery of the Ursulines,** the first order of French nuns to set up shop in Québec, around 1630.

At the end of rue du Parloir, turn right on rue Donnacona, and then left on rue des Jardins. Follow this street to rue Ste-Anne. On your left, you'll see the **Hotel Clarendon,** the oldest hotel still operating in Québec City, built in 1870. Wander in and check out the Art Deco entrance. If all this history is exhausting you, the **L'Emprise** cafe/bar inside the hotel is a great place to stop for a coffee or beer.

Continue along rue des Jardins, and you'll see Québec City's old **City Hall** (Hôtel-de-Ville), built in 1895. If you're interested in knowing more about the history of urban planning in Québec, the **Centre d'Interprétation de la Vie Urbaine de la Ville de Québec** (City Hall Interpretation Center) is in the basement.

Continue along rue des Jardins to the end of the Place de l'Hôtel-de-Ville, turn right on côte de la Fabrique and you'll see the **Basilique Notre-Dame,** first built in 1647, and then destroyed and built again about five times over until it took its final form around the end of the 1700s. (Well, actually, they were still putting finishing touches on it in 1959.) On the same street, you'll see the **Musée de l'Amérique Française** (Museum of French America), where you can get a thorough history of French colonization in the New World, in Québec, and beyond.

Time for another coffee break? Or maybe some lunch or a light snack? You're not too far from rue de Buade where the **Café Buade** (31 rue Buade) offers pizzas, sandwiches, coffee, and the like at a reasonable price.

Keep going along rue de Buade until you reach **rue du Trésor.** The name (which means "treasury") dates from the French regime, when colonists used to pass along this street on their way to pay their taxes. Now it's a great little walkway where artists hang their paintings, sketching, etchings, and more.

Rue du Trésor takes you to rue Ste-Anne right in front of Place d'Armes. Turn left, and you'll see the **Infotouriste Center.** Cross Place d'Armes, and you'll be standing in front of the majestic, castle-like **Château Frontenac,** built in 1893 by the Canadian Pacific Railway Company.

Historical Highlights of Vieux-Québec

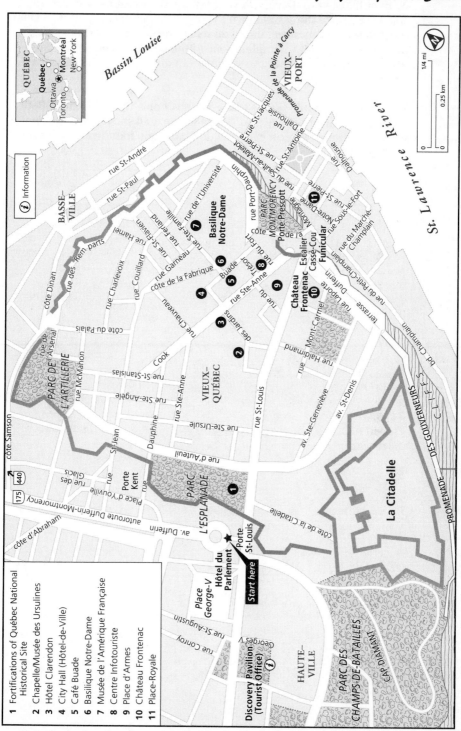

1 Fortifications of Québec National Historical Site
2 Chapelle/Musée des Ursulines
3 Hôtel Clarendon
4 City Hall (Hôtel-de-Ville)
5 Café Buade
6 Basilique Notre-Dame
7 Musée de l'Amérique Française
8 Centre Infotouriste
9 Place d'Armes
10 Château Frontenac
11 Place-Royale

If want to see the Basse-Ville from here, walk to the lookout area in front on the Château Frontenac. On your left are the **Breakneck stairs,** there since 1682. Take the stairs down to côte de la Montagne, and then keep going down on this street until you reach the next set of stairs. These take you to **Le Petit Champlain,** one of the oldest streets in the city, where the houses date to the seventeenth and eighteenth centuries — a shopper's delight, to boot.

Your last stop should be the **Place-Royale,** down the hill from Le Petit Champlain (toward the river). This is where it all started. It's the spot where the French explorer Samuel de Champlain founded New France in 1608.

Chapter 19

A Shopper's Guide to Québec City

O n the whole, people in Québec City like things a little classy. Of course, given that tourism is a mainstay industry here, not-so-classy trinket boutiques abound, especially in the Old City. But don't be fooled by the trashy souvenir shops. Unique, high-quality items are available throughout Québec City, from Inuit art to antiques and clothing. Just don't go looking for bargains — you're likely to be disappointed.

Checking Out the Scene

Souvenir stores aside, Québec City is probably best known as a place to buy antiques, art, and crafts. The antiques stores keep their tourist clientele in mind and tend to specialize in smaller, more portable items like lamps, china, and bedside tables and stools. Prices for antiques are reasonable, partly because Québeckers on the whole are not especially drawn to antiques (leaving plenty left over for you).

For a small city, Québec has a lot of art galleries. They run the full gamut of price and style, offering both traditional and abstract works done by new and established artists at both steep and affordable prices. Most of the works for sale are from Québec artists, but not all. If you don't feel up to investing in art, the city has plenty of stores featuring less expensive crafts and creations from local artisans.

If shopping for clothes, books, or CDs is more your style, you'll find plenty of ways to spend your cash — believe us. Québec City residents are known for stylish dressing, and while you won't find the quantity of local designers available in Montréal, the clothing selection here reflects

Québeckers' flair. Most books for sale in the city are French, but plenty of English books are available, as well. The city has a decent selection of music, but if you're looking in particular for French music, the selection is excellent.

Outside of the Old City, stores hours in Québec City are similar to those throughout Canada. Most stores open at 9 or 10 a.m. and close at 5 or 6 p.m., Mondays through Wednesdays, and Saturdays. Thursdays and Fridays, stores usually stay open until 9 p.m. Many stores open Sunday from around noon until 5 p.m. In the Old City, however, hours are very seasonal. During the high season, you're likely to find shops open long hours, pretty much every day.

Remember to keep track of your purchases. You have to come clean at the border and fork over the details of your purchases to customs agents before you leave. If you stay in Canada more than two days, you can bring back US$400 in goods without paying duty. This includes 200 cigarettes, 100 cigars, and one liter of an alcoholic beverage. If you stay less than two days, your limit drops to US$200. If you buy more than this, no one will throw you in jail — you'll just have to pay a small percentage of the amount that surpasses your limit. Check Chapter 7 for more details on what you can bring back.

Before you commence your Québec City shopping frenzy, don't forget the Canadian tax man (or tax woman; these are modern times). You must pay taxes adding up to roughly 15% of your purchases. For information on how to get a refund on the Goods and Services Tax (which is about half the 15%), see Chapter 3.

Seeking Out the Big Names

Downtown Québec City has only one big name store, and that's **Simons** at 20 côte de la Fabrique (☎ **418-692-3630**). This slightly upscale department store, which opened in 1840, offers a good selection of clothing and accessories for men, women, and children, plus fine bed linens. This is the place to come if you unexpectedly find yourself in the middle of a cold spell and need a hat, scarf, and gloves — not a likely event until at least mid-October, but you never know.

The other big department store you find in Québec City is **La Baie** (The Bay, short for the Hudson's Bay Company), but you have to leave the confines of the downtown area and head out to the shopping malls in the 'burbs. You can find La Baie stores at **Galeries de la Capitale, Place Fleur de Lys,** and **Place Laurier.**

Going to Shopping Malls

People really like to shop here, and for a small city, Québec has an impressive roster of shopping malls. Maybe the winter weather drives Québeckers into these indoor havens of consumption.

You have two shopping mall options within walking distance of the Old City:

- ✔ **Les Promenades du Vieux-Québec,** 43 rue de Buade (☎ 418-692-6000). This small complex is just a few steps away from the Château Frontenac and has 12 upscale boutiques, where you can find jewelry, furs, perfumes, gifts, candies, fine art, arts and crafts, and more.

- ✔ **Place Québec,** 880 av. Honoré-Mercier (☎ 418-529-0551). A multi-level shopping complex attached to the Delta Hotel, this mall has 30 boutiques and is a 10-minute walk from the Old City.

Trouble is (for visitors, anyway), the biggest and best of the malls are a fair distance from the Old City. But if mall crawling is what you want (not a bad alternative when the weather works against you), catch a cab and take off to one of the following:

- ✔ **Galeries de la Capitale,** 5401 bd. des Galeries (☎ 418-627-5800). A 20-minute drive from the Old City, this mall has 250 shops and a small amusement park with games, rides, an Imax theater, 12 movie theaters, and assorted restaurants.

- ✔ **Place Fleur de Lys,** 552 bd. Wilfrid-Hamel (☎ 418-529-8128). Winner of the Canadian Maple Leaf Award for the most beautiful shopping interior design, Place Fleur de Lys is a five-minute drive from downtown Québec City and has 250 boutiques plus major chains.

- ✔ **Place Laurier,** 2700 bd. Laurier (☎ 800-322-1828). A good 20-minute drive from the Old City, this is the mother of all shopping centers. It's the largest shopping center in Eastern Canada with some 350 stores.

- ✔ **Place Sainte-Foy,** 2450 bd. Laurier (☎ 418-653-4184). This is a fashionable mall, featuring 130 stores and boutiques; a 20-minute drive from the Old City.

Strolling in the Best Shopping Neighborhoods

You can find loads of great shopping in Québec. We assume you want to spend most of your time in the Old City, or not too far from it, maybe venturing out, at most, to Grande-Allée for a change of scenery. So, for your shopping ease and pleasure, we break the city down into five shopping areas, discussed in the five following sections. Like almost everything else we recommend in the Québec City section of the book, all these areas are within walking distance of each other.

For antiques and art, you can't beat the **rue St-Paul** area in the Basse-Ville. For souvenirs, arts and crafts, and even clothes, we recommend the area around **Le Petit-Champlain** in the Basse-Ville, including Place-Royale and the area around the **Château Frontenac** in the Haute-Ville. For less touristy types of shops, **rue St-Jean** is the place to go, with its books, CD, and clothes stores (and plenty of cafes and restaurants to rest between your shopping sprints). Finally, if you really want a break from the Vieux-Québec experience, we recommend strolling down Grande-Allée to **avenue Cartier,** where you find a small concentration of shops with items like clothes, outdoor items, and home decor.

Rue St-Paul

You can get to rue St-Paul in the Basse-Ville by following rue St-Pierre from Place-Royale. Or, you can start at the other end of the street. On rue St-Jean, take côte du Palais. You pass through the city walls, and then walk down the slope to the Basse-Ville via rue des Vaisseaux-du-Roi.

This is where you find the biggest concentration of antiques stores in the city. But these aren't the kind of dusty cluttered antiques stores you find on rue Notre-Dame in Montréal (see Chapter 12). Instead, most are neat places that specialize in a certain type of antiques. There's definitely something for everyone. This section lists a few places to visit on your stroll down rue St-Paul.

For old and rare books, check out **Argus Livres Anciens,** 160 rue St-Paul (☎ 418-694-2122). If Victorian and Edwardian furniture, silver, porcelain, and paintings are your thing, stop by **Boutique aux Memoires Antiquités,** 105 rue St-Paul (☎ 418-692-2180). For authentic Québec pine furniture, we recommend **Gérard Bourguet Antiquaire,** 97 rue St-Paul (☎ 418-694-0896). The store offers many 18th- and 19th-century pieces, but you can expect to pay a fair penny for them. **L'Héritage Antiquité,** 110 rue St-Paul (☎ 418-692-1681), also specializes in Québec furniture and sells clocks, oil lamps, and ceramics. For engravings, prints, and maps, the best place is **Les Antiquités du Matelot,** 137 rue St-Paul (☎ 418-694-9585). And if you're more interested in curiosities from the 1960s and '70s, don't miss **Décennie,** 117 rue St-Paul (☎ 418-694-0403), for retro chairs, lamps, and decor.

Rue St-Paul's other specialty is art galleries, although you'd be wise to wander off along some of the neighboring streets like rue Sault-au-Matelot or rue St-Pierre to get the full experience. **Galerie Madeleine**

Lacerte, 1 côte Dinan (☎ 418-692-1566), is one of the best-known galleries of the neighborhood. It sells contemporary paintings and sculpture. **Galerie d'art Alain Lacaze,** 131 rue St-Paul (☎ 418-692-4381), sells oils and watercolors.

Other noteworthy boutiques along rue St-Paul fall outside of the art and antiques category. **Vitrine,** 329 rue St-Paul (☎ 418-694-7384), specializes in furniture and other objects made by local designers. For one of the best selections of fur coats in the Old City, visit **Les Fourrures du Vieux-Port** at 55 rue St-Pierre (☎ 418-692-6686).

Rue St-Jean

Rue St-Jean is probably the least quaint, yet most practical, of the shopping areas in the Old City. A busy commercial street, here you find a number of Québec chain stores. It's also a good place to head if you want specialty food items, books, CDs, clothes, or a comfortable pair of walking shoes. We include rue de la Fabrique in this area, which is a continuation of rue St-Jean uphill toward the Hôtel-de-Ville. The same bustling commercial spirit reigns on both streets.

This is the destination for clothes. For comfortable but elegant men's and women's fashions, Québec chain **America,** 1147 rue St-Jean (☎ 418-692-5254), is a good place to start. **Bedo,** 1161 rue St-Jean (☎ 418-692-0623) another chain, carries edgier, urban women's and men's fashions. Another good option for sportswear is **NRJ,** 1121 rue St-Jean (☎ 418-694-0086). **Louis Laflamme,** 1192 rue St-Jean (☎ 418-692-3774), carries stylish menswear. If you're looking for something to keep your feet comfortable (or warm), the Canadian chain **Roots,** 1150 rue St-Jean (☎ 418-692-2000), sells high-quality leather shoes at decent, although not bargain, prices. A little more into the "interesting" category of clothes, **Artisans du Bas-Canada,** 30 côte de la Fabrique (☎ 888-339-2109 or 418-692-2109), offers a wide selection of outdoor garments, gifts, and collectibles.

Food-wise, if you're a chocolate fanatic, you'll love **Choco-Musée Érico,** 634 rue St-Jean (☎ 418-524-2122), where, with two days' notice, *chocolatier* Éric Normand sculpts whatever you like out of chocolate. You can get good ice cream here, too. For maple products and Québec wines and beers, visit the **Marché Je-An-Dré,** 1097 rue St-Jean (☎ 418-692-3647).

You can find plenty of bookstores along rue St-Jean. Although many are principally *Francophone* (French-speaking), you can find English books and magazines at **Archambault,** 1095 rue St-Jean (☎ 418-694-2088) and at the **Maison de la Presse Internationale,** 1050 rue St-Jean (☎ 418-694-1511).

For gifts, souvenirs, and jewelry, check out **Abaca,** 54 côte de la Fabrique (☎ 418-694-9761), and **Collection Lazuli,** 774 rue St-Jean (☎ 418-525-6528).

Le Petit-Champlain/Place-Royale

Although extremely touristy, Place-Royale and Le Petit-Champlain are still your best bets for souvenirs. While cheap trinkets abound, most stores offer high-quality items, and many specialize in handmade and Québec-made clothing and jewelry. Plus, a number of reputable art galleries are located here.

If you're in the market for one of those striped French nautical shirts, you can find it at the nautical store **Le Capitaine d'à Bord,** 63 Petit-Champlain (☎ 418-694-0624). Into leather? **Peau sur Peau,** 85 Petit-Champlain (☎ 418-692-5132), offers leather clothing, shoes, luggage, and accessories from Québec and international designers. **Ibiza,** 57 Petit-Champlain (☎ 418-692-2103), also carries leather goods by Québec designers. **Zazou,** 31 Petit-Champlain (☎ 418-694-9990), sells clothes made by Québec designers.

For wines and spirits, stop at the **Maison des Vins,** 1 Place-Royale (☎ 418-643-1214). Maple products, a true Québec specialty, abound at the **Petit Cabane à Sucre,** 94 Petit-Champlain (☎ 418-692-5875). **Le Jardin de l'argile,** 51 Petit-Champlain (☎ 418-692-4870), carries Québec-made porcelain, pottery, bronze works, and more.

Château Frontenac

Most of the nicer boutiques in and around the Château Frontenac in the Haute-Ville carry objects best qualified as "upscale souvenir."

Among these, don't miss the boutiques that sell Inuit art. **Aux Multiples Collections,** 69 rue Ste-Anne (☎ 418-692-1230) offers a wide selection of Native Canadian carvings in stone, bone, and tusk. You can also find a great choice of Inuit carving at **Brousseau et Brousseau,** 35 rue St-Louis (☎ 418-694-1828). **Kulik Art Inuit,** just inside the Château Frontenac at 1 rue des Carrières (☎ 418-692-6174), has a wide range of Inuit prints and sculptures.

Two other boutiques worth checking out in this area include the highly specialized **Boutique de Noël de Québec** (Québec Christmas Boutique), 47 rue de Buade (☎ 418-692-2457), which is open all year long. It's definitely a good spot to pick up a souvenir for that somebody who has everything. **La Maison Darlington,** 7 rue de Buade (☎ 418-692-2268), specializes in imported woolen garments including merino and cashmere sweaters, caps, ties, scarves, and gloves for children and adults.

If you want to bring back some locally made beer or Québec liqueurs made out of blueberry or maple syrup, the **SAQ Signature** spirits boutique has them. It's located just inside the Château Frontenac at 1 rue des Carrières (☎ **418-692-1182**).

Avenue Cartier

As nice as the Old City is, its intensely touristy and cramped shops can make you feel claustrophobic. Avenue Cartier is a great place to go for a little breathing space. Leave the Old City from the St-Louis Gate and walk along rue St-Louis until it turns into Grande-Allée. Continue walking west for ten minutes and until you reach avenue Cartier on your right.

Avenue Cartier, with its many boutiques, feels like a pedestrian promenade even though cars are allowed to drive through. It's a nice place to stroll about and has plenty of interesting cafes and restaurants where you can take a break. For practical (but stylish) clothes, **Chez Boomer,** 970 av. Cartier (☎ **418-523-7047**), carries items for children and adults; **Paris Cartier,** 1180 av. Cartier (☎ **418-529-6083**), has elegant clothes for women. For home decor items, check out **Zone,** 999 av. Cartier (☎ **418-522-7373**), a great store that's loaded with extremely tempting stuff for the kitchen, bathroom, or living room. **Azimut,** 1194 av. Cartier (☎ **418-688-7788**), is an excellent outdoors store that sells tents, sleeping bags, and hiking boots. A good spot for CDs is **Sillons le Disquaire,** 1149 av. Cartier (☎ **418-524-8352**).

Index of Stores by Merchandise

Art
Galerie d'art Alain Lacaze (rue St-Paul)
Galerie Madeleine Lacerte (rue St-Paul)

Antiques
Argus Livres Anciens (rue St-Paul)
Boutique aux Memoires Antiquités
    (rue St-Paul)
Décennie (rue St-Paul)
Gérard Bourguet Antiquaire
    (rue St-Paul)
Les Antiquités du Matelot (rue St-Paul)
L'Héritage Antiquités (rue St-Paul)

Books/Magazines
Archambault (rue St-Jean)
Maison de la Presse Internationale
    (rue St-Jean)

CDs
Archambault (rue St-Jean)
Sillons le Disquaire (avenue Cartier)

Clothing
America (rue St-Jean)
Artisans du Bas Canada (rue St-Jean)
Bédo (rue St-Jean)
Chez Boomer (avenue Cartier.)
Fourrures du Vieux-Port (rue St-Paul)
Ibiza (Le Petit-Champlain)
La Maison Darlington (Château
    Frontenac)
Le Capitaine à bord (Le Petit-
    Champlain)
Maison Louis Laflamme (rue St-Jean)
NRJ (rue St-Jean)
Paris Cartier (avenue Cartier)

Peau sur Peau (Le Petit-Champlain)
Roots (rue St-Jean)
Zazou (Le Petit-Champlain)

Department Stores

Simons (rue St-Jean)

Food

Choco-Musée Érico (rue St-Jean)
Marché Je-An-Dré (rue St-Jean)
Petit Cabane à Sucre (Le Petit-
Champlain)

Furniture/ Home Decorations

Vitrine (rue St-Paul)
Zone (avenue Cartier)

Gifts

Abaca (rue St-Jean)
Boutique de Noël de Québec (Château
Frontenac)
Collection Lazuli (rue St-Jean)

Jewelry

Abaca (rue St-Jean)
Collection Lazuli (rue St-Jean)

Native Canadian Items

Aux Multiples Collections (Château
Frontenac)
Brousseau et Brousseau (Château
Frontenac)
Kulik Art Inuit (Château Frontenac)

Outdoors Stores

Azimut (avenue Cartier)

Pottery and china

Le Jardin de l'Argile (Le Petit-
Champlain)

Shopping Malls

Galeries de la Capitale (Québec City)
Place Fleur de Lys (Québec City)
Place Laurier (Ste-Foy)
Place Sainte-Foy (Ste-Foy)
Les Promenades du Vieux-Québec
(Château Frontenac)
Place Québec (boulevard René-
Levesque)

Wines and spirits

SAQ Signature (Château Frontenac)
Maison des Vins (Place-Royale)

Chapter 20

Living It Up After the Sun Goes Down: Québec City Nightlife

In This Chapter

▶ Hitting Québec City's best dance floors

▶ Hearing live music acts throughout the city

▶ Finding neighborhood spots filled with locals

*F*or a place its size, Québec City has a booming nightlife. Inside the walls of the **Haute-Ville,** the scene has a resort-like feel, like a misplaced Yesterdayland from a Disney theme park. The maze of main streets within the walls are lined with numerous watering holes. The majority of them are small, dimly lit, and intimate places, often with acoustic acts and flickering candles, exposed stone walls, and wooden beams. Folk music of all sorts suits the setting and is, indeed, the norm.

The **Grande-Allée** is Québec City's most popular nightlife strip, with clubs and bars on a larger scale. Many occupy more than one floor of the converted townhouses where they often dwell, which seem to sway to the music spilling out of their windows. Most places offer a DJ and dance floor, but a few showcase live music.

Basse-Ville offers lots of action, but it's spread out, extending to the west along the cliffside and into the blue-collar neighborhood of **St-Roch.** Because the rents are cheaper, it's where many of Québec City's edgier, more interesting bars have popped up — away from the colonial razzle-dazzle of the tourist areas.

In this chapter, we tell you about Québec City's most popular nightlife destinations; some lesser known, but equally great spots; and some places frequented only by locals. Some are outside the main tourist districts but are definitely worth checking out. Of course, we do point out the best spots in the Upper and Lower cities, as well as along the Grande-Allée.

On the whole, you spend less money going out in Québec City than in Montréal. Drinks are cheaper, distances between hot spots shorter, and cover charges less frequent. Last call is at 3 a.m.; most places don't get going until 11 p.m., and the night peaks at 1 a.m. The legal drinking age is 18. Because of Québec City's quaint size, the dress code is less cosmopolitan than in Montréal. Lots of clubbers dress in jeans and a comfy sweater, but don't let that stop you from looking your best. Ideally, you want to wear something that gets you into variety of settings, from a cozy pub to a swinging dance club.

Finding Out What's Going On

Unfortunately, Québec City's free nightlife listings magazines are in French. But you don't really need to know French to decipher event listings, so if you want to find something in particular, go ahead and take a look. *Le Soleil* and the *Journal du Québec* are the two French dailies, and their Arts and Entertainment sections may prove helpful. *Le Guide Québec Scope* is a free cultural magazine, partially in English, with restaurant reviews, neighborhood profiles, theater, shopping, and nightlife features, as well as event and show listings. Québec City also has an edition of *Voir,* a free weekly that comes out on Thursdays, and probably has the most comprehensive coverage of the city's cultural calendar.

When deciphering French listings, know that they appear, more often than not, in the 24-hour clock notation. An easy technique is to subtract 12 if the number is over 12h (noon). So 8h30 is 8:30 a.m., but 20h30, is 8:30 p.m. Also, the days of the week are listed in French. They are:

- ✔ *dimanche* (Sun)

- ✔ *lundi* (Mon)

- ✔ *mardi* (Tues)

- ✔ *mercredi* (Wed)

- ✔ *jeudi* (Thurs)

- ✔ *vendredi* (Fri)

- ✔ *samedi* (Sat)

Checking Out the Scene

"No coats; no cover" sums up the action in the winter. Shivering teens scurry between the city's nightlife destinations, dressed merely in scant club-wear and no coats. There's no cover at many of the bars and clubs, so many of these brazen partygoers opt to leave their warmer gear behind, despite the sub-zero temperatures. This way, they avoid the hassle of coat check at the front door and can head straight to the dance floor or the bar and bop between as many bars as they choose. Other spots around town offer a more authentic and less rowdy experience, like neighborhood spots where clamorous patrons talk and laugh over the music and pints of locally brewed draught beer.

Musically speaking, you hear more songs played by live bands than dance music tracks spun by DJs. You're likely to hear lots of live blues, rock, Celtic, and French folk music. In the city's popular *boîtes a chanson* (literally, singing boxes), you hear Québec folk songs in the *chansonier* (or folk) tradition.

For each place in this chapter, if you have to pay a cover charge, we tell you how much, but these clubs are few and far between. We also include the opening nights for an establishment, if they're not open all week long.

Dancing the Night Away: Québec City's Best Clubs

Although your choices may be limited, most clubs play a mix of Top 40, hip-hop, R&B, techno, and all the requisite anthems from the '70s and '80s. Here are our top picks to get you moving:

- ✔ **Cartier de la Lune,** 799 av. Cartier (☎ tel 418-523-4011), attracts a 30-plus crowd, who cut loose and rock out to retro-classics Wednesday through Saturday nights. Everyone gets down without any pretense or even a second thought. Attitude? Who needs it? Sunday evenings are a popular blues night. There's a token cover charge of C$2 (US$1.50) Fridays and Saturdays, which includes coat check. Blues evenings cost C$7 (US$5).

- ✔ **Chez Dagobert,** 600 Grande-Allée Est (☎ 418-522-0393), is Québec City's most famous nightclub and always a good bet. Le Dag has a stage on the main floor for live performances. Upstairs, an immense steel dance floor is enveloped by pounding bass, blinding lasers, and swiveling, colored spotlights. The whole set up is really quite elaborate.

- ✔ **Chez Maurice Night Club,** 575 Grande-Allée Est (☎ 418-640-0711), has a main room with several bars that surround a dance floor packed with a dapper clientele that's between 18 and 30 years old. During the summer, there's plenty of action on the front terrace, which is right on the Grande-Allée. The Maurice is open nightly but charges a C$3 to C$4 (US$2–US$3) cover Wednesday through Saturday.

Québec City Nightlife

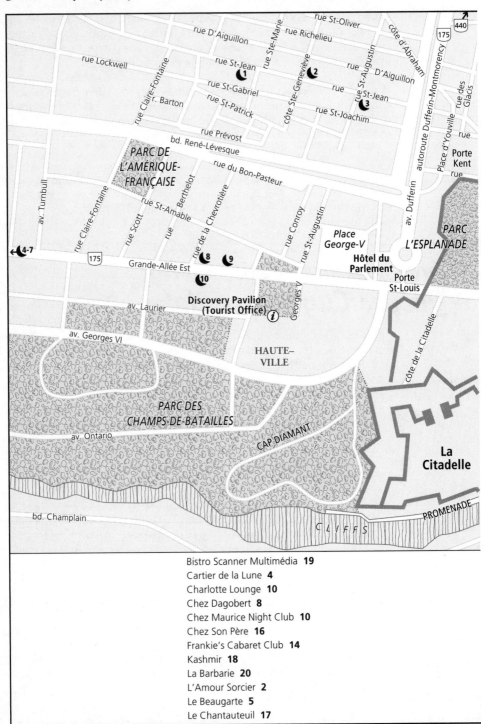

Bistro Scanner Multimédia **19**
Cartier de la Lune **4**
Charlotte Lounge **10**
Chez Dagobert **8**
Chez Maurice Night Club **10**
Chez Son Père **16**
Frankie's Cabaret Club **14**
Kashmir **18**
La Barbarie **20**
L'Amour Sorcier **2**
Le Beaugarte **5**
Le Chantauteuil **17**

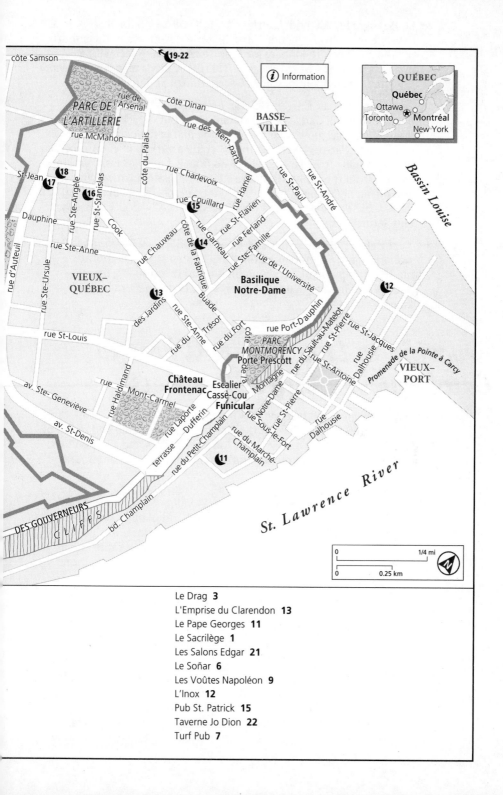

QUÉBEC

Québec
Ottawa
Toronto   Montréal
New York

côte Samson

19-22

rue de l'Arsenal
PARC DE
L'ARTILLERIE

côte Dinan

BASSE–
VILLE

rue des Remparts

rue McMahon

côte du Palais

rue St-Jean

18

17

rue Charlevoix

Bassin Louise

St-Jean

16

rue Ste-Angèle

rue St-Stanislas

rue Couillard

15

rue Hamel

rue St-Paul

rue St-André

Dauphine

Cook

rue Chauveau

rue Garneau

14

rue St-Flavien

rue Ferland

rue Ste-Famille

rue Ste-Anne

côte de la Fabrique

rue Ste-Université

rue d'Auteuil

rue Ste-Ursule

VIEUX–
QUÉBEC

des Jardins

Buade

Basilique
Notre-Dame

13

rue Ste-Anne

Trésor

12

rue St-Louis

rue du Fort

côte de la Montagne

rue Port-Dauphin

côte du Sault-au-Matelot

rue St-Pierre

rue St-Jacques

PARC
MONTMORENCY
Porte Prescott

rue St-Antoine

rue Dalhousie

VIEUX–
PORT

Promenade de la Pointe à Carcy

av. Ste- Geneviève

rue Haldimand

Mont-Carmel

Château
Frontenac

Escalier
Cassé-Cou
Funicular

Porte de la Montagne

rue Notre-Dame

rue St-Pierre

rue Sous-le-Fort

rue Dalhousie

av. St-Denis

rue Laporte

Dufferin

terrasse

rue du Petit-Champlain

rue du Marché
Champlain

11

DES GOUVERNEURS

CLIFFS

bd. Champlain

St. Lawrence River

0 ——————— 1/4 mi
0 ——————— 0.25 km

✔ **Le Beaugarte,** 2600 bd. Laurier (☎ 418-659-2442), in Ste-Foy, is a cab ride away from Québec City's historic downtown in the suburb of Ste-Foy. If you're looking for that frenzied disco feel with a more mature crowd, it's worth the trip. This is the city's mega-club, open Tuesday through Sunday, for 30-somethings and up.

✔ **Le Soñar,** 1147 av. Cartier (☎ 418-640-7333), a basement *tapas* bar with a small dance floor, is an intimate but decidedly modern lounge. The bar glows like a white cube and is the centerpiece in an otherwise dark setting; the DJ spins a variety of electronic beats, ranging from ambient to deep house. Le Soñar is a refreshing change from the otherwise large spaces, indistinguishable decor, and music of Québec City's other dance clubs. Open nightly, but may include a cover charge of C$3 to C$5 (US$2–US$3.75) Friday and Saturday.

✔ **Turf Pub,** 1179 av. Cartier (☎ 418-522-9955), is where many 20-somethings stake out some territory and engage in elaborate mating rituals. By night, the main floor of this pub is a disco — and a bit of a meat market. A sports bar is downstairs in the finished basement.

Grooving to Live Music: Where to Catch Québec City's Best Acts

Live music seems to be Québec City's *raison d'être* in terms of nightlife, especially within the confines of the Haute-Ville. The scale and mood of the establishments seems best fit for lone balladeers and their guitars or small acoustic acts. On most nights, you can find rock, blues, and folk, but not much jazz.

✔ **Bistro Scanner Multimédia,** 291 rue St-Vallier Est (☎ 418-523-1916), is a bar with oodles of street-cred and plenty of urban edge. Local indy rock acts play on a small stage up front and a central bar divides the room. At the back, you'll find a pool table and a computer terminal with free Internet access. Upstairs has more seating and pool tables.

✔ **Charlotte Lounge,** 575 Grande-Allée Est (☎ 418-640-0711), above the main room of Chez Maurice Night Club, has live music most nights. Wednesday, Friday, and Sunday feature a Latin band. On Thursday, it's a '70s rock cover band. But on Saturday, a DJ takes to the decks. Cover is C$3 to C$4 (US$2–US$3).

✔ **Chez Son Père,** upstairs at 24 rue St-Stanislas (☎ 418-692-5308), is one of the more popular *boîtes à chansons,* where solo guitarists belt out ballads from a traditional Québec repertoire, as well as the occasional Bob Dylan cover. The *chansonier* takes the stage nightly at 9 or 10 p.m. The crowd sings, sways, and dances along.

✔ **Frankie's Cabaret Club,** 48 côte de la Fabrique (☎ 418-692-2263), is a new establishment in the upper part of the Old City. Small with an elemental and fiery decor, like an underground lair, it features different sounding nights throughout the week, including urban jazz. Cover: between C$3 and C$5 (US$2–US$3.75).

✔ **Kashmir,** 1018 rue St-Jean (☎ tel 418-694-1648), near the *Porte St-Jean,* within the walls of the Haute-Ville, is a popular venue among 20- to 30-year-old Québeckers. Open seven days, it has erratic programming, which ranges from hip-hop and electronica to alt-rock and punk. Cover: usually between C$6 and C$8 (US$4.50–US$6).

✔ **Le Chantauteuil,** 1001 rue St-Jean (☎ 418-692-2030), has been a venue for traditional folk singers and pub-theater since 1968. This low-key spot attracts an artsy clientele of writers, musicians, painters, poets, and photographers, who gather to commiserate over pints of beer. Open daily.

✔ **L'Emprise du Clarendon,** 57 rue Ste-Anne (☎ 418-692-2480), off the lobby of the snazzy Hôtel Clarendon, this is the one spot where hepcats can swing to live jazz six days a week (closed Monday). It is a small space with the seating arranged around a grand piano, which also accompanies two or three other musicians sitting in for the set.

✔ **Le Pape Georges,** 8 rue du Cul-de-Sac (☎ 418-692-1320), is a small place with a tiny terrace in the Basse-Ville, serving a menu that features many reds and whites by the glass, cheeses, and cold cuts. It closes early during the week (at 9 p.m.), but on the weekend, blues, cabaret, and folk performers play late into the night.

✔ **Les Voûtes Napoléon,** 680 Grande-Allée Est (☎ 418-640-9388), this *boîte à chansons,* set in a downstairs cellar, is very popular for its warm and friendly atmosphere and entertainers who get the crowd singing along.

Drinking In the Local Flavor: Québec City's Neighborhood Bars and Pubs

The following are the neighborhood watering holes where you're likely to find Québeckers — lots of local flavor and character, but not many tourists:

✔ **La Barbarie,** 310 rue St-Roch (☎ 418-522-4373), a brewpub operated as a co-op, makes its own beers. You can get a sampler of eight fine brews, each glass held in a special slot of a wooden carousel. It is a small, cozy pub, with dangling Christmas lights around the bar.

✔ **Le Sacrilège,** 447 rue St-Jean (☎ **418-649-1985**), is a neighborhood bar along rue St-Jean but outside the gates, to the west of the walled Haute-Ville. It is a long and narrow establishment with a beautiful and verdant back terrace during the summer. It's crowded, and groups of friends sit down wherever there's space. Sometimes, this means joining another table and meeting new people. No worries, though; everyone is very friendly.

✔ **Les Salons Edgar,** 263 rue St-Vallier Est (☎ **418-523-7811**), is larger than a typical neighborhood bar, frequented by a young and hip clientele. It has two rooms with extremely high ceilings. The front room has different seating options, along with a long deconstructed bar where patrons mill about. The back room has five pool tables, which you can rent on an hourly basis.

✔ **L'Inox,** 37 quai St-André (☎ **418-692-2877**), is a Québec City brew-pub that makes about a dozen beers. There is plenty of seating in the bar and outside on the terrace May through September. This establishment enjoys a steady flow of regular patrons and hard-core beer lovers.

✔ **Pub St-Patrick,** 45 rue Couillard (☎ **418-694-0618**), a former munitions store during the French colonial period, this pub has a warm atmosphere, made so by the stone hearth and Celtic musicians who almost sit among the clientele as they play. This pub has more than a dozen varieties of beer on tap. If you're feeling homesick, this may be a good place to hear some slurred English. Ah, that's better.

✔ **Taverne Jo Dion,** 86 rue St-Joseph Ouest (☎ **418-525-0710**), located in working-class St-Roch, it is the oldest tavern in the city. You know you're in Deep Québec by the bright florescent lighting, the moose head trophy above the bar, other dated memorabilia, and the stern-faced regulars. Currently, this place is enjoying a revival in popularity among the younger crowd, as the rest of the neighborhood becomes an increasingly hip nightlife destination.

Being Out and Proud in Québec City

The first few blocks of rue St-Jean, to the west of the walled city, just after crossing côte d'Abraham, is Québec City's Gay Village. Along with gay-run cafes, restaurants, and shops, you also find a growing number of nightlife establishments, which also cater to a gay clientele.

✔ **L'Amour Sorcier,** 789 côte Ste-Geneviève (☎ **418-523-3395**), started out as a lesbian bar, but is now popular for gay men, too. Whatever your orientation, check your attitude at the door. This bar is comfortable and unpretentious. It has two rooms, one decidedly more modern and minimalist, finished with corrugated metal as trim.

✔ **Le Drag,** 815 rue St-Agustin (☎ **418-649-7212**), is Québec City's largest gay club with two stories, a drag show, and a dance floor from Thursdays to Sundays. Something for everyone, really. Men cram into the main bar to take in the performances, featuring lip-syncing transvestites. Those who cannot squeeze in can watch the proceedings on closed-circuit TV monitors in the establishment's other rooms. Cover: around C$3 (US$2).

Part V
The Part of Tens

In this part . . .

When in Montréal, do as the Montréalers do. That same wisdom holds true for Québec City. In this part, we give you the essentials to life in Montréal and Québec City. If you're afraid of looking like a tourist, adopt some of these measures, and you'll fit right in.

Chapter 21

Ten Things You *Can't* Live Without in Montréal

*B*eing in the know is a must in Montréal. The cosmopolitan crowds are a discerning bunch, which means that everyone is trying to look fabulous, but in their own particular way. Standing out, rather than blending in seems to be the goal, so lay low, until you get the pulse. In the meantime, this chapter shares some essentials for life in the city.

Hat

Whether it's a chef's toque, or just a hood, six months a year, you'll be happy you have something on your head. Unlike many places in North America, hats here don't mark you as a goof. A bare head marks you as something of a fool, though.

Black

Every year, some fashion authority or another claims that black is being replaced by some new hue, which is then dubbed "the new black." Yet year after year, Montréalers persist in wearing black everywhere, all the time. Whether it's a night on the town, a walk on the mountain, or a trip to the *dépanneur,* black always comes back. Bring whatever you have.

Cigarettes

We couldn't be less politically correct, but smoking is not a stigma in this city. And the line between smokers and non-smokers is, well, hazy. If you're a closet puffer, you'll feel safe coming out here. The anti-smoking movement is upon the city, but we figure smokers are safe for another couple of years.

Coffee

Montréal may be the only place on the continent where lattes haven't completely replaced the *café au lait*. But what people here really like here are espressos — and strong ones at that. Whether the actual drink drives people or the ritual of going to the cafe to indulge in one, who knows? But popular cafes buzz.

Tickets to a Canadiens' Game

By far, this is the premier sporting event in town. Tickets to see the National Hockey League's Montréal Canadiens are always hot. Getting a good seat is tough, though. See our advice in Chapter 11 on how to score a ticket at center ice.

English-French Dictionary

Think this marks you as a tourist? Don't worry about it. Amateur translation is one of the most popular pastimes in the city. Join the fun. You may say stupid things, but you won't be alone. Montréalers spend half the day messing up their subjunctive verbs.

Walking Shoes

Okay, we need to get one thing straight here: We don't mean white running shoes or even high-tech walking shoes — unless they look really cool, in which case they're fine. Just make sure you have something comfortable to put on your feet so you can put in a couple of miles a day of strolling about, say, in-between culinary pit stops.

Wine Glass

No, you don't have to bring your own, not even to a bring-your-own-wine restaurant. We just thought we'd take this opportunity to remind you that while this is a drinking town, it's not really a beer-guzzling town. Montréalers don't so much "drink to drink" as they eat to drink, or drink to eat — sometimes we can't tell which came first. Food without a bottle of wine here is like shopping without sales tax: practically a fantasy.

Picnic Basket

And speaking of drinking, you're allowed to bring your bottle with you to the park in Montréal, as long as it accompanies a meal. Montréalers like backyard barbecues, but they like eating outside in public, too. In summertime, a picnic in beautiful, peaceful Mount Royal Park is pretty hard to beat, particularly if it's well watered, or as we say in French, *bien arrosé* (see the preceding "Wine Glass" section).

Ice Skates

In winter, when the weather is cold enough, you find outdoor ice rinks all over town. Beaver Lake and the Bassin Bonsecours are two of the more popular spots for pleasure skating. In neighborhood parks throughout Montréal, wooden boards surround some ice rinks, where everyone plays pick-up hockey.

Chapter 22

Almost Ten Things You *Can't* Live Without in Québec City

In This Chapter

▶ Protecting yourself from the elements

▶ Capturing the sights on film

▶ Fortifying yourself with caribou

*H*ere's the inside track on visiting Québec City. No matter what time of year you visit, you want to be prepared for the weather, especially during the winter months when Québec City is a Nordic wonderland.

Warm Coat

If you think Montréal is cold, try Québec City. It goes beyond mere accessories like hats, scarves, mittens, and wool socks — although these are all essential too. Winter is non-negotiable, so make sure you have a warm coat. Down-filled is best, and fur will also do.

Walking Shoes

A mere entertainment enhancer in Montréal, walking shoes are your car in Québec City. If white running shoes are the most comfortable thing you have for scaling the cobblestone hills of this city, don't be shy. Be a tourist, but be comfortable.

Camera

With all that beautiful old architecture, quaint streets and great views of the Old City from hotel rooms everywhere, you'd be a fool not to get it on film or video. Don't worry, you won't be alone.

French-English Dictionary

Québec City is a tourist town, but it's still less bilingual than Montréal. Never hurts to have a pocket dictionary in your pocket — that's what pocket dictionaries are made for, after all.

Reading Glasses

You find historical explanations on plaques, monuments, and in galleries across this city, so don't put yourself in a situation where you can't make them out. As an added bonus, you'll also look more serious — and more at home — wearing glasses while you sit in a cafe reading a newspaper.

Umbrella

You can get away without one in Montréal, but not in Québec City. The weather is unpredictable, but the main activities of your day aren't. You're going to be out walking, rain or shine. Better to be prepared; besides, pocket umbrellas are easy to carry.

Credit Card

People in Québec City love to shop and so will you during your stay. Like the ad says, don't leave home without it.

Map

Québec City is so small that getting lost really doesn't pose any danger. No matter what direction you walk in, sooner or later you hit a wall, walk over a cliff, or into the St. Lawrence River. Among the winding streets, though, you may take awhile to figure out which way is up, so keep a map on hand. Hey, this book is full of them.

Caribou

No, not the mammal, but a strong alcoholic beverage, originally mixed with real caribou blood. First used by the settlers of New France to fortify themselves against the harsh winter. Now, an updated recipe, *sans* blood, is what revelers drink to stay warm and giddy during festivities at the Québec City Winter Carnival. Get yourself a bottle, especially if you forget to bring a warm coat.

Appendix

Quick Concierge

. . . .

Fast Facts

AAA

Montréal's affiliate is the CAA, located downtown at 1180 rue Drummond (☎ 514-861-5111; www.caaquebec.com). It's open Monday to Friday, 9 a.m. to 6 p.m., Thursdays until 8 p.m. The emergency road service number for members in Montréal is ☎ 514-861-1313.

Québec City's CAA affiliate is located at 444 rue Bouvier (☎ 418-624-8222). Business hours are Monday through Wednesday from 9 a.m. to 5:30 p.m., Thursday and Friday from 9 a.m. to 8 p.m. and Saturday from 10 a.m. to 4 p.m. The emergency road service number for Québec City is ☎ 800-222-4357.

If you're a member of AAA, you can pick up maps, tour books, and traveler's checks at these offices at no extra charge; you can also make travel arrangements here.

American Express

In Montreál, offices of the American Express Travel Service are located at 1141 bd. de Maisonneuve Ouest (near rue Stanley), ☎ 514-284-3300. Offices are open 9 a.m. to 5 p.m. There's another office in La Baie (The Bay) department store, 585 rue Ste-Catherine Ouest (☎ 514-281-4777), which closes a half-hour before the store closes.

In Québec City, the nearest office is located at 2700 bd. Laurier in Ste-Foy (☎ 418-658-8820). It's open Monday through Friday, from 9 a.m. to 5 p.m.

Area Code

The area code for downtown Montréal is **514**. For suburbs around Montréal, dial **450**.

The area code for Québec City and Ste-Foy is **418**.

ATMs

You can find ATM services provided by major banks in the heart of downtown and throughout the suburban areas. The Bank of Montréal, Banque Nationale, Royal Bank, and Scotia Bank use the Cirrus system. For Cirrus information, call ☎ 800-424-7787. The Caisse populaire and CIBC use the Plus system. For Plus information, call ☎ 800-843-7587.

Baby-sitters

Most major hotels have someone on staff who can look after your children or can make arrangements for child care if you need it. Be sure to advise them of your child's special needs well in advance. Montréal YMCA, downtown on rue Stanley, offers educational day care for kids 18 months to 5 years (☎ 514-849-8393; www.ymca.ca).

Business Hours

Stores generally open at 9 or 10 a.m. and close at 5 or 6 p.m., Monday through Wednesday and Saturday. Thursdays and Fridays, most stores open at the same time and stay open until 9 p.m. Most stores are also open on Sundays from noon to 5 p.m.

Montréal banks are usually open Monday through Friday, from 8 or 9 a.m. to 4 p.m. In Québec City, banks are usually open from 10 a.m. to 3 p.m. Monday through Friday, but may also have evening hours on Thursday and Friday.

Camera Repair

In downtown Montréal, AFC Camera Service, 1015 Beaver Hall (☎ 514-397-9505) repairs cameras, as does Camera Technic Company, 1218 Union (☎ 514-866-2223). In Québec City, Service Camera Pro, 2042 bd. Père-Lelievre (☎ 418-527-0880), repairs every kind of camera on site: film, digital, and camcorders. Also try Camera Test, 51 bd. René-Levesque (☎ 418-529-2803).

Car Rentals

See Chapter 7 for information on car rentals in Montréal and Québec City.

Convention Centers

Montréal's Palais des Congrès runs between rue Viger and rue St-Antoine for several blocks starting at the corner of rue Jeanne Mance (☎ 514-871-3170). Métro: Place-d'Armes or Place-des-Arts.

Québec City's Centre des Congrès is located at 1000 bd. René-Levesque Est (☎ 888-679-4000 or 418-644-4000)

Credit Cards

To report lost or stolen credits cards, contact the following: American Express (☎ 800-268-9824); Diners Club (☎ 800-336-8472); Discover (☎ 800-DISCOVER); MasterCard (☎ 800-826-2181); and Visa (☎ 800-336-8472).

Currency Exchanges

In Montréal, currency exchange offices (called *bureaux de change*) can be found near airports, at the train station, and at the Infotouriste office on Dorchester Square. The Bank of American Canada, 1230 rue Peel, offers foreign-exchange services Monday through Friday 8:30 a.m. to 5:30 p.m. and Saturday 9 a.m. to 4 p.m.

In Québec City, a bureau de change office is near the Château Frontenac at 19 rue Ste-Anne. It is open Monday, Tuesday, and Friday from 10 a.m. to 3 p.m. and Wednesday and Thursday from 10 a.m. to 6 p.m. You can sometimes exchange money in hotels and shops, or you can simply withdraw local currency at an ATM.

Customs

Canada Customs and Revenue (☎ 800-877-9277, or 514-496-1606) is located at 305 bd. René-Levesque Ouest. The closest U.S. customs office is at Ottawa International Airport (☎ 613-523-8120).

Dentists

Montréal has a hotline for dental emergencies at ☎ 514-288-8888 and a 24-hour dental clinic at ☎ 514-342-4444.

Québec City has two hotlines that refer callers to available dentists. Call ☎ 418-653-5412 any day or 418-524-2626 Monday through Saturday.

Doctors

All major hotels should have a doctor on call or be able to call one for you. Embassies and consulates maintain lists of physicians with good reputations. See "Embassies and Consulates," later in this section.

Driving Rules

See Chapter 8.

Electricity

Canada uses the same electricity (110 volts, 60 Hz) as the United States and Mexico, with the same flat-prong plugs and sockets.

Embassies and Consulates

All embassies are in Ottawa.

In Montréal, the American Consulate General is located at 1155 rue St-Alexandre (☎ 514-398-9695). The United Kingdom has a Consulate General at 1000 rue de la Gauchetière Ouest, Suite 4200 (☎ 514-866-5863).

In Québec City, the U.S. Consulate is located near the Château Frontenac, facing Jardin des Gouverneurs, at 2 terrasse Dufferin (☎ 418-692-2095).

Emergencies
Dial **911** for the police, firefighters, or an ambulance.

Also, in Québec City, the Marine Search and Rescue (Canadian Coast Guard) works 24 hours a day. Call ☎ 418-648-3599 in the Greater Québec area or ☎ 800-463-4393 in St. Lawrence River.

Holidays
The following public holidays are celebrated in Québec:

New Year's Day; Good Friday and Easter Monday; St-Jean-Baptiste Day (June 24); Canada Day (July 1); Labour Day (first Monday in September); Thanksgiving (second Monday in October); Remembrance Day (November 11); Christmas Day; Boxing Day (December 26).

Banks and shops are likely to be closed on these days, although museums and restaurants usually stay open.

Hospitals
The following downtown Montréal hospitals have emergency rooms: Montréal General Hospital, 1650 rue Cedar (☎ 514-937-6011); the Royal Victoria Hospital, 687 av. des Pins Ouest (☎ 514-842-1231); the Hôtel Dieux, 209 av. des Pins Ouest (☎ 514-843-2611); and the Hôpital Notre-Dame, 1560 rue Sherbrooke Est (☎ 514-281-6000).

Hotlines
In Montréal: Alcoholics Anonymous (☎ 514-735-8274); Depressed Anonymous (☎ 514-278-2130); Gay Line (☎ 514-866-0103); Gambling Help and Referral (☎ 514-527-0140); Kids-Help (for children in crises) (☎ 800-668-6868); Parents Line (☎ 514-288-5555); Sexual Assault Line (☎ 514-934-4504); Spousal Abuse Line (☎ 514-873-9010); Suicide Action Montréal (☎ 514-723-4000); Youth Help Line (for children or teenagers in crises) (☎ 514-288-2266); Youth Protection (☎ 514-896-3100); Gas Odor Detection (☎ 514-598-3111).

In Québec City: Alcoholics Anonymous (☎ 418-529-0015); Health Info (☎ 418-648-2626); Tel-Aide, for emotional distress (☎ 418-686-2433).

Information
Montréal's Infotouriste Centre (www.bonjourQuebec.com) is located at 1001 Dorchester Square, one block south of rue Ste-Catherine Ouest (between rue Peel and rue Metcalf). From June through early–September, the center is open daily from 8:30 a.m. to 7:30 p.m. From mid-September through May, it operates daily between 9 a.m. to 5 p.m (☎ 877-266-5687 or 514-873-2015).

Québec City's main Tourist Information Centre is located at 12 rue Ste-Anne, just opposite the Château Frontenac at Place d'Armes (☎ 800-363-7777 or 418-692-2608).

Internet Access and Cybercafes
Most large hotels have in-room dataports for your computer, and more and more are offering access to high-speed lines, as well. Check your hotel for in-room rates for local calls.

If you don't travel with your computer, many hotels now offer Internet access from an on-site computer.

You can find cybercafes throughout Montréal. Two good, centrally located options are the CyberGround NetCafé at 3672 bd. St-Laurent (☎ 514-842-1726), and the Cybermac Café Internet at 1425 rue Mackay (☎ 514-287-9100).

In Québec City, the Musée de la Civilisation has computers with free Internet access in its visitor's lounge on the 2nd floor, but you must pay C$7 (US$5) admission to enter.

Language

Québec's official language is French, which is spoken by 85% of the population.

Liquor Laws

You must be 18 or over to legally drink in Québec. Beer and wine are sold in restaurants, bars, lounges, and taverns. You can purchase alcoholic beverages at the government-controlled Société des alcools du Québec (SAQ). There are two convenient downtown locations in Montréal: 677 rue Ste-Catherine Ouest between rue Université and McGill College (☎ 514-282-9445) and 440 bd. de Maisonneuve Ouest (☎ 514-873-2274). Québec City also offers two locations: in the concourse of the Château Frontenac, 1 rue des Carriéres (☎ 418-692-1182), and near the train station at 400 bd. Jean-Lesage (☎ 418-643-4339).

Mail

Stamps for mailing letters within Canada cost C48¢ (US35¢). Letters to the US cost C65¢ (US45¢) and letters overseas cost C$1.25 (US90¢).

Montréal's main post office (bureau de poste), at 1250 rue Université, near rue Ste-Catherine (☎ 514-395-4509), is open Monday to Friday from 8 a.m. to 6 p.m. In Old Montréal, the post office is at 155 rue St-Jacques (corner of rue St-François Xavier). Some large convenience stores throughout the city have small post offices located at the back of the store. Look for the red and white Postes Canada logo in the window.

Québec City's main post office is located in the Basse-Ville at 300 rue St-Paul (near rue Abraham-Martin) near the port (☎ 418-694-6175). Hours are 8 a.m. to 5:45 p.m. Monday through Friday. Another post office is near the Château Frontenac at 3 rue de Buade (☎ 418-694-6102) with the same opening hours.

Maps

City maps are available for free from city tourist offices, in the Yellow Pages, and as free visitor's guides you find in your hotel room. To find out where specific buildings or sites are located, you can also use Canada's online information service, www.canada411.com, which provides small maps showing the surrounding neighborhood of an address.

In Montréal, the Infotouriste office is at Dorchester Square (see "Information," earlier in this section). Bookstores like Chapters (1171 rue Ste-Catherine Ouest; ☎ 514-849-8825), Indigo (1500 av. McGill College; ☎ 514-281-5549), or Paragraphe Bookstore (2220 av. McGill College; ☎ 514-845-5811) also carry maps. If you want a very thorough street map of Montréal, look for the large yellow books published by MapArt Publishing, widely available in bookstores and convenience stores across the city.

In Québec City, you can pick up free city maps at the Tourist Information office at 12 rue Ste-Anne, just opposite the Château Frontenac at Place d'Armes. You can also find maps at Archambault, 1095 rue St-Jean (☎ 418-694-2088) and at the Maison de la Presse Internationale, 1050 rue St-Jean (☎ 418-694-1511).

Newspapers/Magazines

Montréal's English-language daily paper is the *Montréal Gazette,* which provides good coverage of city news and arts and entertainment listings, as well as some world news. Canada has two national newspapers, the *Globe & Mail* and the *National*

Post, which cover Canadian and world news. You can find these papers at convenience stores throughout the downtown area. English-language papers are hard to find outside the downtown area.

For arts and entertainment coverage exclusively, pick up one of Montréal's weekly alternative publications: *Hour* or the *Mirror.* Both are available in convenience stores and at the entrance of bars, cafes, and some restaurants downtown and in the Plateau neighborhood.

In Québec City, major Canadian and American English-language newspapers and magazines are sold in the newsstands of the large hotels, at vending machines on tourist corners in the Old City, and at Maison de la Presse Internationale, 1050 rue St-Jean.

Pharmacies

Québec's major drugstore chain is Pharmacie Jean Coutu, which has a downtown Montréal location in the Ailes de la Mode complex at 677 rue Ste-Catherine Ouest (☎ 514-289-0800) and another big store at 974 rue Ste-Catherine Ouest (☎ 514-866-7791). The other big chain is Pharmaprix, which has a big store at 450 rue Ste-Catherine Ouest (☎ 514-875-7070) that's open 24 hours.

In Québec City, the Chabot Laurent pharmacy is located in the Basse-Ville at 3A Place Royale (☎ 418-694-1262).

Police

Dial **911** for emergencies. There are three types of officers in Québec: the municipal police, the Sûreté du Québec (comparable to state police or highway patrol), and the RCMP (like the FBI) that handles cases involving federal laws. RCMP officers are required to speak English. The Montréal and Québec City police provide service in English.

To reach the Sûreté du Québec in Montréal, dial ☎ 514-310-4141. In Québec City, call ☎ 800-461-2131.

Radio Stations

CJAD (AM 800) covers news, sports, weather, and traffic. Canada's National Public Radio equivalent is the CBC (Canadian Broadcasting Corporation, 88.5 FM), which plays classical music and has various talk shows on arts, news, and current events. For popular music, try Mix 96 at 95.9 FM.

Restrooms

You can find clean restrooms in hotel lobbies, museums, and shopping malls.

In Montréal, that includes Centre Eaton, 705 rue Ste-Catherine Ouest; Cours Mont-Royal, 1455 rue Peel; Les Promenades de la Cathédrale, corner of rue Université and rue Ste-Catherine Ouest; and Les Ailes de la Mode, 677 rue Ste-Catherine Ouest. There are public washrooms at La Baie department store, 585 rue Ste-Catherine Ouest.

In Québec City, the Tourist Information Centre at 12 rue Ste-Anne has clean and spacious washrooms in the basement.

Safety

For the most part, Montréal is much safer than many American cities of the same size. However, walking around the red light district on rue Ste-Catherine Est, east of boulevard St-Laurent, at night is not advised. Stay alert to your surroundings and observe the usual urban precautions.

Like most Canadian cities, Québec City is relatively safe. Avoid leaving possessions in full view in your car and be aware of the people in your vicinity.

Smoking

Smoking is not permitted in public buildings in Québec. Most restaurants have smoking sections, but more and more forbid smoking altogether. Smoking is allowed in most bars.

Taxes

Canada's Goods and Services Tax (*Taxe de produits et services* or TPS in Québec) is 7% and applies to everything but alcoholic beverages. Québec's *Provincial Sales Tax* (TVQ) is 7.5%, calculated on the price plus the GST.

Taxis

In Montréal, taxis line up in front of downtown hotels. You can also call a taxi company directly and usually have a ride within 5 to 10 minutes. Two major companies are Taxi Co-op (☎ 514-725-9885) and Taxi Diamond (☎ 514-273-6331).

Québec City's two main taxi companies are Taxi Coop (☎ 418-525-5191) and Taxi Québec (☎ 418-525-8123).

Telephone

The phone system in Québec is operated by Bell Canada. To get the operator, dial 0 (he or she will speak both French and English). For directory information, call 411.

Pay phones require C25¢ for a local call, and you can use any combination of coins (except pennies). Pay phones are usually located in glass telephone booths on busy streets, in grocery stores, or in hotel lobbies. Shopping centers usually have pay phones near the restrooms.

Time Zone

Montréal, Québec City, and the day-trip destinations mentioned in Chapter 14 are all in the Eastern Time Zone. Daylight saving time is observed from late April through late October.

Tipping

Waiters and cab drivers should be tipped between 10 and 15 percent. For bellhops, tip C$1 or C$2 (US75¢ or US$1.50) per bag. For hotel housekeeping, count C$1 (US75¢) per person per day. For valet parking, tip C$1 or C$2 (US75¢ or US$1.50).

Transit Information

In Montréal, call the STM (*Société de transport de Montréal*) (☎ 514-786-4636) for information about the Métro, city buses, or parabuses for disabled passengers. For airport transportation, call L'Aérobus (☎ 514-931-9002).

Québec's transit authority is the RTC (☎ 418-627-2511).

Toll-Free Numbers and Web Sites

Major carriers flying into Pierre Elliott Trudeau International Airport (Montréal)

Air Canada
☎ 888-247-2262
www.aircanada.com

Air France
☎ 800-667-2747
www.airfrance.com

Air Transat
☎ 877-872-6728
www.airtransat.com

American Airlines
☎ 800-433-7300
www.aa.com

Atlantic Coast Airlines
☎ 800-361-1970
www.atlanticcoast.com

Atlantic Southeast Airlines
☎ 800-361-1970
www.delta-air.com

Austrian Airlines
☎ 888-817-4444
www.aua.com

British Airways
☎ 800-247-9297
www.british-airways.com

Continental Airlines
☎ 800-231-0856
www.continental.com

Delta Airlines
☎ 800 361-1970
www.delta.com

Japan Air Lines
☎ 800-525-3663
www.japanair.com

KLM Royal Dutch Airlines
☎ 800-225-2525
www.klm.com

Lufthansa
☎ 800-563-5954
www.lufthansa.com

Mexicana
☎ 800-531-7923
www.mexicana.com

Northwest Airlines
☎ 800-225-2525
www.nwa.com

PSA Airlines
☎ 800-428-4322
www.psaairlines.com

Royal Air Maroc
☎ 800-361-7508
www.royalairmaroc.com

Swiss International Airlines
☎ 877-359-7947
www.swiss.com

United Airlines
☎ 800-241-6522
www.ual.com

Carriers flying into Jean Lesage Airport (Québec City)

Air Canada
☎ 888-247-2262
www.aircanada.com

Air Canada Tango
☎ 800-315-1390
www.flytango.com

American Eagle Airlines
☎ 800-433-7300
www.aa.com

Continental Express
☎ 800-231-0856
www.continental.com

Northwest Airlines
☎ 800-225-2525
www.nwa.com

Québecair Express
☎ 877-871-6500
www.quebecairexpress.com

Car rental agencies

Avis
☎ 800-831-2874
☎ 800-TRY-AVIS in Canada
www.avis.com

Budget
☎ 800-527-0700
www.budgetrentacar.com

Discount
☎ 800-263-2355
www.discountcar.com

Dollar
☎ 800-800-3665
www.dollar.com

Hertz
☎ 800-654-3131
www.hertz.com

Sauvageau
☎ 800-463-8800
www.sauvageau.qc.cq

Thrifty
☎ 800-847-4389
www.thrifty.com

Major hotel and motel chains

Best Western International
☎ 800-528-1234
www.bestwestern.com

Clarion Hotels
☎ 800-CLARION
www.clarionhotel.com

Comfort Inns
☎ 800-228-5150
www.hotelchoice.com

Days Inn
☎ 800-325-2525
www.daysinn.com

Delta Hotels
☎ 877-814-7706
www.deltahotels.com

Econolodge
☎ 877-424-6423
www.hotelchoice.com

Fairmount Hotels
☎ 800-257-7544
www.fairmount.com

Gouverneur Hotels
☎ 888-910-1111
www.gouverneur.com

Hilton Hotels
☎ 800-HILTONS
www.hilton.com

Holiday Inn
☎ 800-HOLIDAY
www.basshotels.com

Howard Johnson
☎ 800-654-2000
www.hojo.com

Hyatt Hotels & Resorts
☎ 800-228-9000
www.hyatt.com

Marriott Hotels
☎ 800-932-2198
www.marriott.com

Novotel
☎ 800-359-6279
www.novotel.com

Sheraton
☎ 800-325-3535
www.sheraton.com

Travelodge
☎ 800-255-3050
www.travelodge.com

Radisson Hotels
☎ 800-333-3333
www.radisson.com

Wyndham Hotels and Resorts
☎ 800-822-4200
www.wyndham.com

Ramada Inns
☎ 800-2-RAMADA
www.ramada.com

Where to Get More Information

We mention Montréal's and Québec City's main tourism offices throughout this book, but for a quick reference, we include them here, as well.

Centre Infotouriste Montréal
1001 Square Dorchester
☎ 877-266-5687 or 514-873-2015
www.bonjourquebec.com

Tourist Information Centre of Old Montréal
174 rue Notre-Dame Est
www.tourism-montreal.org

Centre Infotouriste Québec City
12 rue Ste-Anne
☎ 800-363-7777 or 418-692-2608
www.bonjourquebec.com

Greater Québec Area Tourism and Convention Bureau
(Québec City)
835 av. Laurier
☎ 418-649-2608
www.quebecregion.com

Several Internet sites list shows, restaurants, and hotels and offer travel information. Here are our favorites:

✔ www.montrealplus.ca

✔ www.tourisme-montreal.org

✔ www.discovermontreal.ca

✔ www.montreal.com

✔ www.quebeccitytourism.ca

✔ www.quebecweb.com/tourisme/

To find the address or phone number of an establishment not listed in this book, one of the following two Web sites can be helpful:

✔ www.canada411.com (Canada's Internet information site)

✔ www.pagesjaunes.ca (Québec's Yellow Pages site)

You can find up-to-the-minute listings of shows, exhibitions, and concerts by visiting the free Web sites of the following English-language publications in Montréal:

✔ www.montrealgazette.com (the *Montréal Gazette*)

✔ www.hour.ca (the alternative arts weekly, *Hour*)

✔ www.montrealmirror.com (the alternative arts weekly, *Mirror*)

If you need to check transit information before you leave home, you can find it by visiting the following Web sites:

✔ www.admtl.com (Trudeau and Mirabel airports in Montréal)

✔ www.aeroportdequebec.com (Jean Lesage airport in Québec City)

✔ www.stcum.qc.ca (Montréal transit)

✔ www.stcuq.qc.ca (Québec City transit)

✔ www.accesstotravel.qc.ca (wheelchair-accessible transport in Québec)

If you prefer print media, you can get a different approach, but just as much good information on Montréal and Québec City, in *Frommer's Montréal & Québec City* (Wiley).

Making Dollars and Sense of It

Expense	Daily cost	x	Number of days	=	Total
Airfare					
Local transportation					
Car rental					
Lodging (with tax)					
Parking					
Breakfast					
Lunch					
Dinner					
Snacks					
Entertainment					
Babysitting					
Attractions					
Gifts & souvenirs					
Tips					
Other					
Grand Total					

Fare Game: Choosing an Airline

When looking for the best airfare, you should cover all your bases — 1) consult a trusted travel agent; 2) contact the airline directly, via the airline's toll-free number and/or Web site; 3) check out one of the travel-planning Web sites, such as www.frommers.com.

Travel Agency_____ Phone_____
    Agent's Name_____ Quoted fare_____

Airline 1_____ Quoted fare_____
    Toll-free number/Internet_____

Airline 2_____ Quoted fare_____
    Toll-free number/Internet_____

Web site 1_____ Quoted fare_____

Web site 2_____ Quoted fare_____

Departure Schedule & Flight Information

Airline_____ Flight #_____ Confirmation #_____

Departs_____ Date_____ Time_____ a.m./p.m.

Arrives_____ Date_____ Time_____ a.m./p.m.

Connecting Flight (if any)

Amount of time between flights_____ hours/mins

Airline_____ Flight #_____ Confirmation #_____

Departs_____ Date_____ Time_____ a.m./p.m.

Arrives_____ Date_____ Time_____ a.m./p.m.

Return Trip Schedule & Flight Information

Airline_____ Flight #_____ Confirmation #_____

Departs_____ Date_____ Time_____ a.m./p.m.

Arrives_____ Date_____ Time_____ a.m./p.m.

Connecting Flight (if any)

Amount of time between flights_____ hours/mins

Airline_____ Flight #_____ Confirmation #_____

Departs_____ Date_____ Time_____ a.m./p.m.

Arrives_____ Date_____ Time_____ a.m./p.m.

All Aboard: Booking Your Train Travel

Travel Agency_____ Phone_____

Agent's Name_____

Web Site_____

Departure Schedule & Train Information

Train #_____ Confirmation #_____ Seat reservation #_____

Departs_____ Date_____ Time_____ a.m./p.m.

Arrives_____ Date_____ Time_____ a.m./p.m.

Quoted fare_____ First class _____ Second class

Departure Schedule & Train Information

Train #_____ Confirmation #_____ Seat reservation #_____

Departs_____ Date_____ Time_____ a.m./p.m.

Arrives_____ Date_____ Time_____ a.m./p.m.

Quoted fare_____ First class _____ Second class

Departure Schedule & Train Information

Train #_____ Confirmation #_____ Seat reservation #_____

Departs_____ Date_____ Time_____ a.m./p.m.

Arrives_____ Date_____ Time_____ a.m./p.m.

Quoted fare_____ First class _____ Second class

Departure Schedule & Train Information

Train #_____ Confirmation #_____ Seat reservation #_____

Departs_____ Date_____ Time_____ a.m./p.m.

Arrives_____ Date_____ Time_____ a.m./p.m.

Quoted fare_____ First class _____ Second class

Sweet Dreams: Choosing Your Hotel

Make a list of all the hotels where you'd like to stay and then check online and call the local and toll-free numbers to get the best price. You should also check with a travel agent, who may be able to get you a better rate.

Hotel & page	Location	Internet	Tel. (local)	Tel. (Toll-free)	Quoted rate

Hotel Checklist

Here's a checklist of things to inquire about when booking your room, depending on your needs and preferences.

- ❑ Smoking/smoke-free room
- ❑ Noise (if you prefer a quiet room, ask about proximity to elevator, bar/restaurant, pool, meeting facilities, renovations, and street)
- ❑ View
- ❑ Facilities for children (crib, roll-away cot, babysitting services)
- ❑ Facilities for travelers with disabilities
- ❑ Number and size of bed(s) (king, queen, double/full-size)
- ❑ Is breakfast included? (buffet, continental, or sit-down?)
- ❑ In-room amenities (hair dryer, iron/board, minibar, etc.)
- ❑ Other_____

Places to Go, People to See, Things to Do

Enter the attractions you would most like to see and decide how they'll fit into your schedule. Next, use the "Going My Way" worksheets that follow to sketch out your itinerary.

Attraction/activity	Page	Amount of time you expect to spend there	Best day and time to go

Going "My" Way

Day 1

Hotel_____ Tel._____

Morning_____

_____

Lunch_____ Tel._____

Afternoon_____

_____

Dinner_____ Tel._____

Evening_____

_____

Day 2

Hotel_____ Tel._____

Morning_____

_____

Lunch_____ Tel._____

Afternoon_____

_____

Dinner_____ Tel._____

Evening_____

_____

Day 3

Hotel_____ Tel._____

Morning_____

_____

Lunch_____ Tel._____

Afternoon_____

_____

Dinner_____ Tel._____

Evening_____

_____

Going "My" Way

Day 4

Hotel _____ Tel. _____

Morning _____

_____

Lunch _____ Tel. _____

Afternoon _____

_____

Dinner _____ Tel. _____

Evening _____

_____

Day 5

Hotel _____ Tel. _____

Morning _____

_____

Lunch _____ Tel. _____

Afternoon _____

_____

Dinner _____ Tel. _____

Evening _____

_____

Day 6

Hotel _____ Tel. _____

Morning _____

_____

Lunch _____ Tel. _____

Afternoon _____

_____

Dinner _____ Tel. _____

Evening _____

_____

Going "My" Way

Day 7

Hotel_____ Tel._____

Morning_____

_____

Lunch_____ Tel._____

Afternoon_____

_____

Dinner_____ Tel._____

Evening_____

_____

Day 8

Hotel_____ Tel._____

Morning_____

_____

Lunch_____ Tel._____

Afternoon_____

_____

Dinner_____ Tel._____

Evening_____

_____

Day 9

Hotel_____ Tel._____

Morning_____

_____

Lunch_____ Tel._____

Afternoon_____

_____

Dinner_____ Tel._____

Evening_____

_____

Your Cruise & Ferry Schedule

Travel Agency_____ Phone_____

Agent's Name_____

Web Site_____

Cruise Information & Departure Schedule

Cruise Line_____ Ship Name_____

Port of Embarkation_____ Date_____

Boarding Time_____ a.m./p.m.   Departure Time_____ a.m./p.m.

Ports of Call_____

Return Cruise Information

Port_____ Date_____ Time_____ a.m./p.m.

Ferry Information & Departure Schedule

Ferry Line_____ Ship Name_____

Departure Port_____ Date_____

Boarding Time_____ a.m./p.m.   Quoted Fare_____

Departure Time_____ a.m./p.m.   Arrival Time_____ a.m./p.m.

Ferry Information & Departure Schedule

Ferry Line_____ Ship Name_____

Departure Port_____ Date_____

Boarding Time_____ a.m./p.m.   Quoted Fare_____

Departure Time_____ a.m./p.m.   Arrival Time_____ a.m./p.m.

Ferry Information & Departure Schedule

Ferry Line_____ Ship Name_____

Departure Port_____ Date_____

Boarding Time_____ a.m./p.m.   Quoted Fare_____

Departure Time_____ a.m./p.m.   Arrival Time_____ a.m./p.m.

Notes

Index

See also separate Accommodations and Restaurant Indexes following this index.

• N •

• O •

• P •

shopping (Montréal)
  antiques, 160, 167
  books/magazines, 255
  budget for, 29
  clothing, 160, 167, 255
  department stores, 161, 166, 167
  Downtown, 161–162, 164
  duty-free, 161
  food markets, 125
  hours, 163, 277
  by merchandise, 167
  overview, 159–161
  Plateau, 164–165
  St-Henri (rue Notre-Dame), 165
  sales tax, 21, 30
  Vieux-Montréal, 166
  Westmount, 166
shopping (Québec City)
  antiques, 251, 254, 257
  art galleries, 251, 254–255
  business hours, 252
  clothing, 251–252
  department stores, 252
  malls, 253, 258
  by merchandise, 257–258
  by neighborhood, 253–257
shows, Web sites, 286
sightseeing. *See* attractions
Simons (department store)
    (Québec City), 252
skating (Montréal), 19, 140
skiing/snowboarding, 13
smoking, 70, 107, 272, 281
soccer (Montréal), 147
Sociéte de Transport de Montréal
    (STM), 84, 85
speed limit, 50
sports
  jet boat, 136
  rafting, 136
  skating, 19, 140
  skiing, 13
  spectator, 145–147
spring, 16–17
Stade Olympique (Montréal), 139–140
stamps, 280
street terminology (French), 3–4
subway (Métro), 28, 84–85

summer, 15, 16, 18
symphony, 184

• T •

Taillibert, Roger (architect), 140
tam-tams (drum-circle), 155–156, 158
Tàpies, Antoni (painter), 137
tax
  accommodations, 59
  alcoholic beverage, 30
  exported goods, 161
  refund for non-Canadians, 30
  sales and services, 21, 27, 30, 68,
    161, 282
taxi
  airport, 78, 199
  fare, 78, 87, 205
  locating, 28, 282
  Montréal, 78, 87
  Québec City, 199, 205
  tipping, 30–31, 282
  wheelchair-accessible, 39
Taylor, Elizabeth (actress), 100
teenagers, attractions
    (Québec City), 244
telephone, 60, 282
temperature, 12, 15
Tennis Masters Canada, 22
terrasse Dufferin (Québec City), 243
terrior, 106
theater
  Festival de Théâtre des
    Amériques, 20
  Montréal, 183
  off-off-Broadway, 21
Théâtre de Verdure (Montréal), 143
tickets
  airline, 48–49
  Métro and bus, 28, 85
  museum, 29
  for shows, 30
  spectator sports, 146, 147
  Web sites, 69, 146, 147
time (military 24-hour), 87, 260.
    See also business hours
time zone, 282

Restaurant Index
Québec City

Notes

FOR DUMMIES®

The easy way to get more done and have more fun

PERSONAL FINANCE

0-7645-5231-7

0-7645-2431-3

0-7645-5331-3

Also available:

Estate Planning For Dummies
(0-7645-5501-4)

401(k)s For Dummies
(0-7645-5468-9)

Frugal Living For Dummies
(0-7645-5403-4)

Microsoft Money "X" For Dummies
(0-7645-1689-2)

Mutual Funds For Dummies
(0-7645-5329-1)

Personal Bankruptcy For Dummies
(0-7645-5498-0)

Quicken "X" For Dummies
(0-7645-1666-3)

Stock Investing For Dummies
(0-7645-5411-5)

Taxes For Dummies 2003
(0-7645-5475-1)

BUSINESS & CAREERS

0-7645-5314-3

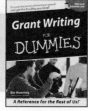

0-7645-5307-0

0-7645-5471-9

Also available:

Business Plans Kit For Dummies
(0-7645-5365-8)

Consulting For Dummies
(0-7645-5034-9)

Cool Careers For Dummies
(0-7645-5345-3)

Human Resources Kit For Dummies
(0-7645-5131-0)

Managing For Dummies
(1-5688-4858-7)

QuickBooks All-in-One Desk Reference For Dummies
(0-7645-1963-8)

Selling For Dummies
(0-7645-5363-1)

Small Business Kit For Dummies
(0-7645-5093-4)

Starting an eBay Business For Dummies
(0-7645-1547-0)

HEALTH, SPORTS & FITNESS

0-7645-5167-1

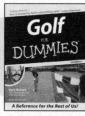

0-7645-5146-9

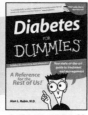

0-7645-5154-X

Also available:

Controlling Cholesterol For Dummies
(0-7645-5440-9)

Dieting For Dummies
(0-7645-5126-4)

High Blood Pressure For Dummies
(0-7645-5424-7)

Martial Arts For Dummies
(0-7645-5358-5)

Menopause For Dummies
(0-7645-5458-1)

Nutrition For Dummies
(0-7645-5180-9)

Power Yoga For Dummies
(0-7645-5342-9)

Thyroid For Dummies
(0-7645-5385-2)

Weight Training For Dummies
(0-7645-5168-X)

Yoga For Dummies
(0-7645-5117-5)

Available wherever books are sold.
Go to www.dummies.com or call 1-877-762-2974 to order direct.

FOR DUMMIES®

A world of resources to help you grow

HOME, GARDEN & HOBBIES

Feng Shui
0-7645-5295-3

Gardening
0-7645-5130-2

Guitar
0-7645-5106-X

Also available:

Auto Repair For Dummies
(0-7645-5089-6)

Chess For Dummies
(0-7645-5003-9)

Home Maintenance For Dummies
(0-7645-5215-5)

Organizing For Dummies
(0-7645-5300-3)

Piano For Dummies
(0-7645-5105-1)

Poker For Dummies
(0-7645-5232-5)

Quilting For Dummies
(0-7645-5118-3)

Rock Guitar For Dummies
(0-7645-5356-9)

Roses For Dummies
(0-7645-5202-3)

Sewing For Dummies
(0-7645-5137-X)

FOOD & WINE

Cooking
0-7645-5250-3

Cookies
0-7645-5390-9

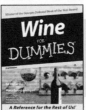

Wine
0-7645-5114-0

Also available:

Bartending For Dummies
(0-7645-5051-9)

Chinese Cooking For Dummies
(0-7645-5247-3)

Christmas Cooking For Dummies
(0-7645-5407-7)

Diabetes Cookbook For Dummies
(0-7645-5230-9)

Grilling For Dummies
(0-7645-5076-4)

Low-Fat Cooking For Dummies
(0-7645-5035-7)

Slow Cookers For Dummies
(0-7645-5240-6)

TRAVEL

Italy
0-7645-5453-0

Hawaii
0-7645-5438-7

Las Vegas
0-7645-5448-4

Also available:

America's National Parks For Dummies
(0-7645-6204-5)

Caribbean For Dummies
(0-7645-5445-X)

Cruise Vacations For Dummies 2003
(0-7645-5459-X)

Europe For Dummies
(0-7645-5456-5)

Ireland For Dummies
(0-7645-6199-5)

France For Dummies
(0-7645-6292-4)

London For Dummies
(0-7645-5416-6)

Mexico's Beach Resorts For Dummies
(0-7645-6262-2)

Paris For Dummies
(0-7645-5494-8)

RV Vacations For Dummies
(0-7645-5443-3)

Walt Disney World & Orlando For Dummies
(0-7645-5444-1)

Available wherever books are sold. Go to www.dummies.com or call 1-877-762-2974 to order direct.

FOR DUMMIES

Plain-English solutions for everyday challenges

COMPUTER BASICS

0-7645-0838-5

0-7645-1663-9

0-7645-1548-9

Also available:

PCs All-in-One Desk Reference For Dummies (0-7645-0791-5)

Pocket PC For Dummies (0-7645-1640-X)

Treo and Visor For Dummies (0-7645-1673-6)

Troubleshooting Your PC For Dummies (0-7645-1669-8)

Upgrading & Fixing PCs For Dummies (0-7645-1665-5)

Windows XP For Dummies (0-7645-0893-8)

Windows XP For Dummies Quick Reference (0-7645-0897-0)

BUSINESS SOFTWARE

0-7645-0822-9

0-7645-0839-3

0-7645-0819-9

Also available:

Excel Data Analysis For Dummies (0-7645-1661-2)

Excel 2002 All-in-One Desk Reference For Dummies (0-7645-1794-5)

Excel 2002 For Dummies Quick Reference (0-7645-0829-6)

GoldMine "X" For Dummies (0-7645-0845-8)

Microsoft CRM For Dummies (0-7645-1698-1)

Microsoft Project 2002 For Dummies (0-7645-1628-0)

Office XP For Dummies (0-7645-0830-X)

Outlook 2002 For Dummies (0-7645-0828-8)

Get smart! Visit www.dummies.com

- **Find listings of even more *For Dummies* titles**

- **Browse online articles**

- **Sign up for Dummies eTips™**

- **Check out *For Dummies* fitness videos and other products**

- **Order from our online bookstore**

Available wherever books are sold. Go to www.dummies.com or call 1-877-762-2974 to order direct.

FOR DUMMIES®

Helping you expand your horizons and realize your potential

INTERNET

0-7645-0894-6

0-7645-1659-0

0-7645-1642-6

Also available:

America Online 7.0 For Dummies
(0-7645-1624-8)

Genealogy Online For Dummies
(0-7645-0807-5)

The Internet All-in-One Desk Reference For Dummies
(0-7645-1659-0)

Internet Explorer 6 For Dummies
(0-7645-1344-3)

The Internet For Dummies Quick Reference
(0-7645-1645-0)

Internet Privacy For Dummies
(0-7645-0846-6)

Researching Online For Dummies
(0-7645-0546-7)

Starting an Online Business For Dummies
(0-7645-1655-8)

DIGITAL MEDIA

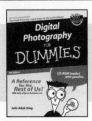

0-7645-1664-7

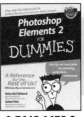

0-7645-1675-2

0-7645-0806-7

Also available:

CD and DVD Recording For Dummies
(0-7645-1627-2)

Digital Photography All-in-One Desk Reference For Dummies
(0-7645-1800-3)

Digital Photography For Dummies Quick Reference
(0-7645-0750-8)

Home Recording for Musicians For Dummies
(0-7645-1634-5)

MP3 For Dummies
(0-7645-0858-X)

Paint Shop Pro "X" For Dummies
(0-7645-2440-2)

Photo Retouching & Restoration For Dummies
(0-7645-1662-0)

Scanners For Dummies
(0-7645-0783-4)

GRAPHICS

0-7645-0817-2

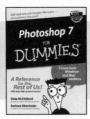

0-7645-1651-5

0-7645-0895-4

Also available:

Adobe Acrobat 5 PDF For Dummies
(0-7645-1652-3)

Fireworks 4 For Dummies
(0-7645-0804-0)

Illustrator 10 For Dummies
(0-7645-3636-2)

QuarkXPress 5 For Dummies
(0-7645-0643-9)

Visio 2000 For Dummies
(0-7645-0635-8)

FOR DUMMIES®

The advice and explanations you need to succeed

SELF-HELP, SPIRITUALITY & RELIGION

Sex
0-7645-5302-X

Parenting
0-7645-5418-2

Religion
0-7645-5264-3

Also available:

The Bible For Dummies
(0-7645-5296-1)

Buddhism For Dummies
(0-7645-5359-3)

Christian Prayer For
Dummies
(0-7645-5500-6)

Dating For Dummies
(0-7645-5072-1)

Judaism For Dummies
(0-7645-5299-6)

Potty Training For
Dummies
(0-7645-5417-4)

Pregnancy For Dummies
(0-7645-5074-8)

Rekindling Romance For
Dummies
(0-7645-5303-8)

Spirituality For Dummies
(0-7645-5298-8)

Weddings For Dummies
(0-7645-5055-1)

PETS

Puppies
0-7645-5255-4

Dog Training
0-7645-5286-4

Cats
0-7645-5275-9

Also available:

Labrador Retrievers For
Dummies
(0-7645-5281-3)

Aquariums For Dummies
(0-7645-5156-6)

Birds For Dummies
(0-7645-5139-6)

Dogs For Dummies
(0-7645-5274-0)

Ferrets For Dummies
(0-7645-5259-7)

German Shepherds For
Dummies
(0-7645-5280-5)

Golden Retrievers For
Dummies
(0-7645-5267-8)

Horses For Dummies
(0-7645-5138-8)

Jack Russell Terriers For
Dummies
(0-7645-5268-6)

Puppies Raising &
Training Diary For
Dummies
(0-7645-0876-8)

EDUCATION & TEST PREPARATION

Spanish
0-7645-5194-9

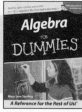

Algebra
0-7645-5325-9

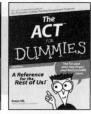

The ACT
0-7645-5210-4

Also available:

Chemistry For Dummies
(0-7645-5430-1)

English Grammar For
Dummies
(0-7645-5322-4)

French For Dummies
(0-7645-5193-0)

The GMAT For Dummies
(0-7645-5251-1)

Inglés Para Dummies
(0-7645-5427-1)

Italian For Dummies
(0-7645-5196-5)

Research Papers For
Dummies
(0-7645-5426-3)

The SAT I For Dummies
(0-7645-5472-7)

U.S. History For Dummies
(0-7645-5249-X)

World History For
Dummies
(0-7645-5242-2)

Available wherever books are sold. Go to www.dummies.com or call 1-877-762-2974 to order direct.